THE
Westminster Pulpit

VOLUME III

THE
Westminster
Pulpit

VOLUME III

The Preaching of
G. CAMPBELL MORGAN

WIPF & STOCK · Eugene, Oregon

Wipf and Stock Publishers
199 W 8th Ave, Suite 3
Eugene, OR 97401

The Westminster Pulpit vol. III
The Preaching of G. Campbell Morgan
By Morgan, G. Campbell
Copyright©1954 by The Morgan Trust
ISBN 13: 978-1-60899-312-3
Publication date 1/15/2012
Previously published by Fleming H. Revell, Co., 1954

CONTENTS

CHAPTER		PAGE
I	THE TRUE FOCUS	9
II	SECRET AND REVEALED THINGS	22
III	SUBMISSION AND RESPONSIBILITY	35
IV	PRAYER OR FAINTING	49
V	SUFFER THE CHILDREN	63
VI	THE VICTORIOUS CHRISTIAN LIFE	76
VII	THE VALUE AND PROOF OF THE RESURRECTION	89
VIII	THE PURPOSE OF LIFE	102
IX	THE CITIES OF MEN AND THE CITY OF GOD	116
X	LIGHT AND DARKNESS	128
XI	THE PROBLEMS OF THE RELIGIOUS LIFE: HAS MAN ANYTHING TO DO WITH GOD?	143
XII	THE PROBLEMS OF THE RELIGIOUS LIFE: CAN A JUST GOD FORGIVE SINS?	157
XIII	THE PROBLEMS OF THE RELIGIOUS LIFE: WHAT DOES GOD REQUIRE OF MAN?	171
XIV	THE PROBLEMS OF THE RELIGIOUS LIFE: THE OPPOSING FORCES OF THE RELIGIOUS LIFE—THE WORLD	183
XV	THE PROBLEMS OF THE RELIGIOUS LIFE: THE OPPOSING FORCES OF THE RELIGIOUS LIFE—THE FLESH	196
XVI	THE PROBLEMS OF THE RELIGIOUS LIFE: THE OPPOSING FORCES OF THE RELIGIOUS LIFE—THE DEVIL	209

CHAPTER		PAGE
XVII	THE PROBLEMS OF THE RELIGIOUS LIFE: IS THE RELIGIOUS LIFE POSSIBLE?	223
XVIII	THE PROBLEMS OF THE RELIGIOUS LIFE: IS THE RELIGIOUS LIFE NECESSARY?	237
XIX	THE PROBLEMS OF THE RELIGIOUS LIFE: IS THE RELIGIOUS LIFE WORTH WHILE?	250
XX	THE PROBLEMS OF THE RELIGIOUS LIFE: THE ALL-SUFFICIENT SOLUTION	264
XXI	HOLINESS: DEFINITION	276
XXII	HOLINESS: A PRESENT POSSIBILITY	289
XXIII	HOLINESS: CONDITIONS	303
XXIV	HOLINESS: ITS FRUIT	316
XXV	HOLINESS: HINDRANCES	328
XXVI	CLEAN, FOR SERVICE	341

THE
Westminster
Pulpit

VOLUME III

CHAPTER I

THE TRUE FOCUS

And I said, This is my infirmity . . . the years of the right hand of the Most High.
                                   PSALM 77:10.

TRUE FOCUS IS ALL IMPORTANT. THIS IS KNOWN TO EVERY person who has looked upon a landscape through a field-glass or has seen its beauties gathered up in a camera. When the instrument is improperly adjusted, the images which it shows are blurred and indistinct; but when, by proper manipulation, the right focus is obtained, how clear, or, to use the technical word, how sharp the picture becomes, with every point clearly and properly defined! So is it with our survey of life. We must view our years from the proper point of vision, or mist and doubt will deceive us.

Reviewing our life, we may look at it in varied ways; but there is only one correct standpoint from which we may do so, and unless we find it there is no explanation of the enigma of life, no vision of things in their true proportion and perspective, nothing is sharp, true, and clearly defined. The life of any man, as he looks back upon it, is perhaps the greatest puzzle which his experience can furnish. His neighbor's life is not so bewildering to him as is his own until he has the right point of vision from which to view it. Sorrows and perplexities, the dispensations of Providence, the new and subtle forms of temptation perpetually appearing, the grief, the anguish, the agony of life, who shall explain these things? What explanation can be found for the mystery of pain, the problem of suffering, and the other dark enigmas which encompass us?

If I can say a word to help some soul who, looking back upon life, finds it shrouded in mist, unshapen and unmeaning; if I can lead that man to a point of vision from which everything shall be sharp, clear, and well defined—the purpose of this sermon will have been answered. In order to do that let me at once say that I believe the one true point of vision is that given in our text: "The years of the right hand of the Most High." For elucidation of this thought we must deal with the text in its context.

This psalm, written by Asaph, is a very remarkable one, and is most clearly divided, as I think the casual observer will have noticed, by the words of my text. The first part of the psalm is of an absolutely different character from the second. When the Psalmist reaches the point where he says, "This is my infirmity; but I will remember the years of the right hand of the Most High," the picture is changed completely. The same man is looking at it, but he has suddenly found an adjustment of the lens by which everything comes into focus, and he sees things as they really are. We shall discover how this comes about if we examine the psalm more closely.

The first ten verses contain twenty-two personal references and eleven allusions to God. The personal pronoun *I* occurs ten times, *my* nine times, *me* once, *mine* twice—twenty-two personal references in all. The Divine name, or pronouns having reference to the Divine, occur eleven times, namely, *God* four times, *Jehovah* twice, *Thou* once, *He* twice, and *His* twice.

This is not an unfair analysis of the psalm. A man's true condition of heart, mind, character, and position is never revealed by the creed (written by someone else) which he recites, but by his ordinary conversation, by the unmeasured words that pass over his lips. A man's real life is not revealed in carefully prepared utterances, but in those which fall from him without his knowledge, and upon which he would have put a check if he could. Thus doth Asaph, in the depth of a grief which is both personal and relative, pour out his complaint. As I hear him I wait for the little words of the speech, disregarding for the moment the great words that tell of his agony and pain, and, lo, personal pronouns come tumbling over each other until they double in number his reference to the Divine.

While the man is in this condition I notice also some of the phrases that fall from his lips. He says, "I will cry unto God with my voice; even unto God with my voice, and He will give ear unto me." Then the first nine verses contain a story of anguish without healing. "In the day of my trouble I sought the Lord. My hand was stretched out in the night, and slacked not; my soul refused to be comforted." He sought God in some way which brought no comfort to him. "I remember God, and am disquieted." The memory of God brought him no peace. "I complain, my spirit is overwhelmed." Complaint brings no relief. "Thou holdest mine eyes watching: I am so troubled that I cannot speak." He charges even his sleeplessness upon God. "I have considered the days of old, the years of ancient times. I call to remembrance my song in the night: I commune with mine own heart; and my spirit made diligent search." Thus he goes back to past experiences; but even out of them he can get no comfort. This contemplation of his need issues in a series of questions which is almost a wail of despair. "Will the Lord cast off for ever? And will He be favourable no more? Is His mercy clean gone for ever? Doth His promise fail for evermore? Hath God forgotten to be gracious? Hath He in anger shut up His tender mercies?"

This is a picture of actual things, but it is out of focus. Asaph has not reached the true point of vision. He is trying to examine his sorrow by taking his stand in the midst of it. He is looking into the bitterness of his own heart, and from his own history he is recalling happy days, only to have the misery of present experience accentuated by the memory of past joyousness and brightness. Sorrow is overwhelming him; and he imagines, in the darkness of his present condition, that God has forgotten him. He asks in the bitterness of his spirit, "Is His mercy clean gone for ever? Doth his promise fail for evermore?"

Suddenly there is an adjustment of the lens, and how great is the difference! "I said, This is my infirmity," this condition of mind. The words, "But I will remember," do not occur in the original. The Psalmist really said, "This is my infirmity—the years of the right hand of the Most High!" He does not announce his intention to dwell upon them, but he announces the character of the years themselves. It is the suddenness of a quick appreciation of the true view of things.

Do you not know what it is suddenly to adjust a picture, by the slightest touch of the hand, so that the whole thing is seen in its true focus? Yes, you have gained the real point of view. So it is here. From the midst of a God-questioning disposition, in which hope is lost, he suddenly says, "This is my infirmity—the years of the right hand of the Most High!" *Now* what do you find? The second half of the psalm is the same picture in focus. Apply to it the same test that we used for the first half. How many personal references are found in the last half of the psalm? Three only: the pronoun *I* thrice. How many references to God? Four and twenty: *Jehovah* once, *Thy* eleven times, the word *God* five times, *Thou* four times, *Thee* twice, and *Thine* once. In the first half the Divine is acknowledged, reverenced, believed in; but the man is overwhelmed with a sense of self and of present grief. In the second half God is the supreme thought in the mind of this man, and self has dropped into insignificance. In the second half of the psalm eight is the multiple of the man's speech concerning God as compared with his words about himself.

I do not propose to enter upon a detailed comparison of the expressions in the second half with those of the first, but there is a remarkable change. In the beginning he said, "Hath God forgotten?" Now he says, "Thy way, O God, is in the sanctuary: who is a great god like unto God? Thou art the God that doest wonders: Thou hast made known Thy strength among the peoples." This is the man who a moment ago was asking if God had ceased to be gracious, and if there were no more deliverance! You cannot take these two parts of the psalm and put them side by side without noticing the marvelous difference between them. One is all darkness, the other is all light; one is blurred and indistinct, the other is clear and sharp. One is characterized by disappointment, by the experience of a man who has almost lost his hold upon God; the other is the song of a man marching with God to victory against all opposition. How comes the difference? Everything depends upon our text. Suddenly in the midst of Asaph's wailing he is reminded, as we believe by the Holy Spirit, that "this is my infirmity—the years of the right hand of the Most High." Bearing in mind the necessity for omitting the words, "I will remember," we have, as I have said, a sudden adjustment of the picture of a man's life and condition; and that adjustment is brought about by his seeing that the years are from the right hand of the Most High.

The years are not the years of God—God has no years; but they are the years of man's own life. We necessarily and rightly mark off days into weeks, weeks into months, and months into years; but when you speak of God you speak of Him who is and has no years. He teaches us this by the words of inspiration. With Him a thousand of our years are as a day; and one day with Him is, in its infinite possibility, as a thousand years. God has no time.

The Psalmist, then, is here speaking of his own years, the measured portions of his existence. He counts them as they come—one, two, three, four, and on. What are these years? They are the years of the right hand of the Most High, the years that are held within the hand of God, the years that are molded, conditioned, and made by that hand. Nothing in the years of the Psalmist's own life is outside the hand of God. That is the force of the figure, which does not appear upon a first reading or upon the reading of the text in its isolation.

The old Hebrew thought concerning the right hand of God is full of meaning. In the song of Moses at the end of his life, as chronicled in Deuteronomy 33:2, he speaks of the right hand of God, saying, "From His right hand went a fiery law for the people," showing that the Hebrew mind thought of the right hand of God as a hand of law, of arrangement. In Psalm 48:10 the right hand of God is spoken of as being full of righteousness, so that here we have not merely law, but equity, law based upon that which is just and true. In Psalm 17:7 the psalmist refers to the right hand of God as a right hand of salvation. In Psalm 20:6 the right hand of God is spoken of as His right hand of strength. In Psalm 118:16 the right hand of God is spoken of as His right hand of action. When you come to the Song of Solomon (2:6), God's right hand is spoken of as an emblem of caressing and tender love. And in Psalm 16:11 you have that magnificent declaration, "In Thy presence is fulness of joy; in Thy right hand there are pleasures for evermore."

The right hand is a symbol peculiar to Hebrew thought and literature, and is used perpetually to mark some great fact in the character and person of God. Law and righteousness, salvation and strength, action and love, and the deep, full satisfaction of every necessity of human life, in pleasures forevermore—all these things, to the mind of the Hebrew, were wrapped up in that magnificent figure of the right hand of the Most High. The years of my life, now says the Psalmist, are years conditioned in law and righteousness—years in which there is the perpetual outworking of salvation and the unceasing manifestation of strength; they are years in which God is active for me, years in which I am perpetually caressed by the love and tenderness of the Divine heart, years which, because they come from the hand of God, are years of the making of eternal and undying pleasure. It was a new light upon his own life, a new point of vision, a new outlook. From this new point of vision the things which had issued in his dirge of wailing and sorrow were suddenly seen to be working together for his good, thus giving a forecast of the New Testament statement. The man had caught a glimpse of the explanation of the mystery of to-day, a glimpse of the outworking into perfect patterns and absolute completeness of the intricacies of the present moment; he had heard his own wail ending in a song of triumph; and all this because he had discovered the fact that his years are from the right hand of the Most High.

Falling back upon our previous statement, that the first half of the psalm and the second are different, and that the difference is wrought by a new vision of life, may we not ask, Wherein does the difference consist?

First of all, self-consciousness is overwhelmed in the sense of God; again, personal suffering is forgotten in view of the divine achievements; and, yet once again, personality is lost in the sense of a God-redeemed society.

Self-consciousness is overwhelmed in a sense of God. One of the most tender, comforting, compassionate methods of God is that which I venture to say you and I never make use of for the comfort of a single broken heart, namely, the exhibition by God of His own overwhelming power and majesty. Again and again is this the way by which God comes with tenderest touch of healing upon broken and bruised hearts. When Job was at the utmost extremity of his pain and desolation God came to him with no word such as I would have attempted to give him, with no word which appeared to have in it the element of explanation or soothing. God came with a display of His own glory. He made His might and majesty to pass before the astonished gaze of the man who sat in the dust; and in that might and majesty of the Most High was the healing which Job so sorely needed. So here Asaph finds his healing and the forgetfulness of himself in a vision of the majesty of God.

Notice the marvelous figurative splendor of the description of the movements of God which you have in the closing verses of the psalm: thunder and lightning, the waters pained, as the Hebrew word expresses it, smitten into agony by the presence of God. This is a graphic picture of the deliverance of Israel from Egypt's bondage and from the waters of the Red Sea. It is the movement of God, the majesty of His march, the magnificence of His power; and as the wounded, broken spirit of Asaph comes face to face with that revelation of power his wounds are forgotten, his sorrow passes away, he is caught up into the excellent and healing glory of the majesty of the great King, and self-consciousness is overwhelmed in a sense of God. If *we* may but get this vision of the years that have passed from us there will be healing for wounds and solace for sorrow in the forgetfulness of self because of an enlarged conception of the majesty of the Most High.

The mightiest influences of God are the most gentle in their touch, and the forces which are most full of majesty and power are the forces that come into contact with wounds and pain in order to heal them. In your knowledge and in mine there is nothing mightier than the sun. The old poetry we learned at school, so simple and quaint, told how the wind and the sun fought for mastery over man. That story of the sun gaining a victory which the wind could not gain has its perpetual philosophy and its undying meaning for the sons of men. The sun, presently smiting the earth upon which the rain and the snow have fallen, will be answered by the hoarded wealth which shall prove that same sun to be the most wondrous of natural forces. Into its light you bring the crushed and faded child which is being nursed back to life, and the kiss of the great sun upon the cheek of the little one makes it also blossom and bloom with beauty. Wounded men and women should not dwell upon their wounds and try to heal them, but should carry them into the sunlight of the majesty of God. They should say of the broken years, the years which are full of pain, the strange, mysterious years. These are the years of the Most High, and upon them shall come the healing of God's uprising in glory.

Notice also how personality is lost in the sense of a God-redeemed society. How different is the last verse of this psalm from the first! The first verse, what is it? "I will cry unto God with my voice; even unto God with my voice, and He will give ear unto me." It is a personal cry. The last verse, what is it? "Thou leddest Thy people like a flock by the hand of Moses and Aaron." To quote once more from the book of Job, "The Lord turned the captivity of Job when he prayed for his friends." How many an individual wound has been healed in this larger outlook upon life, which can come only as we learn that our years are the years of the right hand of the Most High! We look back upon a year that is past, and what is the picture? I cannot answer for you, nor can you do so for me. Shall we not, each for himself and for herself, think of it?

Are there not moments when, looking back upon the year and thinking of your own part in it, you are almost driven to cry out, "Will the Lord cast off for ever? And will He be favourable no more? Is His mercy clean gone for ever? Doth His promise fail for evermore? Hath God forgotten to be gracious? Hath He, in anger, shut up His tender mercies?" How many are saying these things in their hearts, if not with their lips! It is a source of great joy and comfort to know that if we feel these things we need not try to hide them from God. There are expressions with regard to your life which would appear almost blasphemous in the ears of your fellow Christian, but God understands them. I would not say a word to rebuke the anguish and grief that are swelling up in these verses. I dare not. I have no rebuke for such a man or woman, for the soul that has confessed to some awful anguish from which it cannot get away, and is asking, "Has God forgotten?" We must remember that the words of the Psalmist are questions, not affirmations. These words are the cry of a wounded, buffeted, and broken spirit, almost driven to despair by the perplexing facts and forces of life.

But there is something better than this, something beyond it. "The years of the right hand of the Most High." There is a point of vision from which we may look upon the selfsame things, and may catch on them already the light and gleam of morning, an overwhelming sorrow, saying, Yes, that happened, not upon such a day of such a month in such a year, but in one of the years of the right hand of the Most High. It was a part of the fiery law, a method of the divine righteousness, a ministry of the divine love; it had within it the creation of joy forevermore. To-day we can say these things only by faith, not yet by sight, not yet by personal realization, but by faith. There is no agony of heart that we endure, if we know how to take it, that has not in it the element that shall make heaven.

"The years of the right hand of the Most High." I do not see the hand, I have only the years; but I know the hand is there. I know that somewhere beyond this, when the mists have rolled aside, and the life I am conscious of to-day shall have passed into fuller realization, then out of the darkness will the light come, and out of the agony of the moment will heaven's pleasure have been evolved. I hardly like to suggest how this comes about; but some of us are already doing so:

> Ah, then what raptured greetings
>   On Canaan's happy shore!
> What knitting severed friendships up,
>   Where partings are no more!

There is a sense in which, to-day I begin to spell this out, lisping the truth with stammering tongue.

This is but an illustration, but follow me patiently. The year 1894 was a year of His right hand, and there will be more than compensation in the morning of meeting for all the agony of waiting, for I shall see her again, not as a child, but as a fair maiden, in the Father's mansion, grown like Him; and in that transformation there will be all the sweetness which I have lost and missed through the years. The year 1907 was a year of His right hand. I shall see him again, and then the touch of old age will not be upon the brow, but the abiding strength of the age-abiding life. I can only believe it now; but I do believe it. All the years are "the years of the right hand of the Most High." Accidents? There are none. Catastrophes? The word is canceled in the vocabulary of faith. God's covenant is "ordered in all things, and sure." Oh, strange covenant: perplexing mystery of infinite love wrought out through the more perplexing mystery of pain.

May God teach us His lesson of being still and waiting amid the sorrow. All your affliction, all your sorrow, all your disappointment, in God's hand. Oh, the light of it, the glory of it! We do believe; God help our unbelief, teaching us to wait quietly amid the stress and strain of the darkness.

> I cannot see His skies, above,
>   For autumn mists obscure the west;
> But in the shelter of His love,
>   I fain would hush my heart to rest;
> Though some bright hopes have tenderly
>   Been gathered to their last repose,
> This sweet remembrance comforts me—
>   He knows.

For why the summer came—and went,
   He shows not yet to me, His child;
But patience, richer than content,
   Broods softly where the summer smiled;
And where the last bright leaf shall fall,
   The last pale blossom find repose,
Is safe with Him Who loveth all—
              He knows.

Amid the hush of finished things
   He hears His children's feeblest prayer,
The tender shadowing of His wings
   Extends beyond their utmost care;
And loss that ne'er on earth grows less,
   With deep and holy meaning glows,
Since loss, and pain, and homelessness—
              He knows.

I cannot tell if cross or crown
   Lies next within His thought for me;
It matters not, since faith hath grown
   So strong in His dear sympathy;
The clouds that o'er my pathway move,
   The joys beyond its final close,
All rise from His deep heart of love—
              He knows.

So farewell 1907, and let this 1908 bring with it what it may, two years among the many, which with all the rest are "the years of the right hand of the Most High."

CHAPTER II

SECRET AND REVEALED THINGS

The secret things belong unto the Lord our God; but the things that are revealed belong unto us and to our children for ever, that we may do all the words of this law.
DEUTERONOMY 29:29.

THESE WORDS CONTAIN ONE OF THE MOST IMPORTANT PRINciples for the conditioning of all life, and one which constitutes a final anchorage for faith in the midst of perplexities and problems and difficulties which constantly confront the children of faith.

Man naturally resents the unknowable, and one of the chief characteristics of human history has been that of man's determination to unlock mystery, and fathom secrets. This is not wrong. It is right. I do not use the word "natural" in the sense in which we so often use it theologically, as describing the condition of fallen nature, but as proper to essential human nature. Quite apart from the fact of sin, it is a part of human nature as God created it that man everywhere rebels against mystery, and from childhood to the grave in every successive century sets himself to the business of attempting to unlock closed doors and to fathom hidden things. As soon as your child has begun to speak so that anyone can understand, he is making use of these words, I venture to say, almost more often than any other: Why? How? What? In the economy of God every child comes into the world a note of perpetual interrogation. Fathers and mothers, I charge you most solemnly never say to your child, "Don't bother me." You are there to be bothered, and the whole system of Divine education is based upon the curiosity of a little child and answering its questions. I must not follow that line, interesting as it is. But it serves as an illustration at this point. The child is knocking at the closed door, is attempting to fathom the secret. Curiosity is part and parcel of human nature, and apart from it the world would have made no discoveries, would have made no advancement. It is a natural principle in all human nature, and is God-implanted.

This rebellion against the unknowable on the part of man being, within certain bounds, perfectly correct, a part of a Divine purpose, where are the bounds and the limitations to be set? The bounds and the limits are fixed by man's ability to unlock doors and fathom secrets. Anything that a man can discover he has a right to discover, and everything that man discovers is in the last analysis God's revelation to him as he persistently knocks and seeks and works. Every human discovery is a Divine revelation also. When men discovered the uses of electricity they did not create electricity; at the fit time in human history God answered their persistent and patient search by revealing the great secret. The limits are set at the point where man can go no farther, and there are such limits. Every man who has given himself to thought and investigation along any line possible to the human mind has discovered a point of limitation.

A mistake man has made too often, and too constantly, and is making still, when he reaches the limit, is that of rebelling against the mystery that lies beyond it; or the more vital and deadly mistake of denying that there is anything beyond that which he is able to investigate and discover. It is against that twofold danger of man, in his asking of questions and making investigation, that man needs to guard. The words of this wonderful declaration of the Old Testament are fundamental and all-comprehensive. "The secret things belong unto the Lord our God, but the things that are revealed belong unto us and to our children for ever, that we may do all the words of this law." Shall we first of all, then, examine the principle as declared, and, in the second place, make some illustrative application thereof which I trust and pray may be for the strengthening of our faith. Take out the two descriptive phrases of the text and look at them carefully, "The secret things," "The things that are revealed." They are not named in the order of our consciousness. We begin with the revealed thing, and discover that there lies behind it the secret thing. The writer here is beginning from the origin, from the cause, and working out to the effect. "The secret thing," "The revealed thing." For the purposes of following his argument we will reverse the order of consideration, and dwell first upon that which is second but which is first in our consciousness, "revealed things."

The Hebrew word here literally translated means *things that are denuded*, things that are made visible, things that can be seen, things that can be touched and felt, and appreciated by the senses, denuded things. If you keep that in mind for a moment you will see its bearing on that which follows.

Now I need not stay to argue that there are material things, which are obvious. There are mental things we are equally sure of. Poetry, music, philosophy are such. Moral things also we know perfectly well. There are revealed things in the moral and mental and material realms.

Then "secret things." That phrase is exactly the opposite of the other. These words might be translated clothed things, hidden things, things which are, but before which a covering is, so that we cannot see them, or touch them, or handle them, or weigh them. There is no doubt of their existence; but they are hidden. They exist, using the word in its deepest sense, but they are hidden, secret things.

Now let us take the declaration in the order in which it is made here. "The secret things belong unto the Lord our God." The thing secret to you is not secret to God. The thing that is so clothed that I cannot see it is "naked and open to the eyes of Him with Whom we have to do." The revealed thing in the mental realm is the poem or the song, the philosophy or the book. The hidden thing is the process of thought that produces it. I have the poem, the song, the book; but listen to the old Psalmist, "Thou understandest my thought afar off," which does not mean that God is far away and understands my thought at that distant place. God is not far away; for "in Him we live and move and have our being." I cannot lift my hand save in God's energy. I may prostitute God's energy to sin; but I am atmosphered, homed, centred in God, and I cannot escape from Him. What, then, does the Psalmist mean? "Thou understandest my thought afar off," before it is a thought formed in my mind or expressed in my words. Before it becomes a poem or a philosophy, "Thou understandest my thought afar off." He knows the mystery of its genesis and watches the process of its exodus. Thou understandest thought in the making. The revealed thing is the book, the poem, the song. The hidden thing is the working of the mystery of the mind. The book, the poem, the song are mine. The mystery of the mental working is God's. The secret things are known to God. That is the fundamental rock. What an anchorage for faith when you and I once fasten on it for life! The problem that confronts me, and baffles me, does not baffle Him. The mystery that I am attempting to solve, and cannot yet, He knows. The secret things belong unto Him. This confidence keeps the heart firm and steady in the midst of tumult. Some of our fathers used to sing a hymn. One line comes to me,

> Calm on tumult's wheel I sit.

The man who wrote that believed in God. Nobody else could write a line like that. The man who sits calm on tumult's wheel is the man who has the consciousness that over the tumult, around the tumult, knowing it, is the God of infinite peace. "The secret things belong unto the Lord our God."

But now, I pray you, take the next declaration in order: "The revealed things belong unto us." The revealed things and the secret things are closely united. Every revealed thing is united to some secret thing that is hidden. The revealed things are one with secret and hidden forces, and the revealed things express so much of the hidden forces as we are able to know at the time. You may lay your hand where you will upon the commonplaces of life, and I tell you the commonplace thing you touch and see is but the outward and sacramental seal of something that will never be commonplace which you cannot touch and see. Christian Scientists are telling us that there is no matter: that everything is mind, that matter is but *an expression of mind*. And there is an element of truth in it. The absurdity of it I need not argue before an intelligent audience. Christian Science takes hold only where people have nothing else to do. It does not appeal to the average hard-headed Englishman. He has no room for it. Christian Science is characterized by ignorance of science and deficiency of Christianity; but it has elements of truth as has every heresy. When a Christian Scientist tells me that matter is not, it is all mind, what I say to him is this: No, this book is real matter, so are the signs of the music and the letters of the songs, but there is mind behind. This is dust and ashes until mind collects it, and binds, and prints upon it the music. Here is a revealed thing, and a secret thing, and every revealed thing is united to a secret thing. The greater is not the revealed thing but the secret thing that lies behind it.

Have you ever noticed that in our Lord's teaching He made use of figures and symbols, but never hinted that the figure was the fact. He always gives us to understand that, after all, the things seen are only symbols of something else. Let me give you an illustration. He says, "I am the true Vine." Now, we make a mistake if we say that Jesus borrowed the figure of the vine to teach us what He is. The deeper truth is this. God planted the vine in the world and let it grow through the centuries on the pattern of the infinite Christ. Man says, God has taken hold of my name, Father; He has borrowed the human name of Father in order that I may learn how loving He is. Nothing of the kind. God has lent you His name of Father that you may know how loving you ought to be. Do not let us begin at the wrong end of things. Do not let us treat these things as though when we say bread we had said the real thing. Jesus said, "Bread that perisheth; I am the Bread of life." Every loaf of bread is a sacramental symbol. Learn this great truth, and every trailing vine of glory and beauty of vintage is an unveiling of the Son of God and His Church. You tell me the Cross is wooden. I tell you it is spiritual. You bring me to a Roman gibbet, and some of you have the rough, bloody, brutal Cross made out of gold to wear as an ornament—from which thing may God deliver us everywhere

—and you say, This is the Cross of Salvation. No, no; it is not that. What is it? Sin lying across *the heart of God* and wounding Him. That is the Cross. The revealed Roman gibbet of nineteen hundred years ago is something more than men see and understand. Back of it is the secret thing, the infinite and unfathomable mystery. So that, according to this text, all revealed things are united to secret things, and every blade of grass is child of the infinite, and every painted flower by Divinity's fingers is the blossoming out of the essential beauty of God. Revealed things, secret things! The revealed things are ours. What for? To make us possessors of the secret things, to bring us into living touch with the secret things, with the God to whom the secret things belong.

Such is the principle declared. But there is a purpose in all this. What is the purpose? "That we may do all the words of this law." Leaving the local coloring and setting, and taking the principal thought, you find this great truth enunciated, that everything revealed is, if the man will think deeply enough and consider carefully enough, a revelation of law; and the moment a man discovers the law in the revealed thing, and obeys it, he touches and enters into communion with the secret thing behind it. How better can I illustrate at this point than by referring again to that to which I have already referred? Electricity. How is this building lighted to-night? We say by electric light. But how did we get it? It has been developed. But do you know how you developed it? Are you quite sure that in ten years electricians will not laugh at the word developed? That is only a passing word; but it shows us our ignorance. But what do we know? There were revealed things to men who were watching, results accidentally at first, flashing out upon the imagination of the watcher. What did the watcher do? He set himself to discover the law that operated behind the revelation, discovering and obeying which, he found himself in the midst of forces of which man had never dreamed. If I were to say casually to a boy, as though I were trying to catch him, "My boy, tell me, where is there more electricity, in London or in the heart of Africa?" he might be inclined to say, "Oh, in London." But it is not so, and you know it is not so. There is no more electricity here in London than there is in the heart of Africa; but here in London we light our buildings, drive our machinery, flash our messages. In Africa they do none of these things. Why not? Here we have discovered the law, and, obeying it, harness the force, though we cannot understand it. In Africa they have never discovered the law, and the force wraps them about, and they make no use of it. The revealed thing has a law. Obey the law of the revealed thing, and immediately you touch the infinite force behind it.

That is the philosophy of prayer. You tell me to-day that I cannot pray, that God is too much a slave of the universe He made, that He cannot hear me. God is revealing Himself in bird, in storm, in sky, in man, and in movements. Watch, and you will discover a law in everything. Obey it, and you will come immediately into touch with the Infinite Force behind, and you will work miracles; not the miracle of the juggler who amuses a crowd. You must discover the law in the revealed thing; obey it, and you can harness the forces that are infinite to the chariot wheels of your own progress.

Now let us pass to some illustrative applications, beginning among the minor matters and proceeding to the highest. I will begin with the flowers. I take a flower in my hand, and I look at it. There are revealed things. What are they? Form, and color, and fragrance. Are there no secret things here? I need not argue. No scientist, and no botanist, nor any of us has ever yet been able to tell me why the petals of yon chrysanthemum are of that particular tint, or by what strange alchemy things there yellow are here red; why the carbon is but jellyfish there and diamond yonder. Did you think of leaving the Church because of mystery? There is as much mystery in that hymn-book as in all theology, and you had better find your way out of the world as quickly as possible, and even then you will find yourself in the home of mystery. Secret things in the flower! It is impossible to take the illustration without recalling that exquisite little fragment of Tennyson's:

> Flower in the crannied wall,
> I pluck you out of the crannies;
> I hold you here, root and all, in my hand,
> Little flower—but if I could understand
>   What you are, root and all, and all in all,
>   I should know what God and man is.

That is poetic and beautiful in the language of the dead century; but the great flaming principle Moses wrote long before Tennyson wrote it. How did he write it? "The secret things belong unto the Lord our God, the revealed things are for us and our children." Discover the law that lies within the flower, and obey it, and what will happen? The secret will reach you through your obedience, and you will be able presently to work with God in making the old-fashioned garden chrysanthemum into the gorgeous beauty of the flower of to-day. A secret thing, a revelation of a law; a man obeys it, and he is a fellow worker with God in the cultivation of flowers.

Let me move to another realm, and here borrow the words of my Lord Himself in another connection. "The wind bloweth," the revealed thing. "Thou hearest the sound," the revealed thing. The revealed thing in the wind belongs to me. What is it? Sound, strength. The secret thing belongs to God. What is it? "Whence, whither?" Find the law that lies within the wind. What then? Then, that law discovered and obeyed, the wind becomes the messenger of health and of motion; and men will now draw you charts and maps showing you the directions and currents, which are all true; but never forget this, that God still holds in love and wisdom the hidden secret of the wind.

The mind of man. What do you know about the mind of man? Capacity, the necessity for training, the great possibilities of mind when properly trained. What do we not know about the mind? Now hear me and be patient if you do not agree with me. We do not know its nature. We do not know its seat. The whole trend of scientific investigation is along that line at this moment. The age of the physical scientist has given way to the age of the psychological scientist, and as yet they have told us nothing about the seat of the mind. You tell me about brain cells and gray matter. Perhaps! Do you think I am very ignorant? It is because I am not sure. I am a great agnostic in some things. Even if you speak of gray matter and brain cells you do not really think that is all there is of mind. I know men who still have brain cells but no mind! I am still inclined to believe that mind continues when brain cells become dust and ashes. The brain cells may be a medium for today, but there is nothing final about them. Let us say we do not know. Let us say the secret things belong to God. Yet discover the law in the revealed thing, and obey it, and you are coming near to the secret thing. And I for one welcome the psychological movement. It is infinitely broader and sweeter and healthier than the dust of thirty years ago; and men obeying law are emerging into new light.

And now, very reverently let me lift this to the highest plane of all. The Christ Himself. Revealed things. Yes. The historic Person, the Actual Presence in every successive century. Do you question it? I cannot stay to argue it; but I do say that it admits of no questioning. I say to you that the direct presence of Jesus of Nazareth in the world is established without possibility of doubt; and even those questioning the accuracy of our New Testament records at least have to make acknowledgment that there has been a Man named Jesus Who did some things, and said some things which affect this hour. That is all I want. That is the fact. No brilliant Frenchman, or lucid German, or hard-thinking Englishman, has been able to take from us the fact of the historicity of Christ. That is the smallest revealed thing. What is the greater revealed thing? The living Christ, the living message through the centuries, the living Christ in England, doing what none other can do, accomplishing what no philosophy was ever able to do, and no system of education can do. The living Christ, Who passes into the slum, and takes hold of your unfit man, and makes him fit. And while you deny His existence, I show you His miracles; and if you are as honest as the Sadducees you will hold your peace. The revealed things. Thank God I am not speaking of a dead and worn-out Christ. Men and women here who a month ago had not seen the vision have seen it. Men and women who a month ago were in the grip of sin have on their faces to-night the very radiance of heaven's own light and the reflection of the Christ beauty. Revealed things. But there are secret things. What are they? These are some: the method of Incarnation, the mystery of Atonement, the method of Resurrection. Doubt, and doubt very earnestly, any man who tells you these things are not secret things, any man who attempts to formulate, or tabulate, who attempts to tell you of the humanity and Deity of Christ where the one ends and the other begins. He was very God and very Man. Very Man, weeping, tired, weary, tempted. Very God, hushing tempests, casting demons out, healing disease, remaking moral failures. Do I understand Him? I do not. I worship Him, and I say in His presence, "My Lord, and my God." I cannot touch the secret things of the infinite Christ save through the revealed things; but if I will obey the law revealed in Christ I shall come into living touch with the infinite mysteries that lie behind, and Incarnation will bring me into relationship with God; and Atonement will cancel my sin and break its power, and Resurrection will be to me the new enablement for which my weary soul has waited.

And reverently, from this great height, let us descend the mountain again, and let me say to you that God's government of human affairs also has within it these two elements. What are the revealed things? The fact that God is governing. Do we ever see this quite clearly at the moment? I am not sure; I think some do, but I think it is always by faith granted to us. Look back over human history, and if you and I are wise, in the day of densest darkness in history, we shall see God is on the field when He is most invisible. Illustrations crowd upon me. Look out for yourselves at the coincidence of the invention of the printing machine and the Reformation of religion. But you say, Where is God now? God is governing, and the secret things in His government belong to Him.

Let me get from these wide reaches of vision, and take my own life. How do I know God is governing in my life? I look back—and my friends will forgive me—I am not looking back as far as some of you; but I look back and I pick out things to-night, things I cannot speak of, days of my life, dark days; for, as God is my witness, He has given me my share of sorrow's sacrament, days of awful heartbreak, when all the lights along the shore seemed to go out. I would not undo one such day for worlds. I have come at last to see the meaning of them. There seems to be a jumble, when a man is laying the pavement with little bits of blue, and gray, and black, and sand and mortar. But when the building is finished, behold the mosaic. There would have been no mosaic if there had been no apparent jumble in the construction. Already some of the mosaic is shining out for me, and when I have done and passed home, then I shall sing of all the pathway.

Right was the pathway leading to this.
Though it was through blood and tears and suffering.

And so I might go on. Is your experience just now one of sorrow? I am talking to some sorrowing heart, some broken heart. Let me leave everybody else, and talk to you. Is the day very dark, and the way very rough? I cannot understand it. Secret things belong to God. Discover the law that lies within the revealed thing; if it be pain it will be the law of lying plastic even though the hand of the Potter press to pain the clay; and presently out of the process and the ordeal shall come the vessel finished to His glory—a thing of use to God, and of beauty for the infinite ages. May God help us if we forget all the attempts to illustrate, to fasten our faith upon, the great declaration, The secret things are God's as the revealed things are ours.

CHAPTER III

SUBMISSION AND RESPONSIBILITY

I also am a man under authority, having under myself soldiers: and I say to this one, Go, *and he goeth; and to another,* Come, *and he cometh.*

MATTHEW 8:9.

ALL THE SCENES OF NEW TESTAMENT HISTORY LIE IN THE atmosphere of Roman government. Its earliest stories are connected with the decree that went forth from Cæsar Augustus that the world should be taxed. The last definitely historical picture that it presents is that of a notable prisoner, at large in his own house in the imperial city. As we read we grow familiar with Roman armies, with cohorts, legions, and bands; with captains, centurions, and soldiers. We meet with seven centurions. The first one appears in the passage from which my text is taken. He came to Jesus about his servant who was sick; the next one we see at the close of the Gospel narrative, in charge of the crucifixion of Christ; then in the book of Acts we find Cornelius, a devout man, the first Gentile believer to be baptized by the Hebrew apostle; then a centurion placing bonds upon Paul, and, as Paul objects, immediately seeking the advice of his superior officer; then two centurions taking Paul to Felix and protecting him from the threatened hostility of the crowd; then one who took charge of Paul and gave him great indulgence by the direction of Felix; until we come to the last, Julius, who was Paul's custodian on his voyage, and who became interested in Paul, so much so that he saved him from death at the hands of the soldiers in the hour of threatened shipwreck. In all these centurions there is something to admire; in some of them much to admire; and in one of them at least everything to admire. The three first mentioned stand out upon the page of the New Testament, and are remarkable in many ways. This one came to seek the aid of Christ for his slave, and uttered the remarkable words of my text. At the crucifixion another centurion watched the dying of the Man of Nazareth, and so keen and accurate was his observation that he said, "Truly this was the Son of God." Of Cornelius the highest things are written.

How is this excellence to be accounted for? If I were to declare that the military system accounted for it, I am inclined at once to say that would be too broad a statement, yet there is a sense in which it is true. I want to discover that sense, and to make it the method of my appeal to the young manhood of this congregation, to whom this message is to be particularly delivered. The end of the life of the soldier is not in view. I am not dealing with that. Whether that end be war, or whether it be that for which war is waged, I am not discussing that question at all at the present moment. It may be that if I were I should arouse the hostility of some of you, or, rather, I should not find you in perfect agreement with my own standpoint. I think there is a wonderful amount of insight in words which occur in *The Comments of Bagshot*, "There is no peace at any price party. There are only various parties which disapprove of each other's wars." I was recently reminded that so eminent a theologian as the late Dr. Dale once said, "I am for peace at any price, even at the price of war if necessary." I am not discussing that. I am attempting to bring you to a consideration, not of the end of the soldier's life, whether that end be war, or the reason for which war is waged; but of the method of the soldier's life. In understanding that method we shall discover why it is that these men of the old Roman armies had an excellence that attracts us.

That method is declared clearly and simply and inclusively in the words that the centurion uttered to Jesus, "I also am a man under authority, having under myself soldiers." That is a philosophy of life. I wonder if he had ever said that before. I think not. I am inclined to think that it was a sudden expression of a subconscious philosophy. Remember, while he spoke in the first person singular, and while the philosophy was stated in the terms of experience and not in the terms of theory, this declaration was drawn from him by what he saw in Jesus. With an accuracy that should make us very thankful, the revisers have restored to the text a little word omitted in the Authorized Version, "also." You can drop the word "also" and you still have the philosophy, you still have the experience. "I am a man under authority, having under myself soldiers." That is my whole text, and yet it is not my whole text. It is the "also" that attracted me to the text. It is the supreme word. The centurion implied that Christ was a Man under authority and that He had those under Him. He looked at Christ and he saw in Him the fulfilment of the highest ideal of life as He knew it, and so Christ compelled from him the confession of the level upon which he was living his own life, the confession which revealed the philosophy of his life, which I think he had never formulated before.

I shall ask you, first of all, to consider this philosophy of life, "I am a man under authority," that is submission: "having under myself soldiers"; that is responsibility. I am a man under authority: I have soldiers under me. I know how to bend the knee to a throne: I am able to exercise the power of a throne. I have kissed a scepter: I sway a scepter. I am responsible to a throne: I therefore am able to be responsible for those who are beneath me. I am a man under authority, submission. I have soldiers under me, responsibility. That is the highest philosophy of life that can be stated for a young man.

Let us attempt to see a little more clearly what it really means. So far, then, as the method of the life of the centurion is concerned, I borrow the career of such a one as the ideal for young men. First consider the view of life suggested, and then see how the Christian life realizes that ideal at its highest and best.

What is this view of life suggested? This man first said, "I am a man under authority." To illuminate this I will take three simple prepositions: "to," "of," "for." "I am . . . under authority." That is submission *to*, submission *of*, and submission *for*.

Submission *to*. The Roman soldier was submitted to the cause of the Roman Empire, but for the Roman soldier the cause of the Roman Empire was personified in the emperor. The Roman soldier was under authority, and so was submitted to a cause personified in a person. You need not stay with the Roman soldier. It is true all through the ages. For king and country is the motto of the soldier to-day. The king is the personification to the soldier of the larger purpose and issue. The soldier is submitted to the cause of his country as it is personified for him in the king.

Submission *of*. The submission means submission of the central will. Upon enlisting in the army of the emperor the Roman soldier surrendered his will, his property, his relations. From the moment when he enlisted he had no will of his own, no possession of his own, no property of any kind. He could not hold property. Neither could he speak of his relations as any longer being his. He gave up everything. The soldier submitted to a central authority has submitted his will and everything else. His time, his habit of dress, his choice of foods, and all his ability are handed over.

Submission *for*. The Roman soldier was submitted for fitting himself for his work. That meant drill. He was submitted also for his work. That meant war.

The centurion was submitted *to* the service of his country personified in a sovereign; he had made submission *of* his will and of all he had: he had submitted *for* the purpose of his own perfecting, *for* the accomplishment of the work to which he was called.

Turn to the other side of this: responsibility, "having under myself soldiers." I want you very patiently to follow me as I say that the responsibility of the centurion was connected intimately with his submission. He was responsible for the soldiers under him, to the state to which he himself was submitted. He must identify himself with them. He must exert an influence upon them. He must insist upon certain things in their lives. All this for the sake of the state. The state looked to him, held him responsible, for all those who were placed under him, that he should recommend it, utter its requirements, and insist upon the realization of its purpose. So there was the most intimate connection between the soldier's submission and his responsibility. "I also am a man under authority, having under myself soldiers." The first was an upward look to the throne to which he bent; the second was a downward look to the territory over which he reigned. The upward look was in order that he might realize the territory over which he reigned. The downward look was in order that he might satisfy the throne under which he served. In order that we may understand this great philosophy of life, I am more anxious that we should realize the connection between these two things than that we should see either in isolation. This is not a picture of the two sides of a man's nature, the one side subservient to authority, and the other getting satisfaction out of the fact that he was able to make others bend the knee to him. Here is a man who says, For seven years I have been serving a master, now it is my turn. I am going to make someone else serve me! Or here is a man who says, In a certain department of my life I have obeyed; now I am going to compensate myself for the irksomeness of that by making someone else obey me. That is not the picture presented by these words. Let us be careful to draw the distinction. The unifying conception of life to the centurion was the Roman Empire. He said, I am under the empire and of the empire. I submit to its authority and I represent its authority. I look up to a throne in order that I may represent the will of the throne to those over whom I reign. I look down upon the territory over which I reign in order that I may realize in it the will and purpose of the throne to which I am submitted. This is a perfect harmony and interrelationship. There can be no right and perfect government of the territory over which I reign, save as I am in right relationship to the throne over me. The reason why I should perfectly submit to the throne over me is that I may exert its influence among those who are placed under me. I am under authority, submission; I have soldiers under me, responsibility. The responsibility of reigning is intimately connected with submission.

That is a revelation of perfect life. Before I turn to

show that the Christian ideal realizes that, do you see the importance of it? Let me get my sermon out of shape and take the application now. To what throne is your life submitted? What territory are you reigning over? Have you found a throne to which you bend the knee? Have you found a kingdom over which you reign? That is the meaning of human life. Every man is intended to reign, but before a man can reign he must submit. Every man here has found a throne. Every man has found a territory over which he is reigning. You cannot escape it. These are the deep things of human nature which no man can elude. The trouble is that men submit to the wrong throne, and therefore their reign is that of despotism, destruction, death. The influence you are exerting within the circle of your own manhood, the circle of your friends, in your home, your city, is an influence created by your relation to a throne. If the throne before which you bow is the throne of the world, or the throne of the flesh, or the throne of the devil—and these are not separate thrones, that is the trinity of evil—if you bow before that throne, you are still reigning, but it is a reign of devastation, a reign of death. You cannot escape submission to a throne. You cannot escape the exercise of influence, of power. Whether the power be constructive or destructive, for life or death, for lifting or flinging down, depends upon the throne to which you bow the knee. Every man can say, "I also am a man under authority, having under myself soldiers." I am not here to press young men to go forth and find a kingdom. I am here to press them to see to it that they find the right authority, and are exercising the right influence in the place where they reign.

That leads me to the second point. The Christian revelation most perfectly realizes this ideal of life. That ideal was perfectly presented as a pattern in Christ. That is what this man meant, though I do not imagine, or suggest, that he perfectly understood it. Thou art a Man under authority, and Thou hast soldiers under Thee. That is the story of Christ's life. Jesus of Nazareth might have said with perfect accuracy and with far fuller, richer, more spacious meaning than did the centurion, "I am a Man under authority, having under Myself soldiers." Jesus Christ was under authority. He was under authority to the state, the great universal empire of God, which He expressed in that term which we are still using and are only beginning to understand the meaning of, "The Kingdom of God"; and that for Him was personified in God Himself, Who was King, Ruler, Sovereign over the whole empire. He was a Man under authority. "I do nothing of Myself . . . I do always the things that are pleasing to Him." "My meat is to do the will of Him that sent Me, and to accomplish His work." It was a life under perfect and absolute authority. It was a life of perfect and absolute submission. It was a life, therefore, responsible, "having under Myself soldiers," all the forces of the Kingdom of God over which He was appointed to reign. He was under authority and exercised authority. The authority He exercised over the things under Him was the authority to which He submitted, as He yielded Himself wholly to the will of God. The authority of life, light, love, the authority of pure, high, noble ideals; to these things He yielded Himself, for they were in the will of God. These are the very elements of the empire of God. Wherever He exercised His authority it was toward the realization of these things in human life.

Christ did not merely reveal to us the fulness of this ideal as a pattern; He came to call us into submission to it, and to communicate to us the power that would enable us to fulfill that in our life which is essential to it on the highest level and in all fulness and breadth.

To what, then, does Christianity call every young man? To submission and responsibility! Submission to what? To the Kingdom of God personified in Christ as King. I call you in the name of this Christ to submission to the Kingdom of God. I pause because I am so conscious that the familiarity of these terms robs them of their spaciousness and grandeur and beauty. Young men are constantly telling me they are looking for a career. Here is an all-inclusive one, passion for the Kingdom of God. All honor to the soldier who really and truly and deeply loves his country. I ask you to make the master passion of your life not this country of Britain, but the Kingdom of God. If the idea be too spacious, too gracious, as indeed it is, then focus it, localize it, personify it, only remember when you have personified it that that to which you come, or He to Whom you come, does stand for the larger purpose, the Kingdom of God. We call you for this purpose to the Christ, for submission to Him is submission to the Kingdom of God. Come, not merely that you may kiss a scepter and be under a King, but that you may make the Kingdom of God the goal of your endeavor, the passion of your life, that to which you devote all your energies. Here is the true throne. Here is the true state. Here is the true empire to which men should give themselves. The man who can go forth from this chapel saying, I am a man under authority to God's King, and God's Kingdom, is fulfilling the essential necessity of his life on the highest level and in the fullest, best sphere.

Remember that if submission means submission to the Kingdom of God it means submission of the will, and as the Roman centurion in the olden days, having handed over his will and choice, ceased to have property, or time, or relations of his own, so must the soldier who submits to the Christ. If you say I am carrying my figure too far, listen to the King Himself. "If any man would come after Me, let him deny himself, and take up his cross, and follow Me." "If any man cometh unto Me, and hateth not his own father, and mother, and wife, and children, and brethren, and sisters, yea, and his own life also, he cannot be my disciple." This does not mean that the man giving himself to the Christ is to have no love for father, mother, wife, child, brother, sister; but that forever, in every hour of crisis, in every commonplace, in all circumstances, if there should arise conflict between the interest of Christ and that of father, mother, wife, child, brother, sister, Christ must have the pre-eminence, and the Kingdom of God must be first. So that "he that loveth father or mother more than Me is not worthy of Me" is the awful and yet necessary word of the King as men come into contact with Him and desire to submit themselves to Him. Sometimes I think that we lose something of power and force by stating the case in all its widest reaches and its most spacious applications. It means that the soldier is to have no habit unremitted to Christ for approval or disapproval, no hour of his time which he calls his own, no interest in life which is to him vacation from vocation, no single detail of life over which Christ is not supreme, which does not enter into the supreme master passion of bringing in the Kingdom of God. That is the life of the Christian. I know there are a great many people who call themselves Christians who have never come within a million miles of realizing this. Are they Christians? I suggest the question and leave them to their own conscience and the clear teaching of Christ for decision. "Under authority." You have played at life long enough. Begin to live by giving yourself in tremendous submission to this King.

When you have done that, what then? Begin to reign in power. Begin to realize your kingdom. Where shall I begin? says some young man. Give me my work. I give it to you now. "He that ruleth his spirit is better than he that taketh a city." That is in Proverbs. I am not going to preach from that text apart from the New Testament. I long ago gave up preaching the doctrine of self-control. I never say to a man, Control yourself. "The fruit of the Spirit is . . . self-control." You begin to control yourself only as you hand yourself to your King. That is the first empire over which man is called to reign. All the forces and conditions of his own life, the desires and aspirations; the movements of intellect, emotion, and will. I can reign only when I am under authority, when I have kissed the scepter. Enlarge it without my staying to illustrate it. Your home, your class in the Sunday school if you are a teacher. This pulpit is a throne of power for me if I am under authority. If I am not, then it is an awful opportunity for wrecking human life. I am not talking idly. These are the deep and awful and heartbreaking convictions of any man who knows what it is to be called to preach the Word of God. Yet blessed be God, as the apostle declares, the true minister is "led in triumph." If I would reign in this pulpit and bring a territory into subjection to the vast empire of God's Kingdom, then the measure in which I submit is the measure in which I command, and reign in my own life of service. So also in your city, in your country, everywhere. First under authority, and then reigning in power.

I go back to the application which I have already used in the middle of my sermon. Under what authority are you living? What are the sanctions of your life? To what do you remit everything? The lusts and desires of your own life? Is that so? Under what authority are you living? Tell me that, and I will tell you the effect you are producing upon the territory over which you are reigning. The authority to which a man submits is the authority he exercises. Let us break this up. Are you submitting your life to the authority of the flesh, answering its clamant cry, yielding all the forces of your being to whatever your flesh life asks and demands? Then you are exerting the authority of the throne to which you bow. You are spreading a poison and paralysis wherever you go for no man liveth unto himself. Are you bending the knee to the world with its maxims and methods? Then you are exerting the influence of the world in the circle of your friendship, and your friend is becoming worldly because you are reigning over him in the power of the world to which you bow the knee. Are you serving the devil, the devil who was a liar from the beginning and a murderer, the devil who is the prince of compromise and of subtlety? Then you are exerting the influence of the devil wherever you go. Are you serving that great Kingdom of God by crowning Christ? Then you are exerting the influence of that Kingdom and that Christ wherever you go. That which you are under, you transplant into that which you are over. That has a wider application than to young men. Fathers and mothers, that is true of you. It is not the precept which you utter, it is the throne before which you bend that you will see reproduced in your children. It is true everywhere. Let me cease my illustrations and leave the vast, awful sublime truth upon your conscience, and turn to my final word to young men.

Man, you must fulfil your manhood by bowing the knee to a throne and reigning. To what throne are you bowing?

That life of yours, the history and mystery of which I know not, nor could I know if you attempted to tell me, the history and mystery of which you know not, for there are vaster reaches in your manhood than you have ever discovered. God only knows it all. Take that life and hand it over to that One Who out of the eternal ages came into the little spaces of passing time that evil men might know the meaning of life in its richest fulfilment. Hand your life to Him and He will—this is the gospel, the evangel that comes like music to the heart of the man who has failed—He will "restore to you the years that the locust hath eaten." He will give you back the things you have missed. Though the vessel be marred in the hand of the Potter, He will make it again, another vessel as seemeth good to Him. If you, like Jonah, in unutterable folly have paid your fare to try to escape Jehovah, and have gone to Tarshish, if only you will get back, the Word of the Lord will come to you the second time, and He will establish His Kingdom in your life and then you may begin to reign in life.

Is there anything you more desire than a sense of power? Is there anything any man who is a man at all desires more than to be able to say, "I can"? It is the next great word to "I am" on the level of human life. "I am" is the first expression of human personality. If the next be "I think" the outcome is "I can." Do you want to say it? Oh, the scores of men who say to me, "I cannot." They are here to-night. You are here to-night, my brother, you are saying, "I cannot, God knows I would if I could, but I cannot do it. I see the vision, but I have no virtue to win the victory." No, you have bent to the wrong throne, and the influence resulting from your bending to the wrong throne has been destruction of the territory over which you reign, for, remember, your paralysis is your own doing, your weakness is the result of your own yielding.

I pray you turn the deafest of deaf ears to the false and damnable teaching which declares that you cannot help your sin. You can help your sinning. Sin is the rebellion of your will, and it is rebellion against God. You know that you need not have crossed the threshold of the house of sin, or put your life at the disposal of evil things; but you have done it and now you cannot help it, you are poisoned, paralyzed, spoiled. You are saying, I cannot, and you have ruined your kingdom because the throne to which you bent was the wrong throne.

There is a "trysting place where heaven's love and heaven's justice meet," and the trysting place is the Cross where the Christ, Who came to give the pattern, died that you might know how in the mystery of pain God is able to communicate power that makes life over again. If you have been the slave of the awful evil things to which you have yielded yourself, the chain can be broken now. God help you to find the right authority and bow under it, and so find your kingdom and reign over it.

CHAPTER IV

PRAYER OR FAINTING

They ought always to pray, and not to faint.
                                      LUKE 18:1.

SUCH IS LUKE'S INTERPRETATION OF THE MEANING OF THE parable which Jesus uttered to His disciples concerning the unrighteous judge "which feared not God, and regarded not man," but who granted the request of the importunate widow from the purely selfish motive which he expressed graphically and accurately in the words, "lest she wear me out by her continual coming." This is one of the most remarkable things in some senses that the Bible says anywhere about the prayer life, "They ought always to pray, and not to faint." It is one of those statements that stagger, and in the presence of which Christian men and women are always in danger of indulging in some measure of that criticism which is the outcome of unbelief. The first objection raised is to the word "always." It is suggested that this does not quite mean what it says, that the evident intention is that we should be men and women of prayer, having our appointed times, and seasons, and habits of prayer; that believing in the power of prayer, we ought to take advantage of the great possibility whenever we are able so to do, whenever we are in need. That is not what the text says. That is not the interpretation placed upon the parable of Jesus by Luke. The text says, "*always* to pray." If this is one of the most remarkable things said concerning prayer, and one which does undoubtedly challenge the criticism of our unbelief, it does not stand alone in Scripture. There are other passages that indicate the same necessity. When he is closing his letter to the Thessalonians Paul utters in epigrammatic form great injunctions concerning the Christian life. One of them is, "Pray without ceasing." Of this it is also affirmed that he did not literally mean that we are to pray without ceasing. We are to pray every day, two or three times a day, as regularly as possible. We are to be men and women of prayer. But that is not what the apostle wrote. He wrote, "Pray without ceasing." You will not at all misunderstand these introductory words. I recognize the difficulty. You say, I have been too busy to-day with work for God to take time in prayer. I was so pressed with the business cares of last week that I had very little time for prayer. I prayed at morning, noon and night, and often in the midst of the city's rush and din, when some great need crowded on my heart I lifted that heart to God. I prayed often, but I did not pray always, I did not pray without ceasing. I quite recognize the difficulty; but I am so perfect a believer in the inspired infallibility of Scripture that I abide by the words of it, *"always," "without ceasing."* It behooves us, therefore, to ask very carefully what this really means. I submit to you immediately that this particular text of mine in which Luke gives the inspired interpretation of the meaning of the Master's parable lifts the whole subject of prayer on to a very high level, and reveals to us the fact that there is infinitely more in prayer than the offering of petitions, than the uttering of words, than the taking of time, than the attitude of the body or of the mind; that there are deeper depths and higher heights; and that if we would enter into the prayer life with all its fulness of virtue and of victory we must discover what this really means, "They ought always to pray," "Pray without ceasing."

First of all, I would ask you to notice very carefully the slight change in the Revision which is an interesting and important one. The Authorized Version reads, "*Men* ought always to pray, and not to faint." The Revised Version reads, "*They* ought always to pray, and not to faint." To whom was *He* speaking? If you go back to the previous chapter you will see how wonderful a chapter it is, full of solemn warnings and prophetic utterances, strange and mysterious many of them. At its twenty-second verse I find these words, "And He said unto the *disciples*, The days will come when ye shall desire to see one of the days of the Son of man, and ye shall not see it." Then He continues His teaching of the disciples right on to the end of that chapter, and immediately and in that connection, whether uttered at that point or not is of no consequence, in that relationship, according to the placing of the story by Luke, He spoke the parable "unto them," that is to His own disciples, "that *they* ought always to pray, and not to faint." The distinction is an important one, and it is fundamental to our meditation. I am not for a moment suggesting that Jesus Christ had one philosophy of life for His disciples and another for men of the world. On the other hand, I affirm that He had one philosophy of life, and He called all men to accept it. Here, however, He is laying His instructions upon such as have heard His call, and having obeyed it, have become His disciples. They are such as are described in the letter to the Hebrews—which I believe Luke wrote, although the thinking is the thinking of Paul— "He that cometh to God must believe that He is, and that He is a rewarder of them that seek after Him." If a man do not believe these things He will never pray. If these things are indeed believed, if this is indeed the truth concerning God accepted by the heart and mind, then of such as believe, the Lord by His parable affirms that "They ought always to pray, and not to faint."

Having drawn attention to the fact that these words were spoken to disciples, to those who believe that God is and that He is a Rewarder, let us notice the circumstances of this discourse. He is talking to His disciples in view of the fact that the life of faith is a strenuous life, characterized by stress and strain and conflict and difficulty. Mark how He ends His exposition of His parable, "When the Son of man cometh, shall He find faith on the earth?" In the previous chapter I find Him telling these men that to gain their life they must lose it, and to find the real value of eternal things they must turn themselves away from all the allurements of the material and the sensual. He is putting into contrast the life of faith with the life that is lived on the material level. I turn over the pages of the Gospel of Luke a little farther on and I find Him saying almost exactly the same thing. Speaking of the approaching destruction of Jerusalem, and of the fact that in those days men would faint for fear, He charged His own to watch and make supplication. So that the message of this parable and the declaration of this text have application to such as are His disciples, and declare to them the supreme truth concerning the secret of prevailing life in the midst of the stress and strain of discipleship. I need hardly stay to argue the fact that the Christian life is one of stress and strain. I am perfectly well aware that there are senses in which it is a life of peace, and ease, and quietness. I remember the great promises of Scripture concerning peace for the children of God. There is granted to the child of God the peace *from God* our Father. There is granted to the child of God the peace *of God* in the heart, and, moreover, the presence and comradeship of the *God of peace.* Yet these very facts create the strain and stress and difficulty. There is no man in this house who is attempting to live a godly life who does not know the absolute truth of this. Surrounded every day by things material, in the midst of an age which in its outlook is as absolutely godless as any age which has preceded it, it is not easy to live the life of godliness. It is not easy to bear perpetual and prevailing testimony to the unseen things to the ordinary crowd of men and women with whom the man of faith comes into contact, living, as they do, as though there were no God, no hereafter, no spiritual verities. To live the life of godliness in the midst of this age is still to live the life of conflict. Because of the allied forces of godlessness, the Christian life is the strenuous life, and there are scores of men and women in this house to-night—perhaps the affirmation is a strong one, but I believe it to be true—who are weary in the midst of the Christian life, who are tired because of the pressure of the forces of the world upon them—fainting, filled with weariness. To these people Christ says, "*They* ought always to pray, and not to faint."

Before laying further emphasis upon the "always" let me take the terms of my text in order to understand Christ's philosophy of life for His own disciples. What is the real suggestiveness of this word "pray"? If you take it as to its first simplicity and intention, it means—and this is not complete but it will help us to reach the complete thought—to wish forward, to desire toward the ultimate; or if you will have that interpreted by the language of the apostle in one of his greatest epistles, that to the Colossians, it means the *seeking of things which are above.* That does not at all suggest that the Christian is forevermore to be sighing after heaven, and expressing his discontent with the present world, and longing to escape from it; but rather that the Christian is to seek the upper things, setting his mind upon them, and everywhere and everywhen he is to be hoping for, and endeavoring after, the ultimate. That is the simple meaning of prayer. Reaching forward, wishing forward, desiring forward, seeking the upper, the higher, the nobler. So that in prayer there is included, first, always first, the thought of worship and adoration, that content of the heart with the perfection and acceptability and goodness of the will of God which bows the soul in worship. That is the first attitude of prayer. To pray is forevermore to set the life in its inspiration and in all its endeavor toward that ultimate goal of the glory of God, "Being justified by faith, let us have peace with God through our Lord Jesus Christ; through Whom also we have had our access by faith into this grace wherein we stand; and *let us rejoice in hope of the glory of God.*" That is the first quantity of quality of prayer. The vision of the ultimate with a corresponding attitude of life toward it, which is that of perpetual endeavor after it. This means not merely that in the midst of battle and strife and din and smoke, and wounding and blood and tears, that we see a better day, a golden age, but that the soul, seeing that golden age as in the will of God, and realizing that the supreme fact of the vision is that of God Himself, the supreme attitude of the life becomes that of submission, and the supreme effort of the life is that of co-operation with God toward the ultimate upon which His heart is set. That is prayer. Prayer is not merely position of body, or of mind. Prayer is not merely asking for something in order that I may obtain it for myself. Prayer forevermore says when it asks for anything, "Not my will, but Thine be done," which means, if the thing I ask for, however much I desire it, however good it seems to me to be, will hinder or postpone, by a hair's breadth or a moment, the ultimate victory, will be denied to me. Those who know the real secret of the prayer life have discovered the fact that denial is over and over again the graciousness of overwhelming answer. To pray is to desire forward, to seek forward, to endeavor after. It is to have a new vision of God, and of the ways of God, to be overwhelmingly convinced of the perfection of God, of the perfection of all He does, of the certainty of His ultimate victory, and then to respond to the profound and tremendous conviction by petition, by praise, and by endeavor; and so men "ought always to pray" and to "pray without ceasing."

Now notice another term of our text, "to faint." This is our Lord's recognition of the strenuous nature of the life of the believing soul. What is this word, "to faint"? Quite simply, to be paralyzed, to be weak, to be worthless, to feel the force dying and the vigor passing, to be beaten, to be broken down and helpless. I need stay no longer with definition at that point.

We may now consider our Lord's philosophy of life. He puts these two things into opposition. He declares in effect that this is the alternative before every one of us, to pray or to faint. There is no suggestion of a middle course. To pray or to faint. According to this word, this inspired interpretation of the meaning of our Lord's parable and teaching, if men pray they do not faint. If men faint it is because they have ceased to pray. If men do not pray they faint. Men "ought always to pray, and not to faint." Interpret your prayer by the negation. Prayer is the opposite of fainting. Fainting is a sudden sense of inability and helplessness, the cessation of activity, weariness which is almost, and ultimately is, death. Pray, and do not faint. To pray is to have the vision clear, the virtue mighty, the victory assured. To pray is to "mount up with wings as eagles," to "run and not be weary," to "walk, and not faint." Suffer me one moment with that. Have you imagined that the great Isaiah at that point failed in his rhetorical method, and that having said the great thing, there was nothing greater to say, and therefore he climbed down, and there was an anticlimax, and perhaps something of bathos? It is not so. As a matter of fact, he began with the easiest thing of all to "mount up with wings as eagles." Then he took the next thing in the order of difficulty, to run, and the hardest thing last, to walk. In the day when you first caught your vision of God you mounted up with wings like eagles. I am not undervaluing that day. Thank God for the experience. We thank God for it whenever it returns. He gives us the vision ever and anon, and we "mount up with wings as eagles." A defeated and disappointed man once said, "Oh that I had wings like a dove! then would I fly away and be at rest." What a mistake. A man with the wings of a dove could not fly away and be at rest. When the inspired seer speaks of a man flying, he says "wings as eagles." Mark the significance of it. The eagle is forevermore the symbol of Deity. To wait upon God is to use the pinions of Deity, and mount and soar away. Every young believer has those pinions and that great beginning, and God gives them to us ever and anon all the pilgrimage through. Presently, however, there comes a day when there are no wings and no mounting above; we must *run* through. Yet "they shall run, and not be weary." And yet there comes another day, some of you are in it now, it is almost night, so dark has it all become. You cannot run, the way is not clear enough, the enemies are too many, there are difficulties all about you—you must walk, "They shall walk, and not faint." Mark Isaiah's word and Christ's, "They shall walk, *and not faint*," "They ought always to pray, and *not to faint*." Prayer is the opposite of fainting. It is mounting with wings. It is running without weariness. It is walking the uphill, rough and rugged road, and never fainting. That is Christ's great philosophy of life. If men pray they do not faint. If men faint it is because they have forgotten to pray. "They ought always to pray, and not to faint."

How are we to do it? Take the parable and notice carefully one fact about it. It is an exposition of the philosophy of the prayer life by contrast, by contrast all the way through it. The moment you forget that, you miss the beauty and the glory of it. First, all that the judge was, God is not. The judge did not fear God, that is to say, he was not submitted to the highest authority. He did not regard men. He was absolutely careless, and you may sum up the whole thing in Christ's illuminative word, he was unrighteous. All that the judge was, God is not. God regards man. Mark the word of Jesus, "longsuffering over them." God is righteous. "He will avenge," and the word "avenge" there is not the word "revenge." It means to do justice to. The widow came to the unrighteous judge and said to him, "Avenge me of mine adversary," Do me justice in connection with my adversary. He was an unjust judge, an unrighteous man. God is righteous and just and will do justice by all who come to Him. That is the first contrast. There is another contrast, and it is the second contrast that we often miss. In order to persuade the unjust judge importunity was necessary. Importunity is never necessary to persuade God. That is the point where we generally break down in this parable. We make the contrast between the unjust judge and God, but not between the consequent action of the widow and that of the Christian. This parable is constantly taken as teaching that we are to be importunate toward God. It teaches us rather that if we are always praying, importunity in the sense of begging is not necessary. The prayer life does not consist of perpetual repetition of petitions. The prayer life consists of life that is always upward, and onward, and Godward. The passion of the heart is for the Kingdom of God; the devotion of the mind is to His will; the attitude of the spirit is conformity thereto; and the higher we climb in the realm of prayer, the more unceasing will prayer be, and the fewer will be the petitions. It is the opposite of importunity that is taught here. The thought that Jesus gave of God is that of One compassionate, just, mighty, quick to respond to the forward wish of the weakest soul, so that in the midst of the stress and strain and struggle there need be no fainting. The life uplifted in prayer, the whole desire Godward, brings an answer, and there is no comparison equal to showing the celerity of that answer. Quicker than thought or the lightning flash. There is in one of the old prophets an illustration of this in one realm of prayer, where he speaks of God as "a God ready to pardon." This is only an illustration, but notice it. There is a man here to-night while I preach, God grant there may be, who is tired of his sin, broken-hearted on account of it, who determines that without any after-meeting he will seek the pardon of his God. Will he have to be importunate and wait and beg and beseech? No, "ready to pardon." Yonder is a great battleship, the decks are cleared for action, every man is at his post. At last, as the awful moment arrives, the commanding officer says, "Ready?" "Ready, aye ready!" comes back the answer, and he gives the order, "Fire!" You know what happens. That is slow work compared to God's answer. He is ready to pardon, ready to answer your prayer. The unjust judge did not regard God or man. He was selfish and self-centered. Because the widow went and went and went to him, to get rid of her, to save her bruising him, he gave her what she wanted. That is the picture by contrast. God is the opposite of that. Your method in prayer is the opposite of that. Therefore men "ought always to pray, and not to faint." Because of such a God, so full of compassion, so full of might, so full of infinite and strict integrity and justice, the forward wish of the weakest, feeblest, frailest soul brings an answer. He is a God ready to hear and to answer.

If all this be true, if this be what our Lord said to men, and if Luke's inspired interpretation of the meaning be correct, allow me for a moment to lay emphasis upon another word in the text, "They *ought* always to pray." It is a duty, not a privilege. Men ought. All omnipotence is at the disposal of the saint who prays. God is willing, then men ought to pray, which means, men ought not to faint. There ought to be no fainting. You will understand me, I am not preaching to you. I am talking in the presence of Christ's words with you. I have fainted and still do faint: I ought not. Men "ought always to pray, and not to faint." I have no right to faint. Oh, but how strenuous is the life! I know a little of it. Men "ought always to pray, and not to faint." How fierce the battle! I know something of the conflict, but I ought not to faint, because I can pray. All which means that in God there is resource equal to every demand that can be made upon the trusting soul. There is no hour so dark but that if I will *stay upon Him*—once again to use Isaiah's fine language —I shall discover His readiness to support me as I stay. There is no battle so fierce but that if I pray I may not stand, "withstand, . . . and, having done all, to stand." No temptation so swift, so sudden or subtle, but that if I am always praying I may not find at once the wisdom and the might that enable me to overcome. Men ought not to faint, because men ought to pray.

The whole life of the believer should be prayer—and this is the summary and conclusion—every act, every word, every wish. The act that is not prayer in the ultimate, and the word which is not prayer in the last analysis, and the wish that is not prayer in the profoundest depth, are to be put away, they do not become the life of faith. They are things that produce fainting. How can every act be prayer? Ask yourself about your next act, why you are doing it. The Sabbath will soon be over, and we shall leave it behind, for it is the day of prayer. To-morrow morning you will face the calling of the day, in the shop, the office, the school; in professional life, in the Houses of Parliament, in whatever is your calling. What are you rising early and toiling all the day for? The answer of the average man will suit me for the moment. That answer will be, I am working for my living. Perfectly right, but what do you want to live for? Why should you endeavor to support your life and keep it? You have been overwhelmed with the stress and strain of actual physical and mental toil, and you are away to the mountains, to the sea for rest. Why are you going for rest? Why do you want rest? I ask. That I may regain my strength. For what? Cross-examine yourself and see the meaning of your activity. Analyze your own wishing and desire, and see what inspiration lies at the back of it. If by His infinite grace and by the indwelling of the Holy Christ Himself, at the back of all the activity and of all desire and all speech there is the perpetual aspiration, "Thy Kingdom come, Thy will be done," then every act, every thought, is prayer. "To labor is to pray" they say. That depends. If your labor is merely for the making of your own name and fortune, if your labor is to build up your own reputation and to gratify your own sensual desires, then to labor is not to pray. If the reason of this day's toil is the maintenance of a life that is God's, all the forces of which are at His disposal to work His will according to His own appointment, then that life is prayer, and the mountain climb, the rest day by the sea, the toil in the shop and office, the drudgery of professional routine, and the agony of life, all are prayer.

"They ought always to pray, and not to faint." If we do not pray always, we never pray. The man who makes prayer a scheme by which occasionally he tries to get something for himself has not learned the deep, profound secret of prayer. Prayer is life passionately wanting, wishing, desiring God's triumph. Prayer is life striving, toiling everywhere and everywhen for that ultimate victory. When men so pray they do not faint. They mount up with wings as eagles, they run without weariness, they tramp the hardest, roughest road, and do not faint.

My desire to-night has been to arrest irreverent and unintelligent prayer, to indicate a line of contrast which will reveal to men the fact that prayer is infinitely larger than we have often thought it to be. I charge upon you my comrades in this life of faith, do not degrade prayer to a low standard of experience, or make it that by which you attempt to gain things—and mark the startling language of Scripture—that you may spend them on your own lusts. "Ye have not because ye ask not," or "ye have not because ye ask amiss." What is it to ask amiss? To ask for things that I may spend them on my own desires. That is praying that is not answered. Men "ought always to pray, and not to faint." I have come near fainting often. I have fainted mentally, spiritually. The fault is mine. I pray that I may learn the infinite lesson of Jesus that God is other than the unjust judge, and that my method with Him may be other than that of the importunate widow, and that if I do but know what prayer really is, I live homed in omnipotence, and I need never faint by the way. May this strength be ours.

CHAPTER V

SUFFER THE CHILDREN

Suffer the little children to come unto Me; forbid them not: for of such is the Kingdom of God.
                                                    MARK 10:14.

THAT IS THE MAGNA CHARTA OF THE CHILDREN. Its words are of the simplest which ever fell from the lips of our beloved Lord. We are never able to recite them, I think I may venture to say, without feeling some thrill of the tenderness of His great heart in our own. Under whatever circumstances we hear them, they always produce the same result, touching us back from hardness to tenderness. Whenever we hear them recited, or recite them ourselves, there returns a sense of that childhood from which, alas, some of us seem to have traveled far along the dusty highways of life.

And yet, my brethren, if these words of Jesus are characterized by their simplicity, it is not the simplicity of superficiality. It is rather the simplicity of a vast and astonishing sublimity, and I sometimes wonder when I ponder these words—and others like them with which we are all familiar, the simplest things Jesus said—I wonder whether the very simplest of them all are not the sublimest.

To have heard Jesus say this would have been to be saved from misapprehension of the meaning of what He said. A statement like that seems to suggest that we have misapprehended His meaning, and I do think that we have very largely misunderstood that meaning. Not that we have misinterpreted Him, but that our understanding of His meaning has been circumscribed because we did not hear Him utter these words. There are things beyond the fine art of the printer. You cannot print a tone of the voice. You cannot reveal on the cold page, however exquisitely your work may be done, the temper of the speaker. Mark endeavors to save us from that very misapprehension by drawing our attention to the fact of the temper of Jesus at the moment when He uttered these words. "He was moved with indignation." The statement in the connection of these words is almost startling, and we are compelled to pause and consider its meaning. "Suffer the little children to come unto me." All heaven's sweetness is in the great command. It seems, if you will allow me the far-flung and spacious figure of the Bible, as though the very Mother-heart of God were singing itself out in these words. Yes, the voice thrilled in tenderness, but it vibrated in thunder; and when Jesus uttered these words there came together, into the apprehension of the men who heard Him the two things that even to this day it is so difficult to harmonize, and to understand their relation to each other: the goodness and the severity of God. No tenderer thing ever fell from His lips, but "He was moved with indignation." Out of His hot anger came the most gentle and beautiful thing that He ever said about child life.

These things being so, we need to appreciate and study these words the more carefully. Let me, however, say at once that I do not think any exposition can exhaust the meaning of this Magna Charta of the child. What I do hope to accomplish in our brief meditation is to lead you into the atmosphere created by the strong and tender words.

Notice carefully first of all that Jesus made an appeal

and used an argument, and that the two constitute His great charge to His people concerning the children. There is an appeal, "Suffer the little children to come unto Me, and hinder them not." There is an argument, "for of such is the Kingdom of God." If we will take the appeal and the argument together and learn their interrelationship, we come into the atmosphere created by His words, and understand what His charge to His people forevermore is concerning the children.

I take these two first values of the text, the appeal and the argument, but in the other order, asking you to think for a few minutes, first, of the argument of Jesus, "of such is the Kingdom of God," and then, in the light of that argument, to listen to His appeal, "Suffer the little children to come unto Me; and hinder them not."

First, then, as to the argument. I put it first because if we are to understand these words, and become obedient to them, we must catch the profound significance of the argument that the Master used, and His reason for using it on this particular occasion. You will agree with me when I say that an argument is an appeal to conviction. It may be an appeal intended to produce a new conviction, but it is always an appeal to some conviction already held. If I say to a person on any conceivable subject, I want you to do this, because—what follows the "because" will reveal the opinion I hold of the person to whom I make my appeal. I should never appeal to a miser to give on the ground of his generosity! Whatever I make my appeal to reveals my opinion of the person to whom I make that appeal. If we can get back for a moment into the perfect human naturalness of the scene I think you will follow me. Fathers were bringing their children to Jesus. Mothers also, I have no doubt—but all the

Greek pronouns go to prove that they were men who brought their children to Jesus, and the Hebrew law was that fathers were responsible for the religious training of the children. Of course the mothers were there. That goes without saying. These people were bringing their children to Jesus, desiring that He should touch them, and the disciples rebuked them, rebuked those who brought them, and so through them rebuked the children. They felt that Jesus had more important business on hand than that of holding receptions for children. They did not believe for a single moment that He could be troubled with these children. His mind was full of great matters. They knew full well that the deepest passion of His heart was a passion for the coming of the Kingdom of God. They knew perfectly well that those eyes that they loved to look upon were eyes that saw through to the infinite and far distances, eyes familiar with all the beauty of the eternal order; and they knew that He desired, for He had taught them so to pray, that there should be established in the midst of the wreckage and ruin of human conditions all the glory and beauty of the heavenly order. "Our Father who art in the heavens, Thy name be hallowed, Thy Kingdom come, Thy will be done, as in heaven so on earth." They knew, therefore, full well that He was there to teach men the meaning of the Kingdom of God, and to do such work as should bring the heavenly conditions into the earthly life. Therefore they were convinced that He had no time for children. It was a very pardonable thing that the fathers and mothers should desire that the prophet should touch the children, but it could not be. They knew His passion for the Kingdom of God, and so far as they had light they also were men into whom there had entered the selfsame passion. They had caught His enthusiasm because they had seen His vision of the Kingdom of God. This misconception explains the anger of Jesus. He was moved with indignation because, notwithstanding the fact that they had caught His enthusiasm, having seen His vision, and consequently were men who knew something of the coming of the Kingdom of God, they had so little appreciated the real meaning of that Kingdom. Then He said, "Suffer the little children to come unto Me; and hinder them not: for of such is the Kingdom of God." The disciples hindered the children because they thought that the Kingdom of God was a great and weighty matter, and that because He was devoted to it He had no time for children. This misconception He rebuked and corrected by declaring that children are in the Kingdom, and of the Kingdom; and going still further, He declared that they could not enter into that Kingdom, though they had seen its gleaming glory from afar, until they became like the children, for "of such is the Kingdom."

But now mark the graciousness of Christ's assumption. He assumed the devotion of these men to the Kingdom of God. He used an argument that would appeal in their case. He knew perfectly well if they could but come to understand the nature of the Kingdom of God they would never hinder the child coming. They were men in whom the passion and fire for that Kingdom was already burning, and He made His appeal on that ground, "of such is the Kingdom of God."

Thus, when I consider this argument, and note its assumption, I touch the fundamental matter in all our work for the children. I think, brethren, there are many appeals I could make to men and women in order to arouse their interest in, and attempt to compel their work for, children. I think I could appeal to men and women on the basis of the fact that the child nature is full of interest. I think I could make an appeal to men on the basis of the harmlessness of a little child. I think I could make an appeal on the basis of the helplessness of a little child. But Christ made no such appeal, and yet all these were included in His. His appeal is always "of such is the Kingdom of God." Until we have seen that Kingdom at least in outline, and until the vision has captured us, and until a passion for the establishment of it is the master passion of our life, we have no right to try to help the children. I will revise that statement if you will let me. I will not say if it so please you that we have no right, but rather that we have no power to help the children. We can never help our own children, the children in our own home, the children in our schools, the children of the nation, until we have caught Christ's vision of God's Kingdom, and until that has become the master passion of our lives. The Church, spending its strength on disputes concerning doctrines, wasting its time in quarreling about ecclesiastical formulae, becoming worldly and self-centered, always neglects the child. On the other hand, the church, seeking the Kingdom, restless in the midst of everything that is contrary to the will of God; passionately desiring the building of His city, and the bringing in of His rule—that church always seeks the child. A vision of and desire for the Kingdom of God is the master passion in all work for the children.

But while thus looking at the argument as to its assumption note its plain declaration, and consequently its simple revelation. Jesus said "of such." An old hymn is in my mind all the time this morning:

> I think when I read that sweet story of old,
>   When Jesus was here among men,

How He called little children as lambs to His fold,
　I should like to have been with Him then.

I wish that His hands had been placed on my head,
　That His arms had been thrown around me;
And that I might have seen His kind look when He said,
　"Let the little ones come unto Me."

Now let us try with all simplicity to see the actual picture. Those little children of Judæa and Galilee, quite foreign to our children, were yet of the same blood, and the same nature, and the same spiritual essence. Let us, then, look at them in their humanness. See them all about the Christ, some of them timid, clinging and shrinking; and others of them eagerly going forward. Get the human picture, do not buy it, but paint it and look at it. Now, said Christ, "*of such*," of these ordinary children, of these children from the cottage homes, and all the district round, "of such." For I pray you, remember that the children at whom Christ pointed were not even Sunday-school children. They were not children who had been converted in a Special Mission. I am not criticizing the Special Mission for the child, but pre-eminently desiring that we should understand that they were ordinary children. Half an hour after, if I know anything about children, they were playing and quarreling! "Of such" of these ordinary, everyday children. Oh, but you say, He was speaking of the child in the ideal. Ideal nonsense! He was talking about the bairns these disciples wanted to keep back. "*Of such* is the Kingdom of God."

I make two deductions from this word of Christ. The child is the microcosm of the Kingdom. If we really will pay attention to a little child we have before us, focused, condensed, the Kingdom of God. And therefore, as a necessary sequence, the Kingdom of God is the microcosm of the child.

If we take in the larger outlooks, the more spacious conceptions of the Kingdom, then in every little child, the little child you saw this morning, who does not go to Sunday school at all, the child in the gutter, is the picture of the Kingdom of God.

I say, first of all, that the child is the microcosm of the Kingdom. Notice what Christ said to these men. "Of such *is* the Kingdom," not, Of such *will be* the Kingdom, but, "Of such *is* the Kingdom." The child as I find it to-day, is not the microcosm of the Kingdom of God in the ultimate, but it is the microcosm of the Kingdom of God as it is: "Of such is the Kingdom." I think, brethren, that we too inclusively interpret the Kingdom in the terms of consummation. We say, the Kingdom of God, and we attempt at once to take in its vast and ultimate meanings and reaches. There are times when we ought to do it, for the ultimate is the inspiration of the present. But that is not what Jesus said. He who knew more about these children than did their fathers and mothers, declared that the Kingdom of God at the present time *is* as these children are. In a child I find potentiality, imperfection, and therefore, providing always that I have that passion for the Kingdom which is the fundamental necessity, an appeal. All the glory of the oak forest lies in the single acorn which I can hold in my hand. All the glory, or the shame of England, lies in the little child that sits by your side, or that you pass in the street. All the shame of humanity lay in the first child of the race, Adam. All the glory of humanity lay in the young child, in the manger, at Bethlehem. That is potentiality. But in a child there is also imperfection. An acorn is not an oak forest. It is not even an oak. It is imperfect; it is undeveloped potentiality. Finally, therefore, a little child is a perpetual appeal for the treatment that will realize all the things that lie in its personality. The little child is forever saying, So deal with me as to realize all that is in me. That appeal is the true philosophy of education. That perpetual cry of the child should condition all our attitudes toward it, and our relationships with it.

The child is the microcosm of the Kingdom. That Kingdom of God to-day is a great potentiality. The powers of that Kingdom are everywhere. There is no power being used basely, devilishly, but that if it can be redeemed, and put into true operation, is a power making for the ultimate Kingdom of God. But the Kingdom of God to-day is imperfect, not realized. The little child reveals to us what that Kingdom is in its present conditions. Just as having seen in the face of a little child great possibilities, and great imperfections, we hear the appeal of its life for treatment that will correct the imperfections and realize the possibilities, so as we look upon the world to-day we see the possibility, and know the imperfection, and these become the prayer of the world in its need, calling us to active service. Children's Day, did you tell me this was? So it is, thank God. But children's day is London's day, and England's day, and the World's day, and God's day. "Of such is the Kingdom."

Or take the larger outlook, and see how the Kingdom is the macrocosm of the child. We can only think of the Kingdom now in the narrow limit of our own world. Then it means first the right of God by creation, and by redemption. It means consequently that the whole world is crying out after that God Whose it is by creation and by redemption. And, finally, it means the whole world finds eternal life, that is permanence, only in right relationship to God. All these things that constitute your philosophy of the Kingdom of God in its widest application are true of every little child.

The right of God in a child is infinitely more than the right of a parent, for every child is His creation, and every child upon which we look, even if our eyes may not see it, has on its face the mark of redemption. Every child is crying out after God, however we may understand or misinterpret its cry. And hear the solemn word, not now to be dealt with at length, but to be stated of necessity, the child can find eternal life only as it has right relationship with God.

And now I turn briefly to the appeal, "Suffer the little children: and forbid them not." It has three applications. There is the first and simplest. It touches the child, it shows me my duty concerning the child. There is the second and the deepest. It shows me what I must be if I would obey the instruction concerning the child. Finally, there is the third and the widest, the application of this to the world at large, and to the Church's responsibility therein.

As to the first of these, I suppose I need hardly stay to deal with it. It is the old, old story, yet hear His words once more. Said He, "Suffer the little children to come unto Me." That is the positive application. Not, Bring the children to Me, but Suffer them to come. In order that it may be perfectly clear, He interprets His positive by a negative, "and hinder them not." "Suffer the little children to come." See, they are coming! Suffer them to come, and hinder them not! The negative interprets the positive. If we take this positive, and hear the negative interpretation of it, we find that Jesus meant to say that the child will come to Him if we do not hinder it. The Church's responsibility is not that of bringing children to Christ, but of getting things out of the way that hinder their coming. In that matchless picture in the last chapter of John's gospel, of Peter being restored to position and service, when Jesus gave him his work, He said first,

"Feed My Lambs"; He then said, "Shepherd My sheep," and, finally, "Feed My sheep." He did not say, Shepherd My lambs, but feed them. The sheep that has wandered away must be shepherded, but the lamb is here, feed it. I make you this declaration this morning. There is not a child born into the world but that will go straight to Christ unless someone hinders it. I do not know how to go on preaching. I never hear that word of Jesus without having my heart shaken like a tempest. Do not forget it. I would not apportion blame. Original sin, tendency to evil, is in every child; but a Saviour is waiting to receive the child, and if only we will get out of the way, and get everything else out of the way in the child's first home environment, and everywhere else, that child will get straight to Christ. Suffer them, forbid them not! Our business about the children is to see to it that we get out of the way the things that hinder. Hinder them not. Jesus was hot with indignation that men who had seen some vision of the Kingdom should hinder the children. They are trying to come to-day, and we are fooling the time away quarreling about their education. God have mercy upon us! Hinder them not. I would like to have it emblazoned on every hall in which children meet. Hinder them not. That is our responsibility.

And then He turns upon our own souls this great word, Except you become like the little child, you cannot enter into the Kingdom. Unless you are a submitted soul you are bound to hinder the children. And you must be of the child nature also, understanding the child. My brethren, I am content to leave the application of all that. I think it is better made to this heart of mine when I am alone, and better made to yours when you are alone.

Let me take one minute with the last, and final, and widest thought. Make the application of this to the world. "Of such is the Kingdom." He puts the child at the center, and He puts the Kingdom at the circumference, and if we will keep the child at the center the Kingdom is assured; and if we will keep the Kingdom at the circumference the child is safe. "Of such is the Kingdom." He put the child at the center. When shall we learn to do it? May God lead us there. During these weeks of absence from the country things have happened of which as yet I know nothing in detail.

I do not know about the Education Bill, I do not know about the Licensing Bill; I have not yet read the text of either.

But put the child in the midst, and then you will desire to lock Mr. McKenna and the Bishop of St. Asaph up in one room until they have settled this business once and for ever. I am ashamed; in the name of God, I am ashamed! Let us see to it that the child is made the test.

Licensing Bill! Put the child in the midst. That is the test. Vested interest? What do you mean by a vested interest? If for long, long years we have given a right to men for money's sake to harm a child, then in God's name it is time we had done with the business. No vested interest which harms a child can be permitted to remain. Does it harm a child? Oh, fools and blind, if you ask a question like that! Give some of us half a day in the slum, or in the West End! In the name of God, who is there who has not been touched somewhere by the devilry of this traffic in his own heart and life? Put the child in the midst, put the child in the midst, and fling your circumference of the Kingdom of God round it, and then you will have solved your problems.

I am glad to come back on Anniversary Day. It is a new beginning, and consecration, and I make it in the presence of the little child. We read that second chapter in Matthew for one purpose. Take a blue or red pencil, one that you will never fail to see, and put a line under these words, "the young Child." All the way through the great imperial King, the Lord Christ, Son of God, and Son of Man, is designated in that chapter, "the young Child." Thus God, to lead us and help us, makes the eternal King and Priest the eternal Child; and in proportion as we know Him, and are in fellowship with Him, we shall gather every individual child into our heart and our love; and we shall make a child the test of our Church life, and of our political attitudes; and all the things of life and service will be governed by the presence of the child, and "of such is the Kingdom."

CHAPTER VI

THE VICTORIOUS CHRISTIAN LIFE

Having done all, to stand.

EPHESIANS 6:13.

THE WORDS THRILL WITH A SENSE OF POWER EVEN WHEN taken, as I have now taken them, out of their setting. They suggest assured victory. "Having done all, to stand." Considered in their textual relation this becomes far more apparent. I think I had hardly dared to read these words as text if I had not already read their context, that passage toward the close of the wonderful Ephesian letter which the apostle commences with the words, "Finally, be strong in the Lord, and in the strength of His might." Having read the passage, and knowing that it is in your memory, I repeat that these words, "Having done all, to stand," suggest an absolute and an assured victory. In that passage the enemies are all recognized —"against the principalities, against the powers, against the world rulers of this darkness, against the spiritual hosts of wickedness in heavenly places." The equipment of the soldier is perfectly described, the loins girt with truth, the breastplate of righteousness, the feet shod with the readiness of the gospel of peace, the shield of faith, the helmet of salvation and the sword of the Spirit, with prayer and supplication. The clash of conflict is plainly heard. What is the issue? "Having done all, to stand." There is no quaver in the voice. The victory is not hypothetical. The issue is not for one single moment uncertain. The soldier is "to stand . . . withstand . . . and having done all, to stand." He is to recognize the fact that he is not playing at battle. He is to "put on the whole armour of God" and to "take up the whole armour of God." To "put on" may be for military parade. To "take up" is for actual conflict. What is to be the issue of it? "Having done all, to stand." That is a perfect picture of absolute victory.

We are all familiar with the conflict in greater or less degree. I think I am safe in saying that we all desire just such victory as the apostle describes in this great passage. But the question is being asked in a thousand varied ways on every hand, especially by young people who have seen the gleam and desire to follow it. Is that really possible? Is it really possible to live a victorious Christian life? Eagerly and almost in agony the inquiry is made.

How shall I answer that question? Let me say, first of all, there is a sense in which no one can answer it finally for another. The only answer that will be convincing will be that of personal experience when the conditions have been fulfilled and the attempt made. We too often refuse to make the attempt until we have discovered a theory; or, most earnestly desiring victory, we seek for a testimony of other people, and are influenced unduly by it. Seeking for a theory we have found—to use a commonplace expression—that it does not work; or seeking for testimony, we are afraid, discouraged by the exalted nature of it, or by its confession of failure and impotence. There are some things that a man needs to say very carefully, and what I am going to say now is one of them. Scores of young people desiring victorious life have been discouraged by some of the finest books ever written, the lives of the saints of the past. I remember on one occasion having conversation at some length with a young man who had been brought to the verge of despair in his own life by reading that wonderful life of the sainted Fletcher of Madeley. He said: If that be Christianity and if that be the victorious life, it is not for me. If I could gain the ear of the young men and women here to-night who have seen the glory and in the deepest of their heart desire the victory, I would say to them, Do not trust in a theory, do not take as final evidence any testimony, but for yourselves make the great adventure. Learn the conditions as indicated; make your own venture, and come to the final proof in your own life.

I can imagine that some will say, Why are you preaching? Surely you are preaching to declare a theory. Surely you are preaching to utter the testimony of the man who wrote these words, and perchance your own. Yes, I suppose that is true. Yet I desire to deal with a theory, and declare a testimony, only in order to urge and inspire you to make the great adventure for yourself. I will not at the first declare whether or not I hold it to be possible to live this life and gain this victory. If peradventure you think you know sufficient of me and my message to know that I do believe it, try to banish that thought from your mind; and learning the conditions, go your ways to make each for himself and herself the personal adventure.

I want, then, to speak to you of two things. First, the nature of the conflict described in this passage; and second, the conditions of victory as laid down in the theory of this writer and as borne witness to in the testimony of his own life.

I begin with the nature of the conflict. In order to discover it we must first inquire to whom these words are addressed. I go back to the beginning of the letter, "Paul, an apostle of Christ Jesus through the will of God, to *the saints* which are at Ephesus, and *the faithful* in Christ Jesus." The phrase "the faithful" does not mean those who are absolutely true and loyal necessarily; but it does mean those who are living on the principle of faith in Christ Jesus. "To the saints . . . and the faithful in Christ Jesus." All the letter is to such. That is the preliminary condition. This letter, and this passage, and these phrases, "stand . . . withstand . . . and having done all, to stand," have no meaning for, or application to, any other than soldier saints. I am not going to deal at length with this subject of sainthood, but I do desire to remind you of what the writer says in this particular letter concerning those who wrestle against principalities and powers, the soldiers who enter into this conflict. They are, first of all, men and women who are related to Christ by the mystic and mighty ties of actual life. If you read the earlier part of the letter you will find that the apostle is at great pains to teach these people what is their relation to Christ, because they have believed on Him. As he prays for them that they may know God and know perfectly His will, he teaches them that they are men and women in whom the life of Christ is actually present. That is the meaning of the first phrase in the paragraph, "Finally, be strong in the Lord, and in the strength of His might." So that my first statement is that it is impossible to test the accuracy of the apostle's theory and testimony, impossible to find out whether or not it be possible to live the victorious Christian life, until you have become Christ's own. That is the preliminary matter. It is to the soldier saint, already sharing the Christ life, already related to Him, who knows the wrestling, that I speak to-night. There is a sense in which a man never yielded to Christ may be conscious of the conflict, but he knows very little of the strenuousness of it. It was after you had yielded yourself to Christ that you came back to your pastor, teacher, or friend, and said, How is it that since I have given myself to Christ I have been more sorely tempted than ever? You began wrestling against principalities and powers when you became Christ's own. The first thing to be remembered, then, is that the soldier saints are such as are related to Christ by the mystic and mighty tie of actual life.

There is a second matter of equal importance to remember in the teaching of this letter. Those to whom the apostle wrote were called to an ultimate vocation of strange and wonderful grandeur. In the first three chapters the apostle shows that the ultimate meaning of Christian life is not to be discovered in the present life, that it does not lie in the realm of earthly things. By argument and teaching, declaration and illuminative statement, he proves that the ultimate meaning of Christian life lies far out beyond the present age, in those measureless ages that are to come. There the saints are to fulfil their ultimate vocation as they become the messengers to angels and ages of the grace and wisdom of God. These soldier saints in this world are only in preparation for higher, larger, nobler and fuller service.

There is a third matter that must be recognized. The apostle teaches that the saints have present responsibility consequent upon these earlier facts. Let me state that in another form. These soldier saints are such as share the virtue of Christ. I sometimes think that is one of the words a man today needs to pause at. It is one of the discrowned words of our language. We sometimes speak of virtue as though it were a grace and beauty of character. It is that, surely, but that is not the essential meaning of the word. Virtue is strength.

Very accurate and beautiful use is made of that word when in the familiar and beautiful story of the healing of the woman who touched, we read that Jesus knew that "virtue had gone out of Him." That translation of the Greek word, which being Anglicized might read dynamic, is perfect translation. The soldier saint is one of whom the apostle declared that he shares the virtue of Christ. The soldier saint, moreover, is one who is called to a vocation which lies on and out of sight, and for which the life to-day is preparatory. Having revealed these facts of virtue and vocation thus, he shows that in the midst of the present world the saints have immediate responsibilities. Listen to the actual words, "I therefore . . . beseech you to walk worthily of the calling wherewith ye were called." The worthy walk will be, "giving diligence to keep the unity of the Spirit in the bond of peace," growing up "in all things into Him, which is the Head, even Christ." And so the letter runs on, until presently he says, "Finally, be strong in the Lord, and in the strength of His might." The life of the saint is not a delicate softness. It is rather a stern conflict, for the men and women who share the mystic and mighty life of Christ, and are called to ultimate vocation of strange and wonderful grandeur, have present responsibilities, and these create the conflict.

Then notice the apostolic description of the enemies. Strange and mystic words are these, "Not against flesh and blood." He dismisses all carnal thought of conflict as though it were hardly worthy of notice. It is one of those dismissals that sweep out of sight something not to be named by comparison. "Our wrestling is not against flesh and blood." Therefore someone will say the wrestling is a figure of speech, and there is no real meaning in it, there is no conflict. The man who says that has never entered into an understanding of the fulness and majesty of human life. We still imagine that the hero is the man who wrestles with flesh and blood and overcomes. We have yet to come to an understanding of the fact that moral heroism is finer than material. In your house of business, standing behind your counter, sitting at the desk in your office, in your own home circle, in the fellowship of your earthly friends, you may have to fight a far fiercer battle than was ever won upon the field of blood. Paul knew how fierce the conflict is, and in a few sentences he describes the enemies. Notice how they stand over against what we have said. The saint is one who is related by mystic and mighty ties to Christ, and consequently is Christ's own soldier. Therefore, the saint is in conflict with the principalities and powers in rebellion against Christ. With a touch of fine sarcasm, which nevertheless does not underrate the enemy, he says, "the world rulers of this darkness." "This darkness." What does Paul mean? Begin with the smallest circle. Ephesus was a city of light and learning and of wealth; a city in which there existed that strange combination between religion and commerce which had turned the temple of the heathen goddess into the banking house of the merchants. That city was included for Paul in the words, "this darkness." Or take the wider outlook. All the things that were against the Nazarene, all men and forces in the world that were against the ideals of the Christ and the purposes of Christ were included. He stood for the spiritual. All materialized thinking was part of "this darkness." Mark the infinite scorn of the son of light as he looked upon the condition of affairs in the midst of which he and the saints lived, "this darkness"! To the child of God that phrase will constantly recur in the midst of the world's pomp and pageantry, glitter and gaud. "This darkness"! Finally, in a comprehensive phrase that defies our analysis he says, "spiritual hosts of wickedness in the heavenly places." This is the picture of the spiritual antagonisms by which the life of the saint is forevermore surrounded. This man at least believed that the saint has to battle not with flesh and blood, not against men; but against subtler and more terrible forces that lie behind the visible foes, driving them, and making them the instruments of a devilish onslaught. Paul's picture of the conflict is that of conflict between the saints and devilish forces that touch the spiritual life and wrestle with men in order to prevent their realization of the ultimate.

If these are the combatants, soldier saints, related to Christ, called to ultimate vocation in the heavenlies, and having present responsibilities, and principalities and powers, world rulers of this darkness, what is the issue? Inevitable, real, strenuous conflict. Some of you have known the battle so long that it is almost needless that I dwell upon it; but I want to say to every young man and woman here, saintship means definite conflict with spiritual forces, spiritual powers of the air.

> Christian! dost thou see them
> On the holy ground,
> How the powers of darkness
> Compass thee around?

This is the meaning of temptation. This is the reason why on the morning when you rose with hope and consecration, before noon had come, the shadows were about you and the siren voice of evil had spoken to your soul. Principalities and powers. It is against these that we wrestle.

What is the final issue to be? That is the question I want you to ask and decide. In order to do that, let me speak of the conditions of victory as suggested by this whole letter.

Stated in brief language, what are they? First, complete surrender to Christ; second, patient and persistent training under the control of Christ in order to carry on the conflict: finally, determined conflict.

Complete surrender to Christ. Admiration, patronage, imitation are each and all insufficient. You may genuinely and honestly admire Jesus Christ and never be like Him. Patronage may be in this case, as it is so often, a studied insult. Imitation is useless save as at the center of the life there has been submission, and Christ Himself is enthroned. I sometimes wonder if other of my brethren who preach the Word of God feel as I do the enormous and almost appalling difficulty of making some commonplace thing living and vital. Submission to Christ. We have heard it so often that it has become a phrase, a clangor of words with little or no meaning. Submission to Christ means that there must be no choice made anywhere or anywhen save after consultation with Him, that all knowledge must be submitted to the mastery of His mind, that emotion, whether it express itself as hate or love, must be purified in the hot fire of His infinite love.

All choice submitted to Him. How easy it is to sing about consecration and yet live hour after hour, day after day, without ever consulting Christ. So to do is to insult Him. If I am to live the victorious life it is perfectly patent that I must submit. It is not enough to sing of submission. It is not enough to understand the theory of submission. It is not enough to consent to the declaration of the preacher that choice must be submitted to Him, and knowledge must be tested by the mastery of His mind, and the emotion purified in the fire of His love. These things must be done; and if they are not done there can be no victorious Christian life. This is the first thing, the radical thing, definite submission of the life to Christ.

That issues in the second statement, patient and persistent training under the control of Christ. Readjustment of all relationships because He is consulted in the choice. The formation of habits. I wish I could get young men and women to understand that the habits of the Christian life need forming just as the habits of the evil life do. Do not imagine that here by some mechanical action you come into the Christian life. You do in less than a moment come into the possession of the dynamic and the virtue, but you have to form new habits, and you have to be as persistent in your repetition of the good thing that is not habitual, until it becomes habitual, as you were in the repetition of the evil thing that was not habitual until it became habitual. Patient persistence also means cultivation of the neglected spiritual areas of your own personality. I am told that I no longer need to tell men they must be born anew, and in defense of the statement it is declared that many people are now refined, cultured and beautiful, apart from Christ. I admit it. In the narrow circle of what they are apart from Christ they may be in large measure —to use the language and to measure by the standards of the age—cultured, refined. That which is lacking is the consciousness of the spiritual areas of their own being. They never pray, I am told, and yet they are beautiful. I answer, So much less than beautiful, in that they do not pray. Prayer is the final attitude of life. Worship is the last expression of humanity's perfection. If there be no prayer, and no commerce with the eternal, no light of the flashing splendor of eternity on the brow, then life is vulgar, though you may refine it with the refinement of the latest university. There must be cultivation of the neglected spiritual areas of life in order that there may be victorious life.

All this means that there must be determined conflict, the perpetual battle of surrender, the refusal to act apart from Christ. Let me give you the word of Jesus in this connection, "If any man would come after Me, let him deny himself, and take up his cross daily, and follow Me." Not once and for ever, but "daily"! Once and forever, in the sense of the radical denial of self that puts Him on the throne. That is the first thing, and it ought to be such a denial that the attitude is to be maintained; but in the maintenance of the attitude there is to be perpetual taking up of the cross. For those living the Christian life no day will dawn, until that last day that has no eventide shall break upon the astonished gaze, in which it will not be necessary to come to a new cross, and bend to a new surrender. The refusal to act apart from Him is the beginning of the conflict. This is ever followed by the struggle with old claims, old habits, and the toil of cultivating the neglected areas of the being. When a man gives himself to Christ these spiritual areas of his own being are desert, and in order that they may blossom as the rose, and run with the rivers of God, and be beautiful with the light of the eternal morning, there must be cultivation and patience. All this is part of the conflict, and a small part of it. The larger part is that the soldier saint is forevermore pledged to engage in conflict against all that exalts itself against Christ, not only in his own life, but in his home, in his city, in the world.

I am not in the humor to say to young men and women that Christianity is easy, and that for two reasons. First, because I know it is not. Second, because I do not believe that doctrine makes any appeal to young life. I do appeal to those of you who have already put on the armor to take it up, and "stand . . . withstand," and find out whether it be possible, "having done all, to stand." I do appeal to those of you who tremble, and say, This is a serious message: according to this, Christianity is a serious and strenuous business; I am afraid of it. I make my appeal to you, Make trial for yourself of the possibilities.

I have a theory. I have a testimony. What is my theory? That Christ cannot fail. That if I am submitted to Him, obedient to Him, definitely fighting under His direction, I cannot fail. That is my theory. I have a testimony. What is it? That my theory works. Do not imagine I am boasting. I know how I have failed and still do fail. I have to say with the man who wrote this letter, I have not yet attained. I am not yet made perfect. I have not yet apprehended that for which I was apprehended. In these things I am almost ashamed to take Paul's words as my own. I fall so far behind what he knew experimentally of victory. I look back and there is the battlefield where I was beaten, but I know this, that when I was beaten it was my own fault; where I ought to have been surrendered, I had kept back part of the price; or I had grown weary of the discipline and the training for conflict; or I quietly, stealthily, devilishly let in one of the enemies of my Lord, and gave him room in my life. I have never failed since I gave myself to Christ except when I have been to blame. That is my testimony.

I will end as I began. I do not ask you to take my theory, to accept my testimony. Theory and testimony was valuable so far, but you must make your own trial of the possibility of this victorious life. Suppose that it be true that no one yet has lived such a life. I do not admit it actually, but for the sake of argument, and for the moment only. That is no reason why you should not make the adventure. If the world proceeded on the assumption that what no man has ever done no man can ever do, what would be done? Mountains would remain unclimbed. Pictures would remain unpainted. Poems would be unwritten and discoveries unmade. I pray you have done with this content with the experience of the average. Stand alone, and say, I will make this great adventure, I will give, so far as I am able, this Christ His chance of victory in me. I will, so help me God, put on this armor, take it up, stand and withstand, and find out whether having done all I can still stand.

Dwight Lyman Moody, long years ago in this England of ours, when he was unknown, heard it said that the world has yet to see what God can do with one man utterly and absolutely at His disposal. That statement turned all his life. Said Moody, If that is true, I will be that man and give God His chance. Now measure the rich, generous, gracious measure in which he made of his own life, and how he influenced other lives. The story has its disparity from my appeal, but it has its similarity. Make that adventure. Let every man who has seen the gleaming glory, and asks is this thing possible, say, I have heard the theory, I have heard the testimony, they interest me, but I will dismiss them, and for myself I will make this great adventure, and then presently, when the mists have melted, and the ultimate light is shining, there is no doubt that you will be able to say, "I have fought the good fight, I have finished the course, I have kept the faith"; and having done all, I stand.

CHAPTER VII

THE VALUE AND PROOF OF THE RESURRECTION

If Christ hath not been raised, then is our preaching vain, your faith also is vain.
I CORINTHIANS 15:14.

STRAUSS, WHO WAS ONE OF THE MOST BRILLIANT OF THE critics of Christianity, and one of the most unbelieving of the apologists of Christ, declared the resurrection to be the center of the center. That declaration harmonizes with the view of the greatest exponent of the Christian faith in apostolic times. "If Christ hath not been raised, then is our preaching vain, your faith also is vain. Yea, and we are found false witnesses of God; because we witnessed of God that He raised up Christ: Whom He raised not up, if so be that the dead are not raised. For if the dead are not raised, neither hath Christ been raised: and if Christ hath not been raised your faith is vain; ye are yet in your sins. Then they also which are fallen asleep in Christ have perished. If in this life only we have hoped in Christ, we are of all men most pitiable." No language can be clearer. The resurrection is the groundwork of faith because all else in connection with the affirmations of Christianity must be interpreted by it. If Christ hath been raised, then evangelical Christianity is true. If Christ hath not been raised, then all other matters of our faith are misinterpretations. If Christ hath not been raised then God was no more manifest in flesh in Christ than in other men. If Christ hath not been raised then the teaching of Jesus has no other authority than the authority of His own personal conviction, and must be tested by subsequent thinking and speculation. If Christ hath not been raised then the Cross of Calvary was nothing more than the tragic ending of a mistaken, if noble life. All the values of evangelical Christianity are dependent on interpretations of the person and mission of Jesus resulting from acceptance of the central fact of His resurrection.

I desire to speak first of the place of the resurrection in the economy of redemption, as revealed in the Scriptures of Truth; and second, of the values of the resurrection as a basis of faith for all such as are crying out after purity, and after God.

First, then, the place of the resurrection in the economy of redemption. The Christian religion is pre-eminently a religion of redemption. Its whole message may be summarized in the words of our Lord concerning Himself, "The Son of man came to seek and to save that which was lost." That tells the story not merely of the mission of Jesus, it reveals the real meaning of the Christian religion. It begins with man as incompetent, and has to do with the method of his saving, his remaking. That is the distinctive note of Christianity. In that it is differentiated from any and every other religion of which the world has ever known anything. Other religions are ethical, and attempt to interpret to men the higher ideals of life. In so far as they do so they also have Divine authority. Yet others insist upon the necessity of man's culture of his own life, and almost invariably tell him with strange, weird, awful honesty, that his endeavor will be of no avail. The Christian religion comes to man everywhere, and says in effect, Thou art lost, but mayest be found. Thou hast failed, but thou mayest succeed. Thou art ruined, but thou mayest be redeemed. The content of the Christian religion is the declaration of pardon, and of power, and of peace.

In the Bible there is one central figure, and one central truth. The central Person in the Bible is Jesus of Nazareth, called as to person, Son of man and Son of God; bearing as supreme title, indicating the meaning of His mission, the Christ of God. There can be no intelligent study of the Bible that does not show the pathways since His life in the world started with that life, and owe their direction to His indication and His impulse.

The Christian religion may be summarized in one very brief sentence, "God was in Christ reconciling the world unto Himself." I therefore take the life and ministry of Jesus and divide it into four parts. First, there is the fact of incarnation. Second, there is the ministry of His life, His teaching, and His deeds. Third, there is the Cross. Ultimately, there is the resurrection. Let us interpret these facts by the supreme word, "God was in Christ reconciling the world unto Himself." To do so is to recognize that the whole life and ministry of Jesus of Nazareth was an unveiling of the truth concerning God. God was speaking out into speech that men could understand the infinite and eternal things concerning Himself. In the incarnation God did not come any nearer to humanity than He had been before. I go back into the twilight of the Old Testament, and I find the stupendous recognition of the nearness of God to human life. When the prophet at the Babylonish court charged the king with sin, he said, "The God in Whose hand thy breath is, and Whose are all thy ways, hast thou not glorified." The Psalmist declared, Thou knowest my downsitting and mine uprising, Thou understandest my thought afar off. . . . Whither shall I go from Thy Spirit? Or whither shall I flee from Thy presence? If I ascend up into heaven, Thou art there: If I make my bed in Sheol, behold, Thou art there." The singers and the writers of the past were thus conscious of the nearness of God. Paul speaking in the midst of the culture of Athens, said to the philosophic Greeks, "In Him we live, and move, and have our being." Men knew the nearness of God, but they did not know the God to Whom they were near. The incarnation was not the method by which God came nearer to humanity, but the method by which He came into the observation of humanity, and took the speech that man was able to understand. The Word, inarticulate through the far-flung splendor of the ages, became flesh, became articulate in human speech and human accents and human tones, in order that men might hear in their own language the infinite truth concerning God. By way of the incarnation God came into human observation; came into such form and fashion that the men who had ever lived in His presence, whose breath had been in His hand through all their lives, might listen and understand, might see and comprehend. That is the first fact in the ministry of Christ.

The second fact is exactly true to the same underlying principle. I follow Him through all the years of His private life, along the pathway of His public ministry; and as I do so I am coming to the knowledge of God. God is revealing to me His thought for me, His purpose for me, the meaning of the breadth, beauty, and beneficence of His government. I do not wonder, as I ponder the words of Jesus that have been preserved for me by the inspired writers, that men exclaimed, "Never man so spake." Was the message a new message? Was God giving us a new thought? Had God changed His mind?

By no means. In Christ He said the thing that He always thought and intended, but He so said it that man might understand it. Through all the ministry of Christ I have the unveiling of the will of God for human life. Observe Him, moreover, in His attitudes toward men. His awful severity against sin, His gracious tenderness toward the sinner, unveil the attitude of God toward sin, and toward the sinner. The words that passed His lips, that scorch me even until this hour, are the words of God about sin. The words that passed His lips, and which woo and win me toward His heart for rest and healing, are the words of God toward me the sinner.

Now, reverently, one step further. As I stand in the presence of the Cross, I must recognize that the Crucified One is the same Person that I have looked upon in the years of public ministry, the same Person Who is described as the Word made flesh. If "God was in Christ reconciling the world unto Himself" when He came into human life, and as He passed along the pathway of human teaching, it is still true that "God was in Christ reconciling the world unto Himself" in the Cross. In that Cross is unveiled before humanity the grace of God, operating through suffering, toward the restoration of man. The Cross of Jesus Christ, according to the interpretation of the New Testament, was not the place where one Jesus of Nazareth, Who was also God in Christ, wrought out into human visibility the infinite and unfathomable mystery of that passion and pain whereby it is possible for God to take back the sinning man and remake him.

So, finally, when I come to the final fact of the resurrection, it is the revelation of the strength of God accomplishing the utmost purpose of His will. I go back to some of the ancient words concerning Him. Hear this, for instance, "In all their affliction He was afflicted." There are those who believe that from that passage a negation has been omitted and that what was actually written was this, "In all their affliction He was *not* afflicted." I do not say that is an accurate statement, but admitting it for the moment, see what is said. "In their affliction"—He was in it, He shared it, He passed through it with them—but He was not afflicted, He was not beaten down, overcome, defeated. Even if we take the gracious statement as it stands it has the same significance. "In all their affliction He was afflicted. . . . He bare them, and carried them all the days of old." I reverently come to the Cross and there I see unveiled the mystery I can never explain. I will not attempt to interpret it by the words of Scripture. The great herald of Jesus Christ said, "Behold the Lamb of God which taketh away the sin of the world." The apostolic writer said, "His own self bare our sins in His own body upon the tree." Still believing that this is God in Christ, I am face to face with the tremendous declaration that God is bearing the sin of the race. The resurrection demonstrates the fact that He was equal to the burden; that He carried it; that He dealt with it as He intended to deal with it; and therefore the writers of the New Testament invariably when they speak of the resurrection speak of it as the manifestation of the might of God. The apostle declares to us that He was "declared to be the Son of God with power, according to the Spirit of holiness, by the resurrection of the dead; even Jesus Christ our Lord." The Resurrection is the revelation of the strength of Deity; the revelation of the fact that if He was oppressed, burdened with the passion of human sin, He was not overcome thereby; that in the process of bearing the burden He accomplished His purpose, and came at last to ultimate victory. Peter had the same vision of it when He declared, "It was not possible that He should be holden of it." So that the place of the resurrection in the economy of redemption is that of demonstration of the fact that all God thought for human redemption, all God attempted in the mystery of His own being for human redemption, He accomplished.

In the incarnation the fact of God was manifest. By the pathway of Christ's public ministry the will of God was interpreted. In His crucifixion, the grace of God was unveiled. In the resurrection, the victorious strength of God was manifest. The importance of the resurrection is at once evident. Take the first three facts away from the fourth, and what is the result? He claimed identity with the Father, "I and the Father are one." He claimed authority from the Father for all He taught, "I do nothing of Myself, but as the Father hath taught Me, I speak these things." He claimed co-operation with the Father in His work, "My Father worketh even until now, and I work." I come to His Cross and I see Him die. I watch them as they bear Him tenderly and reverently, and place Him in the rock-hewn tomb, and I stand outside that tomb in the garden, and see the great stone rolled to the entrance and the seal of the Roman government placed upon it. Now, what of His claim to identity with the Father? What of His claim to authority from the Father? What of His claim to co-operation with the Father? "If Christ hath not been raised, then is our preaching vain, your faith also is vain." If there was no resurrection all the things declared are discredited. If there was resurrection these things are demonstrated. The whole Christian religion depends upon the fact of the resurrection of Christ. If He never rose, then the story of the incarnation is a myth. If He never rose then I have no demonstration of the authority of

His teaching. If He never rose, then His dying was no more than the dying of Thomas Cranmer. If He rose, then by that resurrection His Person is revealed as other than the person of Thomas Cranmer, His life as different from the life of other men, His teaching as having Divine authority, and His Cross as having some infinite value and meaning. Everything depends upon the resurrection.

Paul did not end with a hypothesis. His ultimate word is, "But now hath Christ been raised from the dead, the firstfruits of them that are asleep. For since by man came death, by man came also the resurrection of the dead. For as in Adam all die, so also in Christ shall all be made alive." The infinite music of the Gospel singing itself through Paul's heart, he declares the possibility of human redemption, basing his conviction, his testimony, upon the great and gracious fact that Jesus Christ rose from among the dead.

Degrade Christ from the place that He has occupied in evangelical Christianity, from that conception which has made the Church what she has been through the centuries; speak of Him merely as on the level of other men, and you have lost your revelation of God, and your ethical authority, and your salvation by passion and suffering and death; and in order to do this you are compelled to deny the actual historic fact of the resurrection. Let that fact of actual resurrection be admitted, and it interprets all the other facts, and explains the history and mystery of the conquest of Christianity through the centuries. "God was in Christ reconciling the world unto Himself," revealing His nearness in the fact of incarnation, interpreting His will in the teaching of Jesus, making visible the awful mystery of His passion in the presence of sin, by the Cross; demonstrating the might by which

He accomplishes the redemption, in the greatness and glory of resurrection.

Now let me turn to the second line of consideration, which is the personal application of that already taken. What is the value of the resurrection as a basis of faith? In order that we may see that let me ask you to think of Jesus before the resurrection as to the claims He made in the presence of human life, as to the purpose He declared He had in view, and as to the promises He definitely made to men as He taught amongst them.

Of His claims, I will refer to only one. In differing ways He deliberately claimed that He and He alone could lead the soul of man to God. There are many texts. Let me take you to that oldest and most familiar, which we generally begin to recite thus, "Come unto Me." That is not the commencement of the declaration. Jesus did not begin there. He began thus, "All things have been delivered unto Me of My Father: and no one knoweth the Son, save the Father; neither doth any know the Father, save the Son, and he to whomsoever the Son willeth to reveal Him." To whom will the Son reveal the Father? In a moment the answer to our inquiry comes, "Come unto Me." By all of which Christ meant to say, first of all, that what humanity needs in its restlessness is to find God. If you would cure the feverishness of life you must lead men to God. Now, mark His claim. "Neither doth any know the Father save the Son." Blasphemous audacity, or Divine Gospel, one of the two! He claimed to be the Revealer of the Father. He declared that His mission was that of leading souls to God.

What did He say concerning His purpose? He declared that He could accomplish His purpose only by dying, and whenever He referred to His dying He referred to His rising again. By many a hint in earlier days of His ministry, by clear and definite declaration in the midst of hostile crowds, by careful and patient instruction to His own disciples, He affirmed the necessity for dying, and declared that if He died He would rise again. I say by many a hint in the earlier days of His ministry. Take two illustrations. When He cleansed the temple and they inquired, "By what authority doest Thou these things?" He answered them, "Destroy this temple, and in three days I will raise it up"; referring to His body, as the inspired writer declares later. On the housetops at night, with the wind sighing through the streets of Jerusalem, an inquiring soul said to Him, "How can these things be?" Jesus said, "Ye must be born anew." This man asked, How can a man blot out the past and begin again? Jesus said in answer, "As Moses lifted up the serpent in the wilderness, even so must the Son of man be lifted up: that whosoever believeth may in Him have eternal life." Life shall come through death was His answer to the inquiry of Nicodemus. If you question the interpretation of these particular passages then come to the set and definite discourse chronicled in the tenth chapter of John's Gospel. There is nothing more wonderful in all the discourses of Jesus than that. He said, "I am the good shepherd: the good shepherd layeth down His life for the sheep. . . . I lay down My life, that I may take it again. This commandment received I from My Father." Or if you turn from the public declaration, which perhaps has in it still something of mystery, then follow the last weeks after Cæsarea Philippi, and listen attentively. "From that time began Jesus to show unto His disciples, how that He *must* go unto Jerusalem, and suffer many things of the elders and chief priests and scribes, and be killed, and the third day be raised up." How often we read that carelessly. If you tell me that was simply the conclusion of a far-seeing soul, if you tell me that Jesus was such as I am, a child of His own age, blundering His way on with great honesty, and seeing that at last these men would kill Him, and that He is now taking His disciples into His confidence and saying, Well, I see how it will all end, they will kill Me. I have been true to My teaching, and when I go to Jerusalem I know they will kill Me—then how do you explain the last thing, "and the third day be raised again"? If you study your New Testament carefully you will discover that He never spoke of His death to His disciples but that He also spoke of His resurrection. I challenge you to find a single exception. In those last weeks, over and over again, He called them to Him and always seems to have been seeking their sympathy, as He told them of the Cross; but He always told them also of the resurrection. Of course, if you question the accuracy of the records, and tear up the New Testament, do not come and hear me preach. I have nothing to preach but this Book. I have no authority other than this. I am not here to defend its authority. That is demonstrated by nineteen centuries of victory in the moral realm.

I come once more to the tomb. He is dead. He is in the tomb. I come as a sinning man. I come as a man who has to say, "The good which I would I do not; but the evil which I would not, that I practise . . . to me who would do good, evil is present." I come as a man who would say to all philosophers: do not discuss how the poison came into my blood; it is here, mastering me; I have sinned; I have seen the fair vision of His teaching and I desire it, but I cannot realize it; I am a sinner with guilt and pollution upon me. This Man said He would lay down His life for me, and take it again that I might share it. This Man said I might be born again by the mystery of His dying. He declared emphatically that He must die and be raised again. He is dead. If He do not come out of that tomb I will not say that He was a deceiver, but He was deceived. If He do not come out of that tomb, the thing He thought to do He has been unable to do. I cannot put it less reverently than that, but I must so put it. I stand in the presence of that sealed tomb of Jesus and say, Is He coming back? If He do not come forth, then though He laid down His life, He cannot take it again; the burden has been too much, the desire too mighty, the great dream of redemption of man by the laying down of His life and taking it again that they may share it, a great dream, but nothing more. If that stone remain there, and Jesus is held captive, then there is no pardon for my guilty soul, and no life for my paralyzed humanity. "If Christ hath not been raised . . . your faith also is vain, void;" yea and it is true in my heart and life.

"But now hath Christ been raised from the dead?" In the moment of that resurrection all the claims of His life and teaching are vindicated. When I see Him come back from the grave I know full well that what He said is true. I know He laid down His life and has taken it again. In the mystery of that death, I cannot enter into the awful chambers of its loneliness, I am forevermore excluded. I cannot understand it or explain it, but I know there has been—

> One death grapple in the darkness 'twixt old systems and the Word.

Between the Lord of life, and death, and sin. If He did not rise again, then death won, and sin won. If He hath been raised, then He won and death is vanquished, because sin is spoiled. Then the sinner has found his Redeemer. If He took

His life again, to share it, then I know that His dying was victorious dying; and the value of His dying He makes over to me for pardon; and the virtue of His life He makes over to me for power, and the presence of my risen Lord shall forevermore be the method of my victory.

I make the application of the great fact of resurrection in the words of this selfsame apostle in his epistle of salvation. Hear them, "If thou shalt confess with my mouth Jesus as Lord, and shalt believe in thy heart that God raised Him from the dead, thou shalt be saved: for with the heart man believeth unto righteousness; and with the mouth confession is made unto salvation. For the Scripture saith, Whosoever believeth on Him shall not be put to shame." Why does the apostle put the resurrection there, why not the Cross? Why did he not say, If thou shalt confess with thy mouth Jesus as Lord, and shalt believe in thy heart that He died for thee, thou shalt be saved? Because that will not satisfy reason, and so creates no basis for faith. Death apart from resurrection makes no appeal to my confidence. Death in the light of the resurrection is that in which I put my trust. I come into the presence of the death of Christ while the light of His resurrection plays upon it, and I say, He loved me and gave Himself for Me; He was wounded for my transgressions, He was bruised for my iniquities; the chastisement of my peace was upon Him and with His stripes I am healed. It is all night if He rose not. It was a tragic death, awful death, a death of failure, as other deaths have been. In the light of resurrection I know it was a death triumphant, a death of accomplishment, a death of victory in the process of which He procured for me the pardon that my sinning heart needs, and the power my weakened life demands.

CHAPTER VIII

THE PURPOSE OF LIFE

Every one that is called by My name, and whom I have created for My glory; I have formed him; yea, I have made him.

ISAIAH 43:7.

THE FIRST APPLICATION OF THIS TEXT WAS TO GOD'S ANCIENT people Israel. The whole message of which it forms a part was delivered to the chosen nation. The opening word of the text indicates the fact that the prophet was thinking, not so much of the whole nation as of the individuals who made up the nation. "Every one" is a distributive by use of which the thought passes to individual life, and the great purpose of its being. "Every one that is called by My name, and whom I have created for My glory; I have formed him; yea, I have made him."

My purpose in taking this verse is not at all to deal with it in its application to the nation of Israel. Neither is it my purpose to deal with it in its application to individual members of that nation only. It is my purpose rather to take it as a revelation of the principle that has application in the case of every individual life; for while there are special ways in which Israel was indeed the chosen nation, and special ways in which the members of that nation were the chosen people of God, yet we must ever remember that all the things said concerning them, in their deepest intention, reveal the thought and intention of God for all men. I have taken this verse out of the ancient prophecy, then, because I conceive it to be a remarkable declaration of the real purpose of human life. "Every one that is called by My name, and whom I have created for My glory; I have formed him; yea, I have made him."

The whole burden of the message of the verse, and consequently the burden of the message I bring you to-night, may thus be expressed in briefest words, *Man is created for the glory of God.* The Bible makes clear to us that this is true, not only of the elect people, but of all humanity. The charge made by the prophet in the ancient days against the king of Babylon was couched in these remarkable terms, "The God in Whose hand thy breath is, hast thou not glorified." We should have charged neglect of his kingdom; with encouraging vice. He was guilty of all these things, but the spokesman of the eternal purpose and the mouthpiece of the Divine message to the profligate king said nothing of these manifestations. He at once struck at the root of the trouble, "The God in Whose hand thy breath is hast thou not glorified." It is equally evident that the principle has application to all men when we come to study the New Testament argument of salvation. Paul, in his letter to the Romans, having shown that the Gentile failed because he held down the truth in unrighteousness, and the Jew because he failed to be obedient to the revelation of God, sums up the whole situation in these striking words, intimately related to the thought suggested by my text, "All have sinned, and fall short of the glory of God." So whether it be the ancient Babylonish king, or whether it be humanity, both Jew and Gentile, the Bible declares that human failure consists in failure to glorify God. That brings us back to our text, with its simple central declaration, "whom I have created for My glory."

A right understanding for the purpose of human life will give us the true standard by which to measure our lives. That is the supreme difficulty, we so perpetually measure ourselves by wrong standards. When Robert Burns sang,

> O wad some power the giftie gie us
> To see ourselves as ithers see us,

he did not touch the deepest thing in human life. It would be a great advantage to us sometimes if we could see ourselves as others see us, but it would be a temporal and passing advantage. If we would find the supreme advantage we must see ourselves as God sees us. When Dr. Jowett was Master of Balliol, on one occasion at dinner a lady, desiring to draw from him some smart witticism, asked him, somewhat flippantly, "Tell us, Dr. Jowett, what do you really think of God?" His answer came quick and sharp: "Madam, it matters nothing what I think of God; it matters everything what God thinks of me." When we allow the Scriptures of Truth to do their work in our lives they always compel us to that judgment seat. We come to the standard of eternity, to the balances of the sanctuary, to the measurements of God.

The declaration of the text is supreme, "whom I have created for My glory." I call you then to quiet meditation on that declaration along two lines. First, man a creation of God; and secondly, man a creation of God, for Himself, and for His glory.

First, then, man a creation of God. In this one brief verse three words are employed to describe that creation. Whereas I am not going to detain you at any length, for detailed examination of them, suggestive as such examination would be, I cannot wholly pass them over. "I have created . . . I have formed . . . I have made." The Hebrew words living at the back of these three English words are as distinct as are the English, and more so; for we may interchange the English words, but we cannot interchange the Hebrew, each one having a separate emphasis and signification. The first word is the essential one, to which I draw your attention specially, "I have *created*." It is an all-inclusive word, which indicates actual causing to be, by the God of omnipotent power and wisdom. At your leisure you will read again the first chapter of Genesis, and you will find these words there used with great accuracy. The word translated "created" appears in that chapter three times only. The word translated "made" occurs over and over again. The word "created" is used only when there was evidently an entirely new beginning, a new departure. If you accept the evolutionary theory of creation you will remember that there are gaps that have never been filled; not a missing link, but many missing links. Three principal links are missing. There is the link between man and the highest form of life beneath him. There is the link between the animal life which is sentient and the vegetable life that lies beneath it. There is a missing link at the back of everything as to origination of the first fact in creation. At those points in your book of Genesis the word "created" occurs and nowhere else. "In the beginning God created," the primal activity of Deity. The word appears again between the vegetable and the animal kingdoms. It occurs again when man appears upon the scene. It is the essential word that indicates the original act of causing to be.

The second word in this particular verse, the word "formed," is a word which indicates a process. It is a word which is perpetually used of the potter at his work at the wheel. By manipulation of things already existing, a new thing is made to be.

The third word, "made," is a word which indicates the outlook on the result. I have made. I have accomplished. I have finished.

I cannot think that it is without signification that the prophet gathered up the three great words used to describe the making of anything when he spoke of what God does in the case of man. *I have created him;* the original essential thought was that of God, and the act by which the thought of God was realized was that of God. *I have formed him;* all the mysterious and hidden processes so full of interest and yet for ever baffling the ingenuity of man perfectly to discover are the processes of God. *I have made him;* when at last he stands upon the earth the completed being the finality of the work is of God.

To me in this great declaration of my text there is infinite comfort. Man in all his complex nature is a thought of God, a work of God. I look out upon nature everywhere, and see in the handiwork of man inventions and improvements, but there is no advance in man, save as man is developed; that is, save as that which already lies within him potentially is realized in the process of human history. All the culture of this age and of every age is simply the development into visibility of powers Divinely bestowed in the original creation of man. How wonderful are the thoughts of men. I see them expressed in architecture, in sculpture, in art, in poetry, in philosophy; but all these are broken lights of that essential thought of God which He wrought out when He made man. Some of you will remember how angry John Ruskin was with the railway train, with what vehement passion he denounced the monster that swept over the landscape and spoiled it. I plead guilty, if guilty be the word to use, to being a disciple of John Ruskin. I owe more than I can tell to his writings, but I never could follow him in that vehement denunciation of the railway train. I stand upon an eminence, and looking out over the landscape see the fields of exquisite green, or, as Ruskin says, the ploughed field which sweeps up the hillside in folds of russet velvet; and as I look a railway train comes thundering across the country. Then I am always inclined to worship the man that made the train, because of the ingenuity that is revealed in it, the wonderful and determined mastership of nature that laughs at mileage and acres, and moves swiftly to its destination. I see in the train, not the smoke, that is a process and will be consumed presently, but rather the power of humanity manifesting itself. Everything that has come from the thinking and planning and working of man is the result of the creation of God. Man is God's thought, and God's creation, and in himself is infinitely more than all his work. Humanity is the creation of God, the crowning creation, the last fact in the wonderful process of creative power. Every human being stands upon that final eminence, and the greatness of man is but evidence of the greatness of God. Man is of Divine creation.

Man is not only of Divine creation in that broadest sense. Every man is a Divine creation. There is an old saying which is used about some outstanding man. I have heard it used on this side of the Atlantic of Oliver Cromwell, and on the other side of Abraham Lincoln. God made Oliver Cromwell and broke the mold; God made Abraham Lincoln and broke the mold. I have no quarrel with the statement. I have a perpetual quarrel with the suggestion. What is the suggestion? That God occasionally makes some remarkable man and breaks the mold, that there may be no repetition. He breaks the mold after He has made every man! Every man is a lonely individuality, a special thought of God, incarnate. When Jesus stood before Pilate, and Pilate challenged Him as to Kingship and as to truth, Christ said, "To this end have I been born, and to this end am I come into the world, that I should bear witness unto the truth." It was a great declaration of conscious individuality, potentiality, responsibility. Every man can say the same in some measure. The trouble is we do not all find out for what we were born and for what purpose we came into the world. In the great economy of God, in the wondrous, matchless marvel of His government it is true of every human being, "whom I have created for My glory."

But it is not only that man is Divine creation; according to the teaching of this book He is a Divine expression, made in the image of God. Perfect personality can only be postulated of God Himself, and that personality is limited in man. Whatever you think of personality, you are thinking finally of the infinite, eternal personality in God. Force, mind, heart, will. Are these elements that constitute personality in man? They are all shadows of the things that constitute the personality of Deity. Man is distinct from all lower creation in this, and herein lies his dignity, that in some way, which perhaps he never perfectly understands, he is kin of God; in His image, made with His likeness, an outworking into visibility of the essential facts concerning God Himself.

Because of these things man is the one link between the material and the spiritual. He is the point in which all lower forms of life touch the highest and become familiar with it. He is the point at which all the highest forms of existence touch the lower, and make them flash and flame with beauty. I pass over all this world and I see everywhere life in creation, but it never becomes spiritual until I see it in man. There is never recognition of the infinite and the eternal until I come to man. I think there is profound significance in the discovery of the opening declarations of John's gospel, where the mystic writer says of the incarnation of the Word, "In Him was life; and the life was the light of men." You cannot say that of anything lower in the scale of creation. You can say "In him was life" of every blade of grass, of every daisy that decks the sod, of every bird that poises in air its wing, and sings the song of seraphim; but you cannot say "the life was light" until you come to man. All else was created by God; but when creation reached man man turned round and looked into the face of God and knew Him. Light flamed with the coming of man. In him the lower orders of creation reach light, and finality. In man earth has traffic with heaven. In man heaven stoops down to earth and makes it beautiful. This is true of every man. Created by God. An expression of God. A link between the material and the spiritual worlds.

Now pass to the second of these thoughts. For what is such a being made? I have created him, said Jehovah by the mouth of Isaiah, for My glory. Here my difficulty begins. I know this is the ancient phraseology of the Church. We are all familiar with it, but how shall we say it so that the declaration may startle us into attention and change the whole order and current of our lives? It ought so to do, and will so do, if we can but hear it as we ought to hear it. Allow me a moment or two with the background of negation. What is the purpose of human life? There is the day of birth, and out there somewhere is the day of death, and these are but human terms, the full meaning of which none of us fully understands. The beginning and the end. What is the real meaning of the interim, of all that which lies between the wail of birth, and the darkness of death? What is the real meaning of human life, its true purpose? I will mention some things to you. The amassing of wealth, the acquisition of knowledge, the pursuit of pleasure. I mention these things only to dismiss them. You have already dismissed them. The deepest in you has said at once, No, it cannot be that a man Divinely created, himself an expression of Deity, a link between the material and the spiritual worlds, has as the purpose of his existence such things as these. Let them be dismissed. I will not stay to argue them for a moment.

Once again. Think of the day of birth. Think of the day of death. Tell me what is the purpose of the life that lies between? Is it the salvation of the soul? Certainly not. That is but the initial activity enabling a man to fulfil the purpose of his being. Is it then sympathy with sorrow? Assuredly not. The day will come—it seems slow in coming but it will come—when God shall wipe away all tears from men's eyes, and sorrow—listen, this is not my imagination, this is inspiration—"sorrow and sighing shall flee away," like black plumaged birds, never to return. Then is the purpose of life the service of humanity? No, that does not touch the deepest. That may be a method by which man to-day will fulfil the purpose of his being, but there is a profounder answer.

What, then, is the real meaning of this strange, complex, and marvelous life of mine; creation of God, expression of God, in itself a link between dust and Deity, between the material and the spiritual? I go back to the ancient prophecy. "Whom I have created for My glory." Allow me to illuminate that declaration by the revelation of the Bible generally, without referring to any particular passage. Man is created first for the knowledge of God. Man is created secondly for communion with God. Man is created thirdly for action with God. Man is created finally for revelation of God.

Man is created first for knowledge of God. There is given to man a consciousness of God which no other being has. The light of the uncreated beam is focussed in the lens of a human spirit. Zophar, in the olden days, said, "Canst thou by searching find out God?" and the answer intended, and the accurate answer, is, By no means. Yet man can know God, although he cannot know Him absolutely and perfectly, just as a man cannot encompass in his thinking eternity. Although eternity as a thought baffles the proud intellect of man, a man can know it. The moment in which a man knows the limitlessness of space he knows that he cannot know it; but in knowing that he cannot know it, he knows it. The moment a man encompasses in his mind the thought of unending duration he knows he cannot know all the meaning of it; but knowing that he cannot know it is to be sure of it, and so to know it. No dog thinks of eternity. No lower form of life thinks of unending space. No other created being can know God, but man is made to know Him. This is the first way in which man glorifies God, by coming to know Him. To this bear witness the words of Jesus Himself, so full of meaning. "This is age-abiding life, that they should know Thee, the only true God, and Him Whom Thou didst send."

Man is made not merely for the knowledge of God but also for fellowship with God, communion with God. In every man there is a desire, and capacity to listen to the voice of God. In every human being there is the possibility of sympathy in thought and feeling with God. It is sadly lacking in all of us, even in the best; yet there is no man or woman in

London but is capable of communion with God; no man or woman but that can desire and cry out after the living God. Where that listening and that crying out and that desire are instructed and directed and obeyed, then God is to be found and known, and communed with. If my assertion is not enough, then in this sanctuary to-night there are hundreds of witnesses who still hear the voice saying amid the city's din and bustle, "This is the way, walk ye in it." For this communion man is made.

All of these are but preliminary and fundamental things. Not merely for knowledge of God and communion with God man is made, but also for co-operation with God. What was it in the beginning? Go, dig this garden and keep it. When the first man began his delving and his digging, his watching and his cultivation, until there came first the blade, then the ear, then the full corn in the ear; first the sapling, then the tree, then the verdure garments, and then the fruit, what was he doing? Working with God. He was partner with God. When the last man delved in your garden, and put in those russet bulbs that had no form or comeliness that you should desire them, and waited and watched until the spring time came and kissed the ground, and out of the russet bulb came the glorious flower, that man worked with God. Co-operation with God is the law of human life, and for that man was created.

I come from Eden and look at the second man, the last Adam.

The whole story of how He glorified God is told in His own words, "My Father worketh hitherto, and I work." Co-operation with God in His case was Redemption and Renewal; gathering the thorns out of the garden and bathing them in His blood that the curse might be removed. It is a metaphor, a figure of speech, but the infinite fact behind is far finer than the figure can ever suggest. The Church in so far as she fulfils the Divine ideal, to use the apostle's words of all its members, is composed of "workers together with God." To-day saintly men and women are in co-operation with God, and presently in those dim and purple distances of the ages to come the ransomed will co-operate with God, for through the Church the kindness of God is to be manifest, and to the principalities and powers in heavenly places is to be made known by them the wisdom of God.

So that man finally fulfils the purpose of his being by such activity with God as results in the revelation of God. Angels desire to look into these things; they bend over, peer into, watch with intense interest the whole process and progress of man. Why? Because, according to that great Pauline teaching, the angels are learning God through His manifestation in humanity as they cannot learn Him anywhere else. Man reveals to man the truth of God, as in the Fatherhood of God he realizes the brotherhood of man. Devils are learning through human history God's righteousness and God's power, and the ultimate doom of evil. For co-operation with God man is made.

Thus man fulfils the purpose of his being. Every man who is living for any lower thing than to glorify God is prostituting God-given powers. It is an ugly word. It is a word that is hardly used in polite society. Yet I pray you remember there is a prostitution as vile as the sin we shudder at; which yet, alas, man seldom trembles at the thought of. It is the prostitution of human life to anything lower than the glory of God. Do I take these hours, these days; these powers, this thought, this mind, this spirit, and use them for any other purpose ultimately than to glorify God? That is prostitution.

Sin is just that, wilful, chosen failure to seek the glory of God. That was the meaning of the word of Jesus when He said concerning Nicodemus, and through him concerning every man, "Ye must be born anew." That was the meaning of Paul when he wrote, "Ye have put off the old man with his doings, and have put on the new man, which is being renewed unto knowledge after the image of Him that created him."

Now I have done; and you will begin. In the light of this consideration, what about our life? God requireth that which is past. Where is it? What of the years that have gone? Yonder the day of birth, I can name it, and date it, and fix it. Somewhere is the day of dissolution. I cannot name it. I cannot date it. I cannot fix it. All these years since then till now have gone. What have I done with them? No such question can be asked, and honestly answered without our having to confess, "We have sinned, and fall short of the glory of God." Yet it is to those who have so sinned, and so come short of the glory of God that He sent His Son. "The Son of man came to seek and to save that which was lost." Here to-night in actual and spiritual presence is that selfsame Saviour. One of the words of my text is the word "formed," the word which I reminded you indicates the activity of the potter. Take that word and let me finish with it. Take that word as I find it in this same Bible. The vessel that the potter formed is marred, spoiled, ruined in the hand of the potter, but *He will make it again another vessel.*

See how you have failed. See how you have groveled in the dust. See how when the golden crown was held over your head, like the man with the muckrake you sought the satisfaction of the glitter of a straw. Behind you are the years the cankerworm hath eaten. The promise is that "He will restore the years that the cankerworm hath eaten." The promise is that "He will make it again another vessel." All He asks is that you will understand another great declaration of this chapter, "I am Jehovah; and beside Me there is no Saviour." Let us come to Him as a Saviour and we shall find Him full of pity, full of power. The past may be forgiven and we may yet live to His glory.

CHAPTER IX

THE CITIES OF MEN AND THE CITY OF GOD

Therefore let us also, seeing we are compassed about with so great a cloud of witnesses, lay aside every weight, and the sin which doth so easily beset us, and let us run with patience the race that is set before us, looking unto Jesus, the Author and Perfecter of our faith, Who for the joy that was set before Him, endured the cross, despising shame, and hath sat down at the right hand of the throne of God.

HEBREWS 12:1, 2.

THERE IS AN IRRESISTIBLE CHARM ABOUT THIS PASSAGE OF Scripture. The suggestions that lie within its compass appeal to us. The mystery of the cloud of witnesses; the strenuous reality of the description of the present experience of the saints under the figure of a race; and, finally, the lonely splendor of the Lord of Faith. It seems a ruthless thing to dissect and analyze a passage so full of beauty as this passage undoubtedly is; and yet this is in part what I propose to do, and that for a very simple reason—that it seems to me that a partial interpretation has robbed it of much of its spacious and far-reaching value. A very common and popular interpretation of the passage is that the writer of the letter is here describing the individual race of a Christian soul through this world toward the mystic and mysterious heaven that lies beyond it; that as the runner presses along his way he is watched in his running by great companies of those who have gone before; and that, in order to win his individual crowning, he is urged to lay aside weights and the sin that doth so easily beset. That interpretation I have referred to as being partial; I am inclined to use a much stronger word, and to say that it is wholly and absolutely inaccurate. I know something of the strenuousness of the individual race. I believe with all my soul in the ultimate glory of the heaven that lies beyond our vision. I am perfectly certain that it is necessary, in order to run that individual race, that there should be the laying aside of weights and of the easily besetting sin; but if the passage be taken, as it ought to be taken, in its contextual relationship, we shall see that the argument is wider in application.

The first word of the passage drives us in honesty to that which has preceded it. A passage commencing with the word "therefore" must of necessity be an appeal based upon an argument already advanced. The argument of this passage lies in all that has preceded it. Let us refresh our minds by passing over the content. The letter opens with a thunderclap. "God, having of old time spoken unto the fathers in the prophets by divers portions and divers manners, hath at the end of these days spoken unto us in His Son." The writer of the letter takes two things for granted—God, and God's revelation of Himself to man. He then immediately begins the specific work of his letter. He is most evidently writing to those whose outlook has been narrow. The Hebrew people had come to think of themselves as the elect people of God, and imagined in their own unutterable narrowness and folly that God had forgotten or neglected the other nations of the earth. When members of this nation passed from Judaism into Christianity, all the things that ratified them in their ancient convictions were broken down and swept away.

They believed that their economy had been administered by angels; that their leaders had been Moses, who led them out of slavery, and Joshua, who led them into the land; that their system of priesthood and religion was lonely and final.

And now mark the method of the writer. He shows them how in Christ are realized the underlying principles which they have so largely lost sight of; and that all the things which they would make their own peculiar possession are fulfilled by Christ. Ministry by angels, he does not deny; but the Son is above the angels, and the new economy means the ministration of the Son. Led out by Moses, he does not deny; but Moses led out, and could not lead in. The new leader leads out and leads in. Led in by Joshua, he agrees; but Joshua, having led them in, could not give them rest. The new Leader leads them in, and, Himself entering into rest, makes rest possible to all who trust in Him. Have they imagined the priesthood was peculiar to them? Let them remember that Melchisedek was not of their tribe or nation, and yet was a priest of God; and the last priest of humanity was after the pattern of Melchisedek, and in His great Priesthood all other priesthoods are forever swept away. So he leads them to see that in the Christ all the things intended in the creation of their national life are realized. But he declares that these things are fulfilled for the sake of the whole world; and gradually, as the argument proceeds, in stately measure and in unanswerable logic, the horizon is put further back, the outlook becomes more spacious, and the light becomes more glorious.

Finally, approaching the appeal on the basis of the teaching, he leads his readers through that wonderful gallery of the heroes and heroines of the past, and comes to the words of my text.

This appeal is that of a master of method. Appeal is made to the whole man. First to the intellect: "Seeing that we are compassed about with so great a cloud of witnesses." At the center, to the will: "Let us lay aside"—"let us run." Finally, with a master touch, to the emotion at its highest: "Looking unto Jesus, the Author and Finisher of faith, Who for the joy that was set before Him, endured the cross, despising the shame."

I propose this evening to bring you especially to the central appeal. Let all the language of appeal to the intellect, and the tender language of appeal to the emotion—both of which we will return to in time—be out of sight. What is it the writer says? Brethren, he says a very simple thing, and this is it: "Let us run the race." What race? The burden of my message to-night is an answer to that inquiry.

In speaking of Abraham, he has declared: "He looked for the city which hath the foundations, whose Builder and Maker is God." Of the others he declared: "These all died in faith, not having received the promises, but having seen them and greeted them from afar, and having confessed that they were strangers and pilgrims on the earth . . ." "God is not ashamed of them to be called their God: for He hath prepared for them a city . . ." "These all, having had witness borne to them through their faith, received not the promise; God having provided some better thing concerning us, that apart from us they should not be made perfect."

Thus it is evident that the race which he urges upon those to whom he writes is not a race toward a heaven out of sight, but a race toward a city. Now let me stand away a little from the letter to the Hebrews and take the whole Bible as an illustration. My Bible opens in a garden, but it closes in a city. To me that fact is suggestive. A city expresses the result of a nation's dealing with a garden. In the heart of man there is a passion for the city. It is there because it is intended that it should be there. God's ideal of man is that he should take the garden and dress it, and bring out its final and ultimate result; and the last result of the garden of man is the establishment of a kingdom, the building of a city, the accomplishment of all the larger reaches of human life. And it is for that ultimate city that the men of the past have always hoped. Abraham left Ur of the Chaldees and set his face toward a city, not a city to be reached beyond the grave, but a city to be built in the world; not a beatific condition of life when the pathway of dust has come to an end, but the establishment in the world of a Divine order. Jesus taught His disciples to pray, "Our Father, who art in heaven. Thy name be hallowed. Thy Kingdom come. Thy will be done" —by men and women who have done with the world and reached heaven? No, a thousand times no! What then? "Thy name be hallowed. Thy Kingdom is come. Thy will be done as in heaven so on earth." The prayer which Christ taught us to pray—which summarizes all prayer, truly understood— is not a prayer that we may be able to pass through the world and win a heaven that lies beyond; it is a prayer that here, in this world, in the midst of its sin and its sorrow and its sighing, the will of God may be done, and the name of God perfectly hallowed by the coming of His Kingdom. In other words, the passion of the man of faith is not to hurry through the world and win heaven. The true passion of the man of faith is that God shall win the world and govern it for the blessing of humanity, for the healing of its wounds, for the ending of its sorrows, for the canceling of its sins, for the establishment of the reign of right and truth, and peace and blessing over the whole world. And as these men of the olden time, according to the writer of the letter to the Hebrews, moved out into loneliness, leaving behind them established orders, they did it in order that they might find a new order—found a new order—in the world, and establish the Kingdom of God on earth. And every great movement and appeal in the history of national life has been in that direction. For, not only among the Hebrews did God work His will; not only them did He guide by the Shekinah; He has guided other nations. Long years ago a band of men went to a land across the sea. For what? So far as they are concerned —I am not dealing with the issue—to establish the Kingdom of God. And, slowly, through all the centuries, men have been looking for that.

I pray you remember the essential things of the final city. It is a city of exclusion and inclusion. What are the things excluded? The conditions. Tears, and mourning, and crying and pain. The character. The fearful, and the unbelieving, and the abominable. The conduct. Murderers, and fornicators, and sorcerers, and idolaters, and liars. Night, the opportunity for evil; the unclean, the occasion of evil; that which makes a lie, the occupation of evil; the curse, which is the outcome of evil. And included within that city I find light, and life, and love, order and radiant beauty. It is a picture of the ultimate establishment of the Kingdom of God in the world. The ultimate of faith's vision and desire is the establishment of the Divine order in the world, the setting up of the Kingdom of God on this earth. The race that we are called on to run is a strenuous race toward the building of His city, the setting up of His kingdom, and the banishing from the broad earth of everything that is contrary to His ideal and contrary to the well-being of those whom He has created and whom He loves.

The appeal of the writer is to rise above everything that is narrow in outlook, to see the broader purposes of God, to gather into the affection all the round world, and to hasten along the line of earnest endeavor, the coming of the day when the city of God shall be built, and when men shall find in His perfect government their own final and perfect social order.

If that be the central intention of the text, I pray you now mark the preliminary word. In order to run that race the writer charges us, "Let us lay aside." What are we to lay aside? "Every weight, and the sin that doth so easily beset." I think I need hardly tarry to speak of the meaning of the passage as to the weights that are to be laid aside. What is a weight? Anything that hinders running toward that goal. Love may be a weight, learning may be a weight. I am mentioning the highest things of set purpose, feeling that it is not necessary to discuss the lower. Anything that dims the vision of the ultimate, that kills the passion, is a weight. "Ye did run well. What did hinder you?" Well, that which hindered you is the weight, and, in view of this large purpose, in view of this ultimate victory, in view of this stupendous intention of God, beneficent, and glorious, and beautiful, the writer charges the men who name the name of Christ to lay aside the weights. Yet, brethren, I think he touches something that lies nearer to the center of the whole necessity, when he says, "and the sin that doth so easily beset." What is the sin that doth so easily beset? I recognize the difficulty of answering the question. I take that word and bluntly translate, "the sin in good standing around." I suggest to you that the word means just exactly that—that the plain translation touches its deepest meaning. Sin in good standing around, sin that is not looked upon as vulgar. The word sin here must be interpreted by its use throughout this letter, and the sin against which he warns those who would run the race is the sin of unbelief. In order to understand what the "unbelief" of this letter is, I must now inquire what is the "belief" that the letter enjoins. Not mental conviction of a truth. That is not the belief of this letter, or of the New Testament. What, then, is belief? The answer of the life to the truth of which a man is convinced. The Greek *εις* with the accusative suggests infinitely more than belief on. I may believe every word of the Gospel of Christ, and be an immoral man. But if I believe into it, if I answer its claim, and walk in its light, and obey its command, and trust myself to its infinite and gracious promises, that is the belief which saves. Unbelief, therefore, is refusal to answer the light, and that is the sin that doth so easily beset. It is sin in good standing around. Now, I say no word against that intellectual attitude that demands a reason, but I do say that if we are to co-operate with God toward the building of His city, we must lay aside the sin of unbelief. Unbelief in what? In God, in man, and in the ultimate building of the city. Kadesh-Barnea still has its lesson. They came to the border, and they sent up into the strange new country spies to spy out the land, and they brought back from Kadesh-Barnea their report. There was a majority report, and there was a minority report, and, as is usual in such cases, the minority report was the true one. What was the difference between the majority and the minority report? The difference in the placing of a "but." Hear, I pray you, the majority report. "The land is a fair land, and a good land; the grapes are luscious grapes; the rivers are beautiful rivers; the hills and the valleys are full of verdure and beauty, *but* there are walled cities and there are giants." The minority report put the "but" a little further on, and it said, "The land is a fair land and a good land; the grapes are luscious grapes; the rivers are beautiful rivers; the hills and the valleys are full of verdure; there are walled cities and there are giants; *but* God will give us the land."

We are going to make no contribution toward the building of the city, and the bringing in of righteousness, if we lose our clear vision of God; but we shall fight our fight, and sing our song, and put in our day of toil with hope and a song of gladness, if the vision of God be kept clear before the mind.

It is equally true that we must lay aside the sin of unbelief in man. The moment we talk about man as being hopeless, we are unfit to build the city of God. We can strike no blow for the delivery of man from the things we lament unless we can see clearly stamped upon every face the hallmark of the Divine image. Unless we see behind the ruin the capacity, unless we see as Christ saw that, however low man is, however broken, however bruised, however spoiled, he is yet worth dying for—unless you and I have that vision, we can do nothing to build the city. There must be belief in the coming of the city. Have you begun to say, It will never come? I remember twenty years ago hearing that prince among our preachers, Alexander Maclaren, of Manchester, say a simple and beautiful thing that has been an inspiration to me through all my work. "Let no man say, because the day seems as though it never would reach high noon, that therefore its light will never be perfect day. Let us, rather, say how fair will that day be on which the twilight dawn has lasted 1,900 years." That is the language of the man of faith. That is the language of the man who knows that at last the victory must be won, and the will of God be perfectly done. If we are to run that race we must lay aside the easily besetting sin of unbelief, and with firm confidence in God and in man, and, in the ultimate, we must give ourselves to the travail and the toil that makes the coming sure.

And now, in a closing word, in order to inspire these people with that faith, the writer of the letter reminds them of the cloud of witnesses. The writer is not describing witnesses who watch us, but those who witness to us. You say to me to-night, It is easy to condemn unbelief, but look at the slow moving of the centuries—the dark places of the earth. No, says the writer, see the witnesses! And I stop there, at the eleventh chapter of Hebrews, which you know so well. Abel worshiped, and Enoch walked, and Noah worked. Abraham obeyed, obtained, offered. Isaac and Jacob foretold. Moses, being preserved, chose. Israel had its Exodus, and came into possession. The writer goes on to say that time would fail him to tell of Gideon and of Barak, and of Samson and of Jephthah, of David also, of Samuel and of the prophets. And the surprising thing is the men he puts in. You would not have put Samson in there. You would not have put Jephthah in that list. O heart of man, take courage! Is there faith in thee? Even though thou dost blunder and seem to fail, thy faith is accounted for righteousness, for faith is something that helps towards the coming of the city. And then, as though deeds were most important, he masses them —"subdued," "wrought," "obtained," "stopped the mouths of lions," "quenched," "escaped," "waxed valiant."

The story is not ended. Saints, apostles, prophets, martyrs, seers, visionaries—the men of to-day at whom we laugh are the men of faith. The vision creates a passion, the passion becomes a mission, and the life is lived till eventide. But the city is not built.

> The fog's on the world to-day,
> 'Twill be on the world to-morrow;
> Not all the strength of the sun
> Can drive his bright spears thorough.
>
> Yesterday and to-day
> Have been heavy with care and sorrow,
> I should faint if I did not see
> The day that is after to-morrow.
>
> The cause of the peoples I serve
> To-day in impatience and sorrow
> Once more is defeated; but yet 'twill be won
> The day that is after to-morrow.
>
> And for me with spirit elate,
> The mire and the fog I press through,
> For heaven shines under the cloud
> Of the day that is after to-morrow.

Seeing the witnesses, I take new heart and hope, and run my race.

But, last of all, looking not at the witnesses, but at the One Witness. Looking unto Jesus, the Author, the File Leader, the One Who goes first, Who takes precedence, and the Vindicator of faith—looking to Him. And if I look to Him, what do I see? I see One Who saw a vision, and for the joy that was set before Him, not the joy of escaping from the earth, but the joy of bringing God's government into the earth; not the joy of being away from the fight and the battle, but the joy of knowing that the issue of the fight and the ultimate of the battle is the establishment of the Divine order, He endured the cross, despising the shame.

Oh for the city of God! Oh for the coming of His Kingdom, for the healing of the wounds of humanity, for the ending of its strife, for the dawning of the last day, bright and glorious! If we would help it, we must run this race. There is no more pregnant or suggestive word in all the Gospel stories concerning our Lord than this. Hear it, I pray you, and I have done. It is a simple sentence, but unutterably sublime. "He stedfastly set his face to go to Jerusalem." What did He see? Jerusalem, hostile, waiting to arrest and murder Him, but "He stedfastly set His face to go to Jerusalem." What did He see? Jerusalem doomed by its own sin—the sword hanging over it, but "He stedfastly set His face to go to Jerusalem." What did He see? Through Jerusalem, hostile and doomed, Jerusalem—the mother of us all, rebuilt—the order established, the victory won, and "He stedfastly set His face to go to Jerusalem."

All the cities of the world to-day are hostile, are doomed, but are to be rebuilt. And it is the work of the Christian Church of whatever name or nation to see that ultimate vision, and then to begin the building just where they are, knowing that He will bring on the top stone, and that we shall join in the shout of the ultimate victory. Amen.

CHAPTER X

LIGHT AND DARKNESS

In Him was life, and the life was the light of men.
JOHN 1:4.

THE TEXT CONSISTS OF TWO STATEMENTS:

First, "In Him was life."
Second, "The life was the light of men."

These are related to a group of ten, with which the seer opens his writing:

"In the beginning was the Word."
"The Word was with God."
"The Word was God."
"The same was in the beginning with God."
"All things were made by Him."
"Without Him was not anything made that hath been made."
"In Him was life."
"The life was the light of men."
"The light shineth in darkness."
"The darkness apprehended it not."

These are not arguments, but affirmations. I do not propose to discuss them, but to proceed on the assumption that they are true.

In the two which I have selected two principal values arrest the attention: first, the Person referred to, and second, the proclamation.

As to the Person referred to, the first demand on honesty is that we should interpret the writer's reference by his own presentation. By that I do not mean that we begin at the mystic distance where he begins. The inclusion of that will be necessary ere we have done with the writing. At first it is enough that we recognize the Person as those who saw Him, who were, in company with the writer, familiar with Him.

This Person, then, is first named in the account of the ministry of John the Baptist, in which the writer declares, "On the morrow he seeth *Jesus* coming unto him, and saith, Behold the Lamb of God, which taketh away the sin of the world." This in itself is an interesting introduction, revealing as it does the human personality—"Jesus"; the Divine relation—"the Lamb of God"; and the avowed mission—"which taketh away the sin of the world."

Adhering closely to the simplest method of observation, this Person is seen as a Man of natural thought, and speech, and habit; Who in the course of His public ministry wrought signs of a supernatural order, and uttered words of stupendous meaning; and Who was brutally murdered, but by resurrection from the dead gave the company of His disciples a new understanding of the meaning of His life and of the nature of His death.

It is perfectly evident that the wonder of that resurrection gave the writer a new conception of the Person, and the prologue of his treatise is assuredly the result of his certainty of that fact.

This leads us to the proclamation of our text. "In Him was life, and the life was the light of men." The demonstration of the first of these was the resurrection. By that it was made certain that in some way Jesus had the power of an endless life. Being so demonstrated, the proclamation is in itself the most stupendous of claims, and can be interpreted only by what has preceded it; that He was the Creator, of which claim it is undoubtedly part, and the final and inclusive affirmation.

The second proclamation reveals the application of this supreme truth to the case of man as the crowning glory of creation. Presently the writer, with his gaze fixed on the Person as visible to the eyes of men, said of Him, "*There* was the true Light, which lighteth every man, coming into the world." By that affirmation he declares that every man has light, that light being the peculiar and distinguishing quality in human life, separating it from all lower forms. In the Person under observation this universally present light came into visibility.

In order to comprehend the light, the whole Person as presented must be seen, and that can be done only as He is observed in all the activities of His life and death as interpreted by His resurrection.

That revelation is unique, stupendous, overwhelming, and affords the one and only explanation of the missionary enterprise of the Church. In the early days of clear, if imperfect, vision, the Church was missionary. Every new unveiling of Christ has been the occasion of new missionary devotion. A supreme illustration is that of the Evangelical Revival, in which the London Missionary Society and nearly all the other great Societies now at work were born. To-day we are in the midst of a process not unmixed with conflict, out of which is coming a yet clearer and more spacious conception of this light, and new missionary enthusiasm and activity are already manifesting themselves.

May we then in reverence, and yet with confidence, attempt to see in broadest outlines the missionary enterprise as explained by this Person and this proclamation?

I propose three lines of consideration of that enterprise as interpreted by the light of the Person of Jesus:—

First, the fundamental conceptions; the ideal-Righteousness.
Second, the impelling motives; the actual-Sin.
Third, the commanding evangel; the possible-Salvation.

I

We begin with the fundamental conceptions of the missionary enterprise. These are created by the light Christ has given us concerning God, and man, and the law of the universe. They may be briefly summarized as conceptions of the unity of God, of the unity of humanity, and of the unity of law. Each of these deserves attention in turn. However, let it be recognized at once that simple and self-evident as these things appear to us to-day, they are so as the result of Christ's revelation, and of His revelation only. In the Hebrew religion there had been insistence on the idea of the unity of God. Its foundation word was, "Hear, O Israel: Jehovah our God, Jehovah is *one*." Yet the mass of the people had been slow to learn the lesson, as a study of their history reveals. The idea of one humanity was totally foreign to humanity, for Judaism had emphasized separation rather than unity. The unity of law was unknown, as is evidenced by the fact that the interpreters of the highest system of law known had divided as between less and greater laws.

As the result of the light which came by Jesus, we now know the one living and eternal God. We know Him as *transcendent*, that is, as being infinitely greater than any creature or the sum total of creation. We know Him as *immanent*, that is, as being near to, and interested in every creature, and the sum total of creation. We know Him as operative, that is, as actually working through all history and all life toward a "far-off Divine event."

This conception of the unity of God has been at once the grandest and most gracious possible. We have not yet discovered all its meaning. Its acceptance has always meant the canceling of terms which, apart from it, are in constant use. To believe it is to cease to know great and small as opposed or unlike; for the smallest is kin of the greatest, and the greatest is co-operative with the smallest. The near and the distant are no longer far removed, for all are held in one consciousness, and upheld by one power. The high and the low are not opposite, and antagonistic; but related parts of the one whole, which lives and moves and has its being in God.

This vision of God is the rock foundation of the thought of those who have come to know Him through Christ.

Closely related to this conception is the conception of humanity which has resulted from the light of the Person of Christ. There is no subject more full of fascination than that of the universality of Jesus. In humanity, apart from Him, different races have had different qualities, and different nations different ideals. In Him all peoples have found the finest fulfilment of all that was best in their peculiar qualities and ideals. Thus, in the very simplicity of His humanity He has brought to light the underlying unity of the race. In Him all the separated notes merge into the one perfect harmony, and therefore in Him there cannot be Jew or Gentile, bond or free. The Man of Nazareth has become the rallying center of men of all races, and thus we have come to recognize that beneath all diversities of race or color or position, humanity is of one blood and one spirit.

This conception of the unity of humanity is awe-inspiring in itself, and in its creation of human interrelationship is most remarkable. To believe it is to be forever unable to be patriotic with the patriotism that thinks only of one's own country; or parochial with the parochialism which has no fellowship with the next parish. It is to see in every man and woman a blood relation, however far they may be separated from us by distance, or temperament, or position. *It is to feel a new joy in the infinite variety which is, after all, but the evidence of the richness of the underlying unity.*

These two conceptions create a third, which the light given by Christ does moreover directly reveal, that, namely, of the unity of law. To grant that unity is at once to recognize law as being love-inspired. There is no other motive for law which holds within itself all the qualities which make for the present realization of order among the members of the one humanity under the government of the one God. This unifying inspiration of law was, moreover, the supreme fact revealed by Christ. His message was delivered, in the figurative language of John, from "the bosom of the Father," and His summary of the true and all-sufficient law of human life was, "Thou shalt love."

This law of love is the severest possible; that is to say, its requirements are most minute and mighty. It can never deny itself by allowing activity which harms and hurts to continue. It makes the standard of action, not what weak and incomplete things are able to enforce in a struggle against strong and complete things; but what strong and complete things are able to do, to ensure the strengthening and perfecting of the weakest and most incomplete. Therefore this law of love is, in its keeping, the condition of perfect joy. Love ever finds its greatest delight in the well-being of all. The mightiest find greatest joy in the measure in which, in love, they care for and make joyful those who are weaker. The weakest find chief joy in the gladness they give to those who in love help them when in love's response to love they gain strength.

All this is but to touch in barest and roughest outline on the great conceptions created by Christ. The application in detail must be left. Nevertheless, these are the fundamental conceptions of the missionary enterprise. They create an impulse which is irresistible under certain conditions. Those conditions are next to be looked at. It is well to remember that these conceptions do not in themselves call for missionary activity. These are the facts of the ultimate order, of heaven set up on earth. When that final goal is reached, missions will cease. The triumphs of Christianity constitute the measure in which missionary operations cease, because these conceptions are realized. The difference between darkness and light is the difference between ignorance of these truths and life lived in obedience to them. When these conceptions have won their ultimate victory in human history our missionary activity will be at an end. Until that hour come, they constitute the deepest reason, and create the most abiding passion for missions.

II

We now turn to the impelling motives of missionary enterprise. These result from that consciousness of the existing darkness, created by the epiphany of light. The apostolic outlook, as revealed in the New Testament writings, was characterized by an almost overwhelming sense of the darkness in which men lived, apart from Christ. Paul wrote of "the works of darkness," "the hidden things of darkness," "the world rulers of this darkness," "the power of darkness." Peter affirmed that the elect race was called "out of darkness." John declared of the loveless man, "The darkness hath blinded his eyes." These men having seen the light were made conscious of the conditions in the midst of which they lived. The contrast was sharp and appalling. Their joy in the light created their agony in the presence of the darkness. Their absolute rest in the perfection of the ideal order was the inspiration of their ceaseless unrest in the midst of the chaos. Thus it has ever been, and thus it continues to be. To walk in the light is to know the darkness. Conditions which are eminently satisfactory to those who have never seen the light are appalling, heart-breaking, disastrous, to the children of light.

The darkness may best be described by contrast with the light. In Christ we have found the One God. In the world we find humanity living without God, having lost its vision of Him. In Christ we have discovered the oneness of humanity. In the world we find humanity broken up and in perpetual conflict. In Christ the one law of love is revealed. In the world we see the mastery of selfishness producing suffering everywhere.

That humanity has lost its vision of God is demonstrated as we watch it at its worship. That there is a light, lighting every man, is evidenced by the fact that the instinct for worship is universal. No human being has been found so degraded that the sense of forces outside the material is wholly absent. We may speak of superstition, and barbarism, but the man with a fetish does by his thought of it demonstrate this sense of the spiritual, and recognize some relation to it. Yet how awfully the light that is in him is darkness. The highest conceptions of God, when held in the light of His manifestation in Christ, are dark indeed. They postulate a being, or a number of beings, hard, cold, distant, relentless, capricious. Descending in the scale, gods of selfishness, of greed, of corrupt, and degrading passions are worshiped, until at last the conception of deity is that of antagonistic devils, who are worshiped by being persuaded not to hurt. Darkness in very deed, but we have come to know it only because we have seen the light.

This lost vision of God has produced everywhere the break up of humanity. We have already referred to the fundamental word of ideal Hebraism as being, "Hear, O Israel: Jehovah our God, Jehovah is one." The immediate outcome of that declaration was the command, "Thou shalt love Jehovah thy God with all thine heart, and with all thy soul, and with all thy might." This is significant in that it suggests that the recognition of One God makes for the unification of every individual life by the one law of love, and thus makes possible the true social order. The words of the Preacher, "Where there is no vision, the people cast off restraint," are demonstrated true in all human history. All anarchy is the outcome of atheism. National strife and bloodshed, social conflict and cruelty, individual bitterness and brutality, alike result from lack of the knowledge of God, which is life and not death, light and not darkness, love and not hatred. Yet these are the conditions in which the greater part of men are still living.

The absence of love as the law of life issues in the mastery of selfishness, and this is the secret of all individual sin, and the source of all the woes and wounds and weariness of the peoples.

That these are the conditions we need not stay to argue. Eyes lifted from the contemplation of the Light of the World, in which have been seen the facts of the unity of God, the oneness of humanity, and the perfection of the law of love, and turned to the great lands in which the families of the earth are dwelling, see with awful distinctness the darkness of the lost vision of God, of the consequent tearing and agony of humanity, and of the cruel and blasting tyranny of the mastery of selfishness.

It is this vision of the darkness as seen by the light which is the impelling motive of missionary enterprise, consuming, and driving like a fire in its almost terrific passion for the passing of the darkness and the victory of the light.

Yet we have not so far found the real secret of the victories won, or the most compelling cause for continued toil. The case is hopeless indeed if there be nothing more to be said. The problems are but suggested by the vision of the ideal, and the consciousness of the actual. How is the actual to be changed into the ideal? That is the supreme question, and all missionary endeavor has been the result of the possession by the Church of the one and only answer. To that we finally turn.

III

The superlative factor in missionary enterprise is its great evangel. That evangel is infinitely more than a revelation of truth about God and man. It is the declaration of an activity of God which is in harmony with His nature, and through which man, notwithstanding his failure, may be restored so completely that all the highest ideals revealed in the Person of the Christ may be perfectly realized. As we said at the commencement, the light of men which came into the world with the coming of Jesus needs the whole of His life and mission through death, if it is to be perfectly understood.

The perfect ideal is not the complete evangel. Indeed, in itself it is not an evangel. It is a glorious presentation of the magnificent and beneficent purpose of God; but if the only light is that of such revelation, then man learns from it only how far he is falling short. But when there is superadded to that unveiling of an ideal the story—awe-inspiring and full of mystery—of a death which is the ultimate of all human woe and anguish, which, nevertheless, merges in a resurrection of unquestioned triumph; and in the claim of the risen One to all authority in heaven and on earth, and in His command to His disciples to proclaim the evangel, then hope springs in the heart, for we realize that through that Person a work has been wrought which makes possible the correction of the false and the establishment of the true.

The truth is the great deposit of the Church, possessing which, she is in debt to every land, and people, and age, until hearing and obeying, the darkness pass and the perfect light of the true order is the brightness and joy of human life in its individual, social, national, and racial experience. Every land where His light is unknown is a reproach to the Church. All the peoples who, sitting in darkness, still sin and suffer, are by their sinning and suffering calling to the children of light to be honest and pay the debt they owe.

May we, then, reverently inquire what are the essential notes of this great evangel? In attempting to name them I shall studiously avoid making any statement in the realm of those unfathomed secrets of the methods of God which are forever beyond human understanding. The things *revealed* are for us and our children.

Taking, then, the whole fact of the Christ—His Being, His teaching, His death, and His resurrection—we find that three declarations constitute the evangel. It may be well, first, to state them in all brevity. They are:

> First, that God cannot deny Himself, and therefore obeys His own law of love at infinite and amazing cost.

Second, that humanity must return to that same law by accepting the grace provided at such cost.
Third, that because of God's action, wherever man makes such return the past can be blotted out, and the highest and most glorious ideal be fully realized.

I am almost painfully aware of how each of these assertions opens the way for very much elaboration, and nothing would be more delightful than to be able to carry it out. That is, however, made impossible by the fact that we are still straitened by the limitations of time. Moreover, it is not absolutely necessary to the present intention, which is that of examination of a great theme in broadest outline. We must content ourselves therefore for the moment with a few brief sentences in each case.

As to the first. By incarnation God did not actually come nearer to man. Neither was the death of Jesus of Nazareth a point of new departure on the part of God. Incarnation was the method by which God revealed to men who had lost their vision of Him the fact of His perpetual nearness, and the nature of His Being. By the death of Jesus of Nazareth He wrought out into visibility, so far as that was possible, an attitude of His nature, and an activity of His grace, whereby, and alone whereby, man could be saved. The eternal and still finally incomprehensible facts are those of the existence and nature of God, and of that suffering of the infinite Love, whereby the very guilt of sin is canceled, and its power broken. In order to have right relation with these facts it was necessary that they should be manifested, and therefore the life and death of Jesus were necessary. The first note of the Gospel is the absolute certainty that God can and does forgive sin and break its power.

As to the second. The messenger of the evangel must

ever be true to the statement of necessity on the part of those to whom the message is delivered. He cannot be true to the message of the Divine pain if he tells men that sin does not matter, or that it is merely part of a process toward its opposite. He forever declares that it is all wrong, and that its ultimate is the distance and the disaster which its direction indicates. The conditions of restoration are those of return to obedience. Here, however, is the matchless beauty and surpassing loveliness of our evangel. God has made the method of return to His law that of accepting as a gift of His grace the forgiveness of sins, and all the resources necessary to the remaking of the broken life. That gift of grace is not a cloak for sin, but a cleansing from it, not an excuse for unfitness, but an energy for fitness. To refuse it is to choose sin and ruin. Thus if the first note of the evangel be that of the grace of God, the second is ever that of the responsibility of man.

As to the third. Far be it from me to seem, by any words now to be uttered, to minimize the value and importance of the things already spoken. They are the profoundest and mightiest, the things rooted in God, and thrilling with His power. Yet this last note is so full of delight that in it one exults, and is constrained to perpetual song. Because of God's action in grace, wherever man obeys, the best can be realized in spite of all the worst.

In the return of man to God through Christ the true God is known, and all the false ones are swept away. It is when God is so found that every wily and sinful Ephraim exclaims, "What have I to do any more with idols?" When man sees the one Lord, and exercises in Him the one faith of submission, and is baptized into life and light and love by the one Spirit, he finds the one God and Father of all, Who is over all, transcendent; and through all, operative; and in all, immanent. In that moment he finds the one humanity, and in that moment self is smitten to the death, and love enthroned. Then begins the healing. Bitterness passes from the heart like a pestilential vapor driven forth before the rush of the wind from the snow-capped mountains. Round the new center of love-governed life all the circles of family, of society, of nation, and of race feel the thrill: and hastened is the day of the new heavens and the new earth wherein dwelleth righteousness. This is our evangel. Its notes are Love, the love of God; Faith, the answer of man; Hope, the certainty of victory. This evangel is not parochial, national. It is Divine, and therefore humane, and wherever it is proclaimed man finds it in very deed the one and only Gospel.

Brethren, my theme is inexhaustible, but my time is not. Those of you who know the Light most perfectly are most conscious of how human expositions of it are ever in danger of dimming its effulgence. For that in this message which has obscured the one Light of life I most sincerely pray the pardon of my gracious Lord. But if in any measure I have been able to speak, so as to be understood, the things that are deepest and most awe-inspiring in my own life, I thank God. Let us remember at least the great text, and so much of the suggestions made as will help us to clearer understanding of the unique and lonely splendor of our evangel.

In Christ to have found God, and man, and the law of Love, is to have become awfully conscious of the gross darkness that covers the people.

In Christ to have found the grace of God, the way of human salvation, and the assurance of the ultimate victory of Love is to be filled with a passing for the proclamation of the glad good news to all lands and peoples for the glory of

God, the healing of man, and the establishment of the Kingdom.

The Vision creates the passion; the passion compels the mission. If we lack missionary devotion it is because we lack passion, and if we lack passion it is because we lack vision.

CHAPTER XI

THE PROBLEMS OF THE RELIGIOUS LIFE: HAS MAN ANYTHING TO DO WITH GOD?

To THE EARS OF THE CHRISTIAN BELIEVER THE QUESTION seems superfluous, and I think I may almost say it sounds grotesque. That fact notwithstanding, to vast numbers of men and women it is the most perplexing of questions, and constitutes the initial religious problem. If that question could be settled the whole attitude of their life would be altered.

The question is full of interest at the present time. It exactly expresses the mental attitude of the scientist to-day. Thirty years ago the scientist was not in the humor to ask questions; he was making affirmations, declaring quite reverently, quite devoutly, quite honestly, but with absolute dogmatism, that God, if there be a God, is unknowable by man. That is not the mood of the scientist of to-day. He is on the much saner and safer ground of asking, not necessarily in this language, but to this effect, and in this spirit, Has man anything to do with God? He may not yet write God with a capital G, indeed he may not use the word God at all, but he is recognizing that behind all material phenomena there is something, and he is now inquiring honestly, reverently, with profound earnestness, what relation has man to this fact?

The question is an interesting one for another reason. It indicates the point at which theology becomes religion or fails to become religion. Theology is the science of God, the truth concerning God, the facts concerning God so far as they have been discovered and recognized. Theology is not religion. I believe it to be quite necessary to religion, but it is not religion. A man may be theological and irreligious. The point where theology merges into religion, or else declines to be religion, is where the question is asked, Has man anything to do with God?

The question is interesting in the third place because it challenges the Bible. When I use the word challenge, I do not mean it attacks the Bible. The Bible assumes an affirmative answer to that inquiry. The Bible never argues for the existence of God. It takes God as granted. From its first stupendous and majestic word to its last glorious refrain it is a book the theme of which is the relation between man and God, defined, enforced. So that when I ask the question, Has man anything to do with God? I challenge the Bible. I do not contradict it, but I inquire as to its accuracy.

This initial question, which is a serious question to hundreds of men to-day, is of interest because it exactly expresses the mental attitude of the scientist to-day, because it indicates the point at which theology becomes religion, and because it challenges the Bible.

Now faith—and by faith I mean for the moment the attitude of mind of the Christian man—recognizes the right to make such an inquiry. It also insists that the right to inquire involves the responsibility to consider the evidence. I want to make that quite clear to my friend who is inquiring. You have a perfect right to inquire. Do not believe any preacher, or any man who claims to be a prophet, who tells you that you have no right to ask questions. You will never find bedrock for religious faith until you have learned how to ask questions. It is equally true that the right to ask questions involves the responsibility of considering the evidence. You have no right to ask questions and then imagine that there is no answer. You must listen to the answer. You are not bound to accept it, but you must listen to it. That is to say, the man who asks a question does by such action indicate the fact that his mind is open, and that he desires an answer. If not, then the man who asks questions is a trickster, and we have no time for him, and no patience with him. When Jesus stood confronting Pilate, and Pilate asked Him questions, Christ said to him, "Sayest thou this of thyself, or did others tell it thee?" Is your agnosticism first hand or second hand? It is a very important question to begin with when you are going to ask a question. If the question you are asking in the presence of the Christian religion is a question you have heard in Hyde Park, and you repeat it glibly because you think it sounds clever, then, in the name of God, I have no time or patience to deal with it. But if the question comes up out of the agony of your soul, as a sob out of your inner life, out of a tremendous, passionate desire to know the truth at all costs, then, because the hand of my Lord has been upon me in ordination, my business is to try to help you. I may not have gotten very far, but as far as I have come I want to show you the way. You remember Tennyson's "In Memoriam," and how he describes the fight of doubt for faith. I know it is an old story, but listen to it again:—

> You say, but with no touch of scorn,
>   Sweet-hearted, you, whose light blue eyes
>   Are tender over drowning flies,
> You tell me, doubt is Devil-born.
>
> I know not; one indeed I knew,
>   In many a subtle question versed,
>   Who touched a jarring lyre at first,
> But ever strove to make it true:

> Perplext in faith but pure in deeds,
>   At last he beat his music out.
>   There lives more faith in honest doubt,
> Believe me, than in half the creeds.
>
> He fought his doubts and gather'd strength
>   *He would not make his judgment blind,*
>   He faced the spectres of the mind
> And laid them: thus he came at length
>
> To find a stronger faith his own;
>   And Power was with him in the night,
>   Which makes the darkness and the light,
> And dwells not in the light alone.

From that I take the one line I endeavored to emphasize, "He would not make his judgment blind," which means not merely that he would not accept a dogma simply because the preacher declared it to be true; but also that he would not accept his agnosticism as final until he had tested it by every power of his mind. If you ask questions you must be willing to weigh the answer.

Suffer me still another word in the preliminary stage. Let those who are honestly inquiring recognize the difficulty of faith in the presence of their inquiry. By that I mean to say there are those who are so certain, so irrevocably certain of God, that it is very difficult for them to argue for Him or for man's relation to Him. I remember my dear old father saying to me over and over again in days when I did not so perfectly apprehend his meaning as I have come to do since, in my own experience, I am far more sure of God than I am of myself. Now, if you are an inquirer you can hardly understand that. Even if you think it false and that we are very foolish, please to remember that it is a conviction, that it is a sincere conviction, and remember also that if the man of faith has to be patient with you, you must learn to be patient with the man of faith. All that is very preliminary, yet I have taken time to say these things, because they indicate, so far as I am able to do, the attitude of my own mind toward the man who is inquiring in the spiritual realm.

In attempting to deal with this question I do so as giving evidence rather than as pleading a cause. Twenty-five years ago I came as a young man into a place of almost unutterable darkness about spiritual things. Two inquiries came to me with forceful power. First, is there a God after all? Second, and if there be a God, have I any personal relations with Him? Has He any personal, direct, immediate relationship to me? I am bound again to pause a moment to say there are, perhaps, some of you here who have been Christians for years who never came to such a crisis as this. I can only say, be patient with those who have been through it. Without undervaluing the quantity or quality of your faith, I still believe that what Tennyson says is true: the man who faces the spectres of the mind comes to find a firmer faith his own, not firmer than yours, but firmer than the faith he had before he faced the spectres of the mind. I want to say as I look back to that period of the eclipse of faith—I think that is a correct description of what took place in my own mind—it was not caused by anything moral. I say that only in order to intensify the testimony I desire to bear to any who may be facing similar inquiries. I believe that Dr. Torrey affirmed that infidelity and immorality are always closely allied. That may be true in some senses, but I do not believe that all infidelity springs from immorality. I do believe that infidelity will work out into immorality, but that is another matter. So far from these inquiries arising out of any moral delinquency, they came immediately following the most definite experience of spiritual blessing that ever came to me. The eclipse swept over me in a day, and hung over me for months, even for two years. I had been brought up in a home where my first slumbers were wooed by songs full of the music of the name of Jesus. The whole atmosphere of my home life was an atmosphere permeated by confidence in God. I never learned to doubt when I was a child. I had no chance. Then suddenly, and apparently without cause, these inquiries came. Is it true that there is a God? And if it be true, has that God anything to do with me? It is the second of those questions which is the real theme of our talk together to-night. The first is intimately related to it, and I choose to begin there.

My answers to these inquiries in each case are of the simplest. I propose to give the answers that came into my own experience, and to tell how they came. These answers do by no means reveal the final structure of faith. That is not yet completed. There are a great many things I am not yet sure about; things about God, and about man, and about Truth. The structure is in process of building. The final exposition, the ultimate explanation, I am still waiting for. These first answers constitute the rock foundation upon which faith is being built, and the first stone of the structure of faith laid upon that rock foundation. Twenty-five years ago, when the light came, I began again the life of faith, finding a firmer faith my own, and I did so, first upon the rock foundation of a simple conviction; and from that conviction came a first deduction, which deduction was the first stone in the structure of faith, which is not yet finished.

What, then, was that first piece of rock that I found underneath my feet in the day of faith's conflict, in the day of faith's eclipse?

This: *The consciousness of myself and the universe be-*

came the conviction of God. After a process of inquiry, and of attempt to restate the doctrines of the faith in such terms as would enable me to accept them; and finding myself utterly unequal to the task, there came a moment when, standing alone on the earth in the midst of the universe, I seemed to come to the consciousness of myself and of that universe. That consciousness compelled me to affirm, It is infinitely easier in the presence of myself and the universe to believe that there is a God than to believe that there is not. It was not much to stand on, but it was a bit of rock under the feet of a man who had been sinking. You say, You demonstrated nothing. That is true, but I had a conviction. You cannot demonstrate a great many things of which you are absolutely sure. You are sure that the woman you call mother is your mother, but you cannot demonstrate it. I did not get mathematical demonstration, but I got conviction, and came at last to say: Here am I, here is the universe. I cannot believe that there is no God! There is a God! It was not much, just a bit of rock; but, oh, God, what a bit of rock means to a man who is drowning. I started there. If you can get a bit of rock under your feet, never mind the temple; never mind the Church; never mind the theologians; put your feet down and stand squarely on it.

Now, I should like to describe the process by which the conviction came. That is not easy, but I propose to attempt it with all brevity. That conviction came as the result of a look back, a look around, and a look on.

A look back to origins. I came to realize that everything results, and to ask from what? You remember Mr. Hastings' old riddle. Here is a hen, and here is an egg. The hen results, from what? The egg. The egg results, from what? The hen. Go on, and when you have solved that you have solved the

Christian religion. I only quote it to remind you that everything results. A chair. It results from what? From man's handiwork. On what? Trees. Trees? How did they come? They resulted. From what? Leather, what is that? There were animals once. Whence came they? They resulted. From what? Get on back with your journey.

That is all very childish, is it not? But put your hand where you will; put it on your own thin-veined wrist. It results from what? All that is the beginning of a journey. I do not care how far back you go, through the long centuries, the infinite mysteries, all the evolutionary processes. I do not care anything about them. Back, back. Oh, where did it all begin? The only answer that ever brought satisfaction to my soul is, "In the beginning, GOD." Yes, I can believe that. If you say mighty atom, or tell me about a protoplasmic germ, which John Ruskin translates for me and reminds me that the Greek term being translated means, first, stuck together, I ask, What was stuck together? And who stuck it together? I am not playing; my soul went through all this in agony twenty-five years ago, and no theory satisfied my reason until I said, at the back of all results, as originating cause, is God. That was my first bit of rock.

Then there was a look round, first on the vast, then on the minute. On the far-flung splendors of the starry night, on the minutiae of beauty in a handful of lichen, of moss, of dust. I looked out on life, not human life merely, but on all life, and I saw changeless change, and changing changelessness: seasons regularly moving, life repeating itself true to type, types by inoculation with new types making new mysteries and new wonders, but everywhere order, and everywhere law. I said, Who presides over all this? A double-faced something? Nothing; it all happened? I cannot believe that. Then I found that the Christian writings declare of man, the final manifestation of life, In God he lives, and moves, and has his being. I came to see that the infinitely great God is seen in the infinitely little thing, in the dust; and in the infinitely vast thing, the universe; and I said, Yes, that is easier than any other proposition.

Then I took a look on. All mystery; the light is not clear even yet, but the rhythmic order of things convinced me that at the last "that cannot end worst which began best." There is a goal somewhere, to be reached somehow, "one far-off Divine event to which the whole creation moves." I am not talking theology now. Theology discusses how the goal is to be reached. The conviction of the goal brought certainty in my own soul of the one presiding Being.

Then I began to ask about the Being, and I discovered certain things from which I could not escape. Let me only name them: wisdom and might, beauty and beneficence. I came to the conclusion that all these things must ultimately rest in the Being who "spake and it was done," through Whose power all things are upholden, to Whom as the final Goal all things forever move.

Now a few brief words as to what was the result of that finding. I passed immediately to the second inquiry, Has man anything to do with God? I do not think that inquiry can long remain unanswered if God be believed in as a personal Being, having in His own being wisdom, might, beauty, and beneficence. You see, I am trying to omit all the terminology of theology. I am not speaking of righteousness, holiness, love. All these things are there. I am speaking only of the things I found apart from the revelation of Scripture. When the first conviction came to me, I came to the second conclusion, a deduction from the conviction. Because God has everything to do with man, man must have to do with God. If man is of God, and in God, and for God, as a part of creation, it is utterly unthinkable that God, having everything to do with man, man could have nothing to do with God. That was the first stone laid upon the rock foundation.

Think of the process by which I came to that conclusion. Two propositions and deductions made from them. The first proposition. Man is the crowning wonder of creation. Theories and processes matter nothing in this respect. I am not saying what my conviction is, but it does not matter at all whether man was created by a definite, immediate act within an hour from thought to completion; or whether man emerged through long processes. I care nothing. Here is the fact. Man is the crowning wonder of creation. We are all agreed on that, the agnostic, the so-called infidel, the inquiring scientist, the Christian preacher, the most indifferent man who looks about him at all. We are all in agreement. From that proposition I made this deduction. The Creator cannot be unmindful of the crowning glory of His creation. It is unthinkable that if this whole vast and minute universe has come from God, and is of God, and moves toward God, that God should be careless of the highest, most wonderful thing in all creation. You remember the psalmist's inquiry, "What is man that Thou takest knowledge of him?" The psalmist's query and our conclusion may be put together, but they begin at the poles asunder. The psalmist started with revelation, which declared that God is mindful of man and visited him. On the basis of revelation, he inquired what relation there was between man and God. "What is man that Thou takest knowledge of him?" Revelation says, Thou art mindful of him. In the presence of that statement the psalmist asked, What can man be? Our question is not that. Our question is, Has man anything to do with God? We affirm the relation, and we demand to know whether the man who is related has anything personal to do with God.

God is, and He has something to do with man. He sustains him. And man has something to do with God, man receives his life from God, he lives and moves and has his being in God. Now comes the real point of inquiry. Has God anything to do with man's doing, his thinking, his habits, his morality? I submit this to you. The crowning glory of man is moral. I am not quite so sure that I carry you all with me when I say that, nevertheless, I repeat, the crowning glory of man is moral. Is it not so in a little child? You love the child when it is not immoral, but non-moral, before it has come to a knowledge of right and wrong. A child in its mother's arms is not immoral, but it is non-moral. How you watch the day when it begins to be moral, to know right and wrong, making its own choice, defying you. I shall not be misunderstood when I say there is a charm in the defiance of a little child. It needs to be guided, for defiance is but the exercise of the supreme function of life, will. It is the hour of dawning beauty. You have watched all the physical development and the opening mental power, as it looked up and inquired, talking in language no one but a mother could understand; but the crowning hour comes when the child becomes moral. What is true of the child is true of the nation. I read this morning a very remarkable article in the *Daily News* on W. J. Bryan; one of the most *inseeing* articles, if I may be allowed that word, that I have ever read. In the course of that article I read these words:

> His appeal is always to the moral conscience. The name of the Almighty is as familiar on his lips as it was on the lips of Mr. Gladstone, and it is the highest tribute to his sincerity

that employing it he never gives you the sense of canting. The truth is, he lives in an atmosphere out of which our politics have passed. No one to-day in the House of Commons ever dares to touch the spiritual note. When we say that oratory is dead, we mean that faith, which is the soul of oratory, is dead. Oratory fell to earth when Gladstone and Bright ceased to wing it with spiritual passion. Our wagon is no longer hitched to a star.

The proportion in which that is true is the proportion in which this nation has lost its greatness and its grandeur and its glory. The proportion in which the highest spiritual emphases of morality are reckoned out of court in the legislative assembly is the proportion in which we are under eclipse. I put it that way, for God grant that the touch of ultimate spiritual morality may be felt yet again in all our national life. You know it is true. Morality is the supreme thing, the greatest grandeur in the child and the man, in the people and the nation.

Get back to the beginning. If the child, the man, the people, and the nation, are the creation of God; and if it be unthinkable that He is not interested in that which He has made its crowning glory, can it be thinkable that He is not interested in the highest glory of that which He has created, which is moral? To me it is utterly unthinkable.

Let me repeat the three things I have tried to say. First: It is easier for me to believe God is, than that He is not, when I stand in the midst of the universe. Second, I cannot believe that, man being the crowning glory of creation, God can be unmindful of him. Finally, when I look on man and know that the ultimate, most wonderful thing in him is morality, I cannot believe that God is careless about morality. Consequently, I believe that this God, Whom I have never felt with the touch of sense, upon Whom these eyes can by no means look, can reveal Himself to man, and I believe man can receive the revelation. The ability in each case is obligation. In the case of God the obligation is fulfilment.

I have attempted to go over the ground which I trod, not thus easily, but in tears and in pain and anguish, twenty-five years ago. I bring to you, in conclusion, a word from the most ancient of the Scriptures of our Bible, "Acquaint now thyself with Him and be at peace." My friend, inquiring at this the very beginning, the threshold of religious problems, let me say to you in all sincerity, that no man of intellectual power can rest in agnosticism. He may find himself there, but he cannot find rest there. The man who says, I am an agnostic, in an agony, and is inquiring, will find his way through; but the man who is smug and satisfied, and imagines he has reached the highest plane of intellectual greatness because he is an ignoramus will never arrive anywhere. There is no rest for an intellectual man in agnosticism. I charge you, if you are making inquiry, put your blood into it, put your life into it. "Acquaint now thyself with Him, and be at peace." Do not stand on the edge of great questions and indulge in the dilettante fooling with them. Get down to the business, and so far as you have ability, ask honestly, persistently, determinedly. It was Eliphaz who said to Job, "Acquaint now thyself with Him, and be at peace." Job was agnostic, but never rested in his agnosticism, and he said, "Oh, that I knew where I might find Him." Someone says, That is exactly where I am, where I have been for a long time. Now, you must be patient with me as I bring you the Christian message. "No man hath seen God at any time. The Son Who is in the bosom of the Father, He hath declared Him." That God, infinite, mysterious, present everywhere, came "out of the everywhere into the here"—to borrow reverently George Macdonald's description of the baby—and tabernacled—may I be more blunt in my translation, 'pitched His tent' among us, "and we beheld His glory, glory as of the only begotten of the Father, full of grace and truth."

Man, my brother, there is no escape from God. Get to Him through the Son and you will find rest. You say, What of the problems of the Incarnation, the Atonement, the Resurrection, theologies old and new? In God's name do not begin with these things, but begin with the God of Whose existence you are convinced. Put your feet on the one bit of rock, and you will find it not so small as you thought it was; but rather the strong and mighty rock of ages. Then begin to build the superstructure of faith by handing over your life to the light so far as it has come to you, to the truth so far as you have come to see it.

CHAPTER XII

THE PROBLEMS OF THE RELIGIOUS LIFE: CAN A JUST GOD FORGIVE SINS?

IT WILL BE ADMITTED AT ONCE THAT THE POSSIBILITY OF the forgiveness of sins has been believed in and proclaimed by the Christian Church for nineteen centuries.

False deductions have been made from the central doctrine, and false presentations of that doctrine in the process of the centuries. By false, I mean untrue to the earliest teaching of Christ and His apostles as that teaching is recorded for us in the Scriptures of the New Testament.

Perhaps the most glaring of the false deductions was that which was known as the Antinomian heresy, which was that because God has in His grace provided perfect redemption it does not at all matter how a man lives.

Perhaps the supreme illustration of what I mean by false presentations was to be found in that most remarkable movement which preceded the reformation, and had its head center of exposition in Tetzel, who preached that by certain payment on their part men might receive indulgence to sin. These false deductions, and false presentations, as well as the simple proclamation of the New Testament declaration, do prove that the idea of the forgiveness of sins has obtained in the Christian Church from the beginning until now.

This belief is based on belief in the government of God, the conviction of righteousness, and the consciousness of sin.

The idea of forgiveness of sins cannot be present to the mind of the man who does not believe in the existence and government of God. Therefore, all we said last Saturday night must be taken for granted as we take up this second problem of the religious life. God is, and God governs. If you deny these things then you deny sin, and this inquiry as to whether God can forgive sins is absurd. Unless we find common ground in this premise we certainly shall not find a common resting place in the conclusions that I shall draw. To admit the government of God is to be convinced of His righteousness, and that conviction is ever followed by the consciousness of sins. Do you quarrel with me at that point? Do you question the accuracy of what I am now taking for granted? If for a moment you grant the idea of righteousness, measure yourself by that idea, and tell me if you have realized the ideal. I do not care, for the moment, whether your father was a sinner, or whether Adam fell. I care very much about these things on other occasions and in other directions, but not now. See God, and righteousness, and immediately, if you are honest, you will say I have failed. I think there is no man here who knows what righteousness is, who has had the first faint idea of the ideal of perfection and of beauty, but who is compelled to say, While I see it, and believe in it, and admire it, I have not realized it. That is the consciousness of sin. It may bring no terror to the heart, but it is there. It is only as these things are recognized that we make such an inquiry as the inquiry of our subject to-night. Taking these things for granted, I inquire, Can a just God forgive sins?

Seeing that the forgiveness of sins is a Christian doctrine, it is necessary that we inquire what the doctrine really is that the Church teaches. I think you will agree with me that this is a fair proposition. Suppose I had no Bible and no Christian body of truth, and no Church which for nineteen centuries had been proclaiming the possibility of the forgiveness of sins, and someone should suggest a question such as this, I should have to approach it from a different standpoint altogether, and answer it in a different way. Even then I should say to my questioner, What do you mean? There are two or three words in your simple question that I want you to define. What do you mean by "just," by "forgiveness," by "sins"? Exactly as I would ask these questions if this inquiry came to me without the light of the Christian revelation, seeing that the idea conveyed by the inquiry is a Christian idea, I must still ask these questions. What is the Christian meaning of the terms "just," and "forgiveness," and "sins"? Let us then proceed along three lines. We will define our terms. We will state our problem. We will attempt to formulate the answer of the New Testament.

First of all, for the definition of terms. The terms are very wide, having racial applications. We will, however, endeavor to confine ourselves to the individual applications. Understand from this moment I am attempting to deal with these questions as though I were the only man involved in the inquiry, as though I made the question pertinent to myself, and entirely and absolutely personal, as though I said, Can a just God forgive *my* sins? In dealing with the inquiry in that way we will first define our terms. I am going to attempt a rapid definition of words used and ideas conveyed in that question.

First, the words, *just, forgiveness, sins*. What does the word *just* mean? If you take the word that lies behind it, and examine it, and attempt to discover, as you always will do if you are a careful reader, its root significance, I am not at all sure that you will not at first be somewhat surprised. The word out of which this comes is a word which means *seeing*.

Let me suggest another word, *observing*. You say at once that these two words mean the same thing, and yet the second of them is constantly made use of in a slightly different sense from that in which the first is always used. Seeing suggests a view. Observing also suggests a view, but it often means more. For instance, you say to a boy, Here is a rule of conduct, observe it; by which you mean to say, You are not only to see, but to act in harmony with the thing you see. So if the root idea of the word translated *just* be *seeing*, its use means acting in harmony with the thing seen. *Just* means activity in conformity with things as they really are. Can a God who acts in conformity with things as they really are forgive sins?

Let us be as simple and childlike with our next word, *forgive*. What does *forgive* mean? To let go is the simple meaning. It suggests the idea of unlocking a prison house so that the prisoner is set free. The sense in which the word is used always means to treat sins as though not committed, to let them go, blot them out, pardon them, forgive them. Let me repeat my inquiry in the light of these definitions. Can a God Who acts in conformity with things as they really are treat sins as though they had not been committed?

For the third time let us follow this line of definition. From the Christian, Biblical standpoint it is almost more difficult to define words translated *sin* or *sins* in our Bible. I am content to take the word that is most often translated sin, which suggests the simplest fact in the mind of the writers. It is a word which means "missing the mark." It is the word used of a man standing with his rifle and shooting at a bull's eye and missing it. It is a word which indicates the failure of the man who sets himself to realize, and never realizes. He misses the mark. To fail, whether wilfully or unwittingly, is, in the broadest sense of the word, sin. Let me make my inquiry again. Can a God Who acts in conformity with things as they really are treat missings of the mark as though the mark had not been missed? That is the problem of this inquiry.

Once again, take the two ideas suggested here for definition. First, the idea of the justness of God. What is justness? We have already said it is seeing things and observing them in the sense of being true to them. Let us now put it this way. Justness in God is undeviating conformity to truth, in Himself, and in His dealings with all others. Take the phrase *forgiveness of sins* and the idea suggested by it. What is meant by the forgiveness of sins? The treating of failure as nonexistent, and the treating of the one who fails as though not having failed. That is forgiveness in the Bible sense. If you try to understand what forgiveness means by what you do with your children you will never understand it at all. If you begin to argue that just as you say to your child, I forgive you, so God does with the sinner, you do not begin to know what the Bible teaches about the forgiveness of sins. That is not the forgiveness of the Bible. You cannot make the sin of your child as though it had not been, and that is what the word really means. Someone is saying, You are making the problem more difficult than it seemed. I hope I am. In order to persuade ourselves that God can forgive, we are losing the amazement that ought to fill the heart in the presence of the meaning of the Cross and His infinite grace in forgiveness. The thing that first overwhelms me is the problem. Then the thing that overwhelms me more is the solution of the problem which the Bible teaches and for which the Christian Church really stands.

Having spent so much time with the definition of terms, let me now try to state the problem. Here are certain self-evident things that I submit to you and pray you to follow me, and not to be afraid. As to God. To treat sin committed as not committed is to act out of conformity with truth. That is unjust. As to the universal order. To treat sin committed as not committed is to establish and confirm sin. That is unjust. As to the sinner. To treat sin committed as not committed is to establish and confirm sin as a power in the life, and that is unjust. Now, the problem can be stated by only first making a fundamental affirmation. *A just God can forgive sins only by basing His judicial action upon absolute truth.* If the forgiveness of sins means the violation of truth, then God can never forgive sins. Can God so deal with sin as to enable Him to forgive it on the basis of absolute truth?

You say to me, Of course God can forgive sins, because He loves. I say, Yes, but then in God's name remember what love is. Love is not a sentimental softness that overlooks the poison in the blood. Love is not an anæmic weakness that weeps over cancer and refuses to cut it out. There is nothing we are suffering from to-day more than this weakened conception of the meaning of love. We begin to understand love only when we understand that at its heart, at its center, are purity, and eternal righteousness. Let me say the thing as I feel it. If you could persuade me that forgiveness, which simply says, Oh, never mind, say no more about it, pass it over, could satisfy God, then I say it could not satisfy me. It does not get to the depth of my own being. It does not touch the heartache and anguish of my conscience. Before I can know forgiveness as experience in which I dare rejoice, there must be, somehow or other, blotting out, canceling, making not to be. I tell you honestly that it does not seem to me that there can be a solution, until I open my Bible and begin to read it.

Now I want—and as God is my witness I feel the almost appalling difficulty of it—I want to state the Christian answer to this great inquiry. I do not propose to state the answer in the terms of my own ideas of how God might do this thing. I will tell you why. It is honest for me to say only what I have already said, that there appears to be no solution. What, then, does Christianity affirm? The Bible teaches the forgiveness of sins. The Church has taught the forgiveness of sins. We are still—in proportion as we are true to the doctrine of the Catholic Church for nineteen centuries, and to the doctrine of the Word of God—proclaiming the possibility of the forgiveness of sins. Upon what grounds?

First of all, let me attempt in a very few sentences to state the process by which God can forgive sins so far as that is stated in the New Testament; then let me speak of the provision He has made for sinning men who turn to Him, and, finally, of the great proclamation which is entrusted to us in the presence of sin.

What is the process? We must begin where the New Testament begins. First of all, there is presented to our view a Person, Jesus of Nazareth, Jesus the Christ; or, to give Him the full and dignified title with which the apostolic writings abound, and which culminates all other suggestiveness, the Lord Jesus Christ. What is this Person according to New Testament teaching? God incarnate. I know perfectly well that you may say that is not granted. I am not dealing with the question as to whether this Person is God incarnate or not, apart from my Bible. That is an inquiry which every man may make, but that is not the one with which I am now dealing. All I now say is, and I say it quite carefully, if that Person, the Lord Jesus Christ, is not God incarnate, then some part of the New Testament is untrue. It is quite impossible, absolutely impossible, and those of you who differ most widely from my own position will agree with me here, to retain your New Testament and deny that. You may deny it, and deny it honestly, but if you do, then there are certain parts of the New Testament which you say are not true. I respect your conviction, though I do not share it. I want you to see this. I stand asking what the Church has taught for nineteen centuries upon the basis of Biblical revelation, and my first answer is, that, first, a Person is presented to me, God incarnate. I see Him living. I see Him dying. I see Him rising.

Then, in the second place, will you remember that this New Testament teaches that this Person is a manifestation. In His life there is manifestation of righteousness. In His death there is manifestation of substitution. In His resurrection there is manifestation of victory won in and through and out of death.

Now, a manifestation is never all. A manifestation means that all cannot be seen, and therefore it must have a medium through which men may come to see it, though they cannot see it all. The moment you speak of this Person as a manifestation, using, if you will, the actual phrase of your New Testament, "God manifest in flesh," you recognize the spiritual and essential fact behind the manifestation, which is more than the manifestation, which is superior to the manifestation, of which the manifestation is but the unveiling, the revelation.

Therefore, finally, this whole fact revealed in Jesus is inexplicable. I cannot know all the life, even though I see its lines and lights, and movements. I cannot know all the death though I see its suffering and brutality and tragedy. I cannot know all the resurrection, though I see its triumph and hear its song. Behind the manifestation is a great spiritual and essential fact, yet not a contradiction to the manifestation. That is to say, I am to interpret the spiritual, essential, eternal facts in the terms of the manifestation. When I look at the life of Jesus I see righteousness incarnate, and in that manifestation I learn, as nowhere else, the holiness and righteousness of God. In the same way, when I look at that death interpreted by all the declarations of the New Testament, I see death for others, death in which He bore our sins in His own body on the tree, in which He was the Lamb of God bearing the sin of the world. In that death I see manifestation of something in God, infinite, mysterious, overwhelming, appalling, which cannot be shown in any other way than by such a death as that. In the terms of that human death I come to understand something that lies back in Deity which I cannot fully understand, but which apart from this death I never could have dreamed of.

Looked at on human levels, what was this death of Jesus? Suffering undeserved. Suffering on behalf of others out of pure love and compassion. At the back of it, what is there? The suffering of God out of pure love on behalf of those who do not deserve such suffering. You say that does not explain it, and I admit I have never yet had it explained. It lies beyond me, surging upon my spirit in billows of unfathomable love that almost break my heart, yet eluding the grasp of my mind. I come back to the terminology of human manifestation, "By His stripes we are healed. The chastisement of our peace was upon Him." That old prophetic word was carried out to the letter in the human life of Jesus. But this was manifestation in order that human eyes might see the infinite and unexplored reaches of the pain of the being of God. So I see through Christ the activity of righteousness, of expiation, and, finally, of victory. In His life God's righteousness revealed. In His dying, God's expiation by suffering of man's guilt unveiled. In His rising, God's victory over all the forces of darkness made manifest.

What is the result of this according to the New Testament teaching? Think for a moment of the provision. The New Testament declares that there is now forgiveness of sins through the shed blood of Christ, that by the shedding of His blood remission has been made. Blood is the symbol of what? I veil my face, and take my shoes from off my feet. God knows I do not. So much as blood says, I know. Blood shed is not life lived, but life laid down. Blood shed is not merely the strength of a great ideal. It is the bruising and battering of that ideal. It is agony, and pain, and defeat. That is the symbol. God help us to tread reverently when we go beyond it. The issue of sin realized in God, gathered into His heart, to His own suffering, to His own pain, to His own wounding. That is the ultimate significance of the old word in the Hebrew economy, "In all their afflictions He was afflicted."

The New Testament never teaches that a man named Jesus tried by dying to persuade God to love. The New Testament never teaches that God was impassive, and never felt pain, while some person other than Himself endured it, in order to appease Him. There is no such teaching from Matthew to Revelation, from Genesis to Revelation. The New Testament does teach—and quarrel with all I say, but hear this—"God was in Christ." Every word He spoke was a word of God, and every work He wrought was a work of God, every tear He shed was a tear of God. The very blood He poured out was in that sense symbolical of the very blood of God. So that we are in the presence, not of a unit out of the vast multitude of humanity, pure in himself, trying to deal with God so as to make God love men. We are in the presence of God, in the One in Whom dwelt all the fulness of the Godhead corporeally, that men might see a suggestion of it, and come to an understanding of it. In Him I see how God has taken hold of guilt, and made it not to be, curing the pain in His own pain, ending the issues in His own agony, taking all the responsibility and the mysterious harvest into His own nature and bearing it. Thus a God of absolute truth, without violation of truth, makes sin not to be, and thus forgives the sinner. Whether these things are so or not, these are the things the New Testament teaches. These are the things for which the Christian Church has stood, and must stand, if she would remain. The doctrine of the forgiveness of sins is a doctrine that a just God can and does forgive, not by putting the issue upon someone outside Himself, but by gathering up into His own heart and life and being the weight of sin, by suffering in Himself.

Consequently, the proclamation of the Christian evangel is that God can be just and the Justifier—mark well the condition—"of him that *believeth* in Jesus." What does that mean? To believe in Jesus is to return to the government of God at the point of His grace. Never miss out government when you think of grace; never miss out grace when you think of government, for in Christ the two have met. In the universe, measureless to us but measured in God, in the pain and passion of God my sin has been canceled, made not to be, but put away. Now God says, By the Man Whom I have ordained, through Whom the eternal things are manifest, in Him put your trust. That is a command. Master, "what must we do, that we may work the works of God?" said the cynical men of His day to Jesus. "This is the work of God, that ye believe on Him Whom He hath sent." That was

His answer. It is the first word of the new law. Believe. A man says, I will not believe. Very well, then there is nothing for you but the harvest of your own wrongdoing, the hell to which sin sends you. Remember, if you will proceed along the path of your own disobedience all that it involves here and forever of darkness and death is the issue of refusing to believe. I am talking in London. I am talking to men and women who know the evangel. You cannot begin there for the dark nations of the earth until you have preached the evangel. I am talking to men who know it. God comes in Christ, through Christ, revealing His righteousness, His expiatory suffering, His victorious life over and through death.

> Grace there is my every debt to pay,
> Grace to wash my every sin away.

That Grace is government, and God says, Now get back into My government and yield yourself to Me by obeying Me at the point of trusting Me. I come at the point of His grace and I find not merely the value of the Cross, but the virtue of the resurrection, and ultimately the victory of a realized ideal. If a man will not, then to refuse is to remain unforgiven. God is a God ready to pardon. I love that word of the ancient prophet, because ready does not mean merely willing, but fully equipped, to pardon.

So I come to Him in Christ, I come to Him with my sin—or put it in the plural my sins, I bring them all to Him—and I say, He cannot be just and forgive them unless He can find a basis for His judicial action in absolute truth, He cannot treat the sin as never committed unless He can put it away as to its virus, and as to its issue. That is what He has done, and because He has done it, He can pardon sin.

My final word is this. The experience of men for nineteen hundred years witnesses to the truth of the Christian proclamation. I know my sins are forgiven. If I say that all alone you must at least believe me to be honest in my conviction. When I multiply my testimony by the company in this house to-night who can say the same; and when that company is multiplied through this city and land, by the numbers who are singing the song of assured forgiveness, and when that testimony is multiplied for nineteen centuries, in which men have confessed their certainty of the forgiveness of sins; you have a weight of evidence that is overwhelming. You dare not charge all the men who have made this claim with hypocrisy or with lunacy. Through nineteen centuries men have sung this song, and the testimony and burden of it has been, "I know my sins are all forgiven. Glory to the blessed Lamb."

Hear me again. The evidence of life rising to higher levels of righteousness witnesses to the truth of the experience. The man who really knows his sins forgiven is the man who rises and begins the life of conquest over sin. If a man say his sins are forgiven, and goes on deliberately sinning, he is a liar. The language is vigorous, but it is Johannine, that of the apostle of love. The man who tells me he knows his sins are forgiven, and continues in sin, is lying. That is not the normal experience of the Christian Church. If you deny me this affirmation, I ask you, Where have you been living? And on what have you been looking? You may quarrel with the Salvation Army; you may not like their flag and their big drum and their Hallelujah; but their one message is the forgiveness of sins, and the perpetual result of their preaching through all the years of their existence has been that sinning men have been saved from the power of sin. The demonstration, I repeat, of the truth of the experience affirmed is in the remade lives of men and women who go out to sin no more. I do not mean that forgiveness brings immediate victory. I do say that forgiveness creates the passion not to sin, and inspires the endeavor to be obedient, and presently realizes absolute victory.

So if we are sinners and know it, there are two things concerning which we need to be most careful. First of all, to remember that God sets up the Cross of His Son as the trysting-place to which we are to come, and the place at which we are to turn our back on wilful sin. Then we are to remember that by that Cross uplifted, or by that for which it stands—all the infinite mystery that lies behind it—it is possible, to use the apostolic language, for God to be just and the Justifier of him that believeth in Jesus. So when all has been said, we sing the old song, and know the answer is ours as we sing:

> Rock of ages, cleft for me,
> Let me hide myself in Thee!
> Let the water and the blood
> From Thy wounded side which flowed,
> Be of sin the double cure;
> Save me from its guilt and power.

CHAPTER XIII

THE PROBLEMS OF THE RELIGIOUS LIFE: WHAT DOES GOD REQUIRE OF MAN?

THIS INQUIRY IS THE OUTCOME OF THOSE WHICH HAVE preceded it. If it be granted that man has to do with God, the inquiry is natural and necessary: What does God require of man? If it be granted that God can forgive sins the inquiry is urgent and vital: What does God require of man? If it be true that I have to do with God, what does God require of me? If it be true that when I realize I am a sinner He can forgive sins, what does God require of me?

The inquiry is of supreme importance because it deals with fundamental matters; it gets back in human life, behind the incidentals, to the essentials; down in human life beneath the ripples on the surface, to the still majesty of the underlying tides. It is the first question of all life. It asks: What does the God in Whom I live and move and have my being, and Whose are all my ways, in Whose hands my breath is, require of me—His creation, over whom He still maintains the right of government in the material, mental, and moral realms? Because the inquiry deals with the foundations of life, it deals also with the whole superstructure.

The answer to the inquiry is contained in the writings which—accepting the facts of God as dealt with in our first study—interpret His will for men and His methods with them. These writings declare the requirements of God in terms of the ideal, and in terms of the actual. In God the ideal and the actual are identical. He is what He ought to be. All you postulate of Him which is true and high and noble, He is. In man they are not identical. The ideal and the actual are not the same in human experience. A man who was transparently honest before he met Jesus Christ and after, said, "To me who would do good, evil is present," by which he meant that the ideal was seen but the actual was out of harmony with it. On the other hand, Jesus said, "I do always the things that are pleasing to Him." In that claim the ideal life is expressed in the words, "things that please Him," and the actual in the declaration, "I do." Jesus alone in human history united the ideal and the actual in His experience.

The ideal and the actual are not identical in human experience. Therefore I propose to answer our inquiry in two parts. First, the ideal requirement of God; second, the actual requirement of God. His actual requirements are that we may at last fulfil the ideal; but we look at them in separation in order that we may understand what the requirements of God for men really are.

The ideal requirement of God. I want first to state the terms of revelation, and having done so to consider the revelation of the terms. I go back to Deuteronomy, and to Micah; and then coming to the New Testament, listen to Jesus. My quotations are selected from the great books of authority. Deuteronomy is law in the terms of love. Consequently, it is the supreme book of authority in the old covenant. Micah was pre-eminently the prophet of authority. From these two great books of authority I take my selections from the Old Testament. Then I turn to the New, and come to Matthew, because therein I have the King, always speaking in tones of absolute and final authority.

In the first we find what the law says that God requires. In the second we find what grace and truth say that God requires. "The law was given by Moses; grace and truth came by Jesus Christ." In these quotations from the law by Moses, and from grace and truth by Jesus Christ, we shall find the terms of the revelation of the ideal requirements of God.

I go back to Deuteronomy and find that God requires of man that he should love Him and serve Him, and keep His statutes. I come to Micah and I find that God requires that man should "do justly, and love mercy, and walk humbly with God." In each of these declarations the word "require" is used in our translation, but the Hebrew words are different. They both convey the same idea, but there is a difference of emphasis. The Hebrew word in Deuteronomy means, This is what God *inquires;* this is what God *asks.* When Micah wrote he used another word with more fire in it, more force in it, which we may safely translate, This is what God *insists upon.* When the law was given it declared, in our simplest sense of that word, what God *requires.* But the law having been broken, Micah, calling the people back from their sins, used another word with another emphasis: God insists. The things that God insists upon are that a man shall walk with Him, shall do justly, shall love mercy. In the New Testament I find the requirements of God in words of Jesus, spoken in answer to a cynical inquiry by a lawyer, "Thou shalt love the Lord thy God with all thy heart, and with all thy soul, and with all thy mind. This is the first and great commandment. And a second like unto it is this, Thou shalt love thy neighbour as thyself. On these two commandments hangeth the whole law, and the prophets." Everything that Moses and Micah said lies in this, "Thou shalt love the Lord thy God. . . . Thou shalt love thy neighbour." Hear one other word of Jesus in answer to our inquiry. It occurs in the middle of the manifesto. More criticism has been spent on it than on any other of the sayings of Jesus, criticism of an order more perilous than all higher criticism, criticism which attempts to accommodate the great words of Jesus to the low level of the living of people who think they are Christians and are not "Ye therefore shall be perfect, as your heavenly Father is perfect." What does "perfect" mean? The exact opposite of sin. Sin, the word most commonly used in the New Testament, means *missing the mark*. The root idea of perfect is *hitting the mark*. "Ye therefore shall be perfect." You shall not miss the mark, but hit it. You shall not fail, but succeed. You shall be all God meant you to be. Whether that is a promise or a command does not at all matter. Whether the mood be indicative or imperative is of no consequence. If it be a command, all His commands are promises. If it be a promise, all His promises are commands.

But what is the revelation of these terms? That God requires from every human being perfection, the realization of the ideal. That is God's first requirement. God expects me to be what He made me to be. That is perfection. God does not expect us to be angels, because He has not given us the angelic nature. He expects a man to be a man. He expects a woman to be a woman. He expects a child to be a child. There is nothing more out of harmony with the will of God than a child that ceases to be a child before it has ceased to be a child. There is nothing more out of harmony with the will of God than a man who does not come to manhood when he does come to manhood. Nothing insults high heaven more than a woman who does not become a woman even when she becomes a woman. Your perfection and mine will be as different as are our different lives in outward expression; as identical as are our two lives in life principle. I am not attempting to deal with the outward expression. In a congregation like this there are as many different expressions as there are people; but the inner essential thing in all life is likeness to God, that is, perfect love and perfect truth. Under the command of these two, all the things of the life are to be realized, the artistic, the mechanical, the business; whatever is in us to be realized at its profoundest and its best. That is the will of God.

The passion for perfection is common to humanity. You cannot find a healthy being but that has a passion for perfection in some form. The only people who seem afraid of the word are Christian people. I am constantly asked, Do you believe in Christian perfection? It is a most absurd question, and I am always inclined to reply to it with another question, Certainly I do. Do you believe in Christian imperfection? The passion for perfection is in every healthy soul. Did you ever know a boy or girl who did not dream dreams and see visions of what he or she was going to be and do? Perhaps you in your folly sneered at them, and hindered them. That was a Divine passion in their heart, a desire to reach the goal, to hit the mark. The passion for perfection is indicative of the possibility of perfection. No man ought ever to be satisfied to be less than he is intended to be in the economy of God. God expects that every man shall be that. If you are satisfied with anything less than that, God is not. He requires, He asks, said the ancient lawgiver; He requires, He insists, said the thundering prophet of the closing days of Hebraism, that man shall walk with Him, do justly, and love mercy; that men shall realize their own lives, and realize them by living in harmony with Himself. That is what I mean by the ideal requirement.

All, so far considered, is related to our first inquiry, and the answer concerning man's relation to God. The requirements of God thus understood result in the conviction of sin. Can anyone stand in the presence of his own life, the ideal possibility, and say, I am perfect? You say the instruments were imperfect to begin with. I am not discussing that at all. I admit it. If you admit it, you admit the thing I am asking you to admit, failure, sin. Because the instruments were imperfect to begin with, all the activities have been imperfect. When a man says, If that be the Divine requirement, I have failed, then he begins to ask the new question, What are the actual requirements of God for me? If there were nothing other than what I have been saying, then where are we? Where am I? Where are you? If the demand of God is realization of my life, and perfect realization, I have failed. When Pilate looked into the eyes of the Jewish priests, and said to them, "What I have written, I have written," he was giving expression to his own obstinacy, but he gave expression to a fact far more profound than he knew. What you have written you have written, and you cannot unwrite it. I cannot undo the failure of the past. There lie behind me the years that the cankerworm hath eaten. There lie behind me wasted opportunities. I care nothing if you tell me there have been no vulgarities in your life. My reply to you will be, What do you mean by vulgar? If you are measuring yourself by the ordinary man you may be a very respectable man, but if we measure by heaven's requirement, we are guilty sinners, every one, vulgar with the awful vulgarity of those who are cultured mentally perchance, but have no commerce with heaven and no traffic with God. No man sees what the Divine requirement really is without having to say, I also have failed, I also am a sinner.

Therefore our inquiry must now follow the terms of the actual. What does God demand of such a man? What does He require of me, a sinner? This brings us back to our previous inquiry. I will but state in briefest words the sum and substance of that message thus, God has provided plenteous redemption: forgiveness of sin through the value of His passion, and the dynamic for purity through the victory of His resurrection. In the light of that, what does God require? Come to the terms of the revelation, and once again I take you back to the words of Jesus, startling words as we read them. The cynical men of His own age asked Him, "What must we do, that we may work the works of God?"—What does God require of us? Christ replied, "This is the work of God, that ye believe on Him Whom He hath sent," or, as I think it should always be read, "That ye believe *into* Him Whom He hath sent." That is what God requires of the man who has failed. Those of you who are not perfectly and experimentally familiar with all the meaning of this will admit that it appears a very surprising thing for Christ to say. Listen to it in the light of much preaching which we hear, "This is the *work* of God, that ye *believe* into Him Whom He hath sent." There are those who tell me that I am to be saved by works. There are others who say, There is nothing to *do, only* believe. Christ says, "This is the *work of* God, that ye *believe* into Him Whom He hath sent." Who is right, they or He? If we say at once, as we do, that He must be right, then what did He mean? He meant unquestionably to claim that He was not King merely, but Saviour also. Realizing the fact of their failure, knowing their sin, He said, if they would believe into Him they would work the work of God. That is to say, God provided in Him for their cleansing, for their new birth, for a gift of new life in the energy of which they would be able to do the thing which God would have them do. Therefore, the initial responsibility is that men believe into Him.

Why do I say *into?* Those familiar with the Greek New

Testament know that the preposition *eis,* whenever used with the accusative, means motion into. It is not believe on—you can believe on Jesus Christ and lose your soul. You can believe everything about Him that was ever written and perish. To believe *into* Him is to hear His claim, and, knowing it true, to obey it. This is what God requires of men who have sinned and failed. Having made perfect provision whereby sin can be canceled and paralysis energized, God's requirement is that we believe into Him Whom He hath sent, that we yield ourselves to the Christ.

The revelation of these terms is that all a man needs for his remaking is provided in Christ Jesus. What does God require of man? That man take what God has provided. "He came unto His own, and they that were His own received Him not. But as many as received Him, to them gave He the right to become children of God, even to them that believe on His name; which were born, not of bloods, nor of the will of the flesh, nor of the will of man, but of God." In that passage John uses two terms, *receive,* and *believe,* and shows that they are synonymous, thus suggesting that whichever helps us most we are free to use. Those who receive Him, who are they? Those who believe into His name. What is it to believe on Jesus? To receive Him.

God requires from me perfection. That is, the ideal. I cannot give it Him. What does He do for me? He provides for me in Christ forgiveness for my sins, and power to go and sin no more. Now what does He require of me? That I take what He provides, that I crown the King He presents, that I trust in the Saviour He sends, that I receive the life He places at my disposal. That is the first requirement for the sinning soul. God presents the one all-sufficient Saviour, revealing the pattern, providing the power, and commanding men everywhere to repent and believe into the Son Whom He hath set forth.

The requirements of God in grace are man's fulfilling of His requirements in law. The actual requirements are realization of the ideal requirements. Am I putting these two things into opposition to each other? By no means. Has God ever given up His ideal requirement for you or for me? Never. Does He by Jesus Christ consent to take something less than perfection in our life? By no means. Is the work of Jesus Christ that of asking God to excuse and let into heaven multitudes of incompetent souls? By no means. Was the work of Jesus Christ the making of a provision by which a man can be hidden out of God's sight in his impurity? By no means—a thousand times, by no means. Did Jesus Christ come to fling a cloak of righteousness over the filthiness of my rags? By no means. A cloak of righteousness, a robed righteousness, surely yes. I can still sing what my father sang.

> Jesus, Thy blood and righteousness
> My beauty are, my glorious dress;
> 'Midst flaming worlds, in these arrayed
> With joy shall I lift up my head.

The robe of His righteousness is never placed upon the filthiness of rags to hide them. The work of Jesus Christ is not that of bringing into the Kingdom of God men who are paralyzed and incompetent; but men made perfect. That is the meaning of the mission of Jesus. God's actual requirement is that man shall believe on Jesus, in order that His ideal requirement that man shall be perfect may be fulfilled. "Now unto Him that is able to guard you from stumbling, and to set you before the presence of His glory without blemish in exceeding joy." Was anything more stupendous than that ever written? That is what God requires. Nothing less than that will ever satisfy

Him. He begins with the actual requirement that we submit ourselves to the perfect Saviour Whom He has provided, in order that that Saviour may realize in us all that we failed of, and all that we have lost.

I pray you remember, however, that in the first submission to Christ the perfect ideal is not realized at once. Saul of Tarsus was smitten down on the road to Damascus by the Lord of love and life, but thirty years after that, writing one of his most beautiful epistles, he said, "Not that I have already obtained, or am already made perfect: but I press on, if so be that I may apprehend that for which also I was apprehended by Christ Jesus." Thirty years of Christian experience and discipline; of fire, nakedness, peril, sword, and yet he had not yet attained, was not yet made perfect. God deliver us from the idea that by some mechanical dispatch we can come into all perfection of Christian character. I pray you remember this perfect ideal is not realized at once, but the perfect force necessary for the realization can be received at once. Before you cross the threshold of this house, before you leave Westminster Chapel, you can have all that you need for the ultimate. If Paul said, I have not yet attained, in the same letter he said, "To me to live is Christ." He had all the forces, as is indicated in the words, "One thing I do, forgetting the things which are behind, and stretching forward to the things which are before, I *persecute* toward the goal." You say, That is wrong. Oh, no, it is quite right. When Paul said, "I persecuted the Church," he used exactly the same verb as we have translated *press*. He meant to say, all the zeal and passion and earnestness which he had put into the business of persecuting the Church he afterwards put into the business of attempting to reach the goal, and be what God would have him be.

I am perhaps speaking in the presence of men and women

who have been Christians more years than I have been in the world, and who in the time of their Christian relation have in all probability been far more loyal to their Lord and Master, and far more simple in their faith than I have been, but these are the men and women who will be the first to say, We have not yet attained, we are not yet made perfect. I am also speaking to men and women who have only recently started the Christian life. Let them remember that they possess everything that is necessary for ultimate perfection, because, having received the Christ, they possess Him in all His perfection, and in all His power; and at last when His work is done they will be like Him, presented faultless before the throne of God. Without these forces perfection is impossible. With them perfection is assured.

Hear me as I utter this last word, applicable alike to those who never yet have answered this actual requirement of God that they should yield themselves to Christ, and to those who longest have been following Him. *Belief into* is the preliminary, and perpetual condition for the realization of perfection. That is to say, belief into Christ is not an act, it is an attitude. I believed in Christ, you tell me, forty years ago. I care nothing at all about that. Do you believe in Him now? That is the question. I am not undervaluing your past experience. Thank God if you have a day about which you sing, a place to which you take pilgrimage. Some of us have neither day nor place. There were years in my Christian life when it troubled me that I could not put my hand on a day or an hour or place. It troubles me no more. Yesterday is gone. Jesus saves me now! Belief is an attitude, and there will never dawn a day upon our failing, sinning, yet trusting souls when we can afford to cease our trusting. There never will come a day so bright in our experience that we can walk wholly by sight, never a day in which we shall be able to cease to believe into the Son of God.

That is God's requirement. The actual requirement includes the ideal requirement. When I believe into Him, what does it mean? I will begin on the lower level. I shall love my neighbor as myself. I am silent because of the rebuke of it to my own soul, and to the souls of all such as are honest. You and I have no right to sing of our love to God unless it is expressed in our love to men. If I see my brother in need, and shut up the bowels of my compassion against him, how dwelleth the love of God in me? "Thou shalt love the Lord thy God. . . . Thou shalt love thy neighbour as thyself." That is the ideal, and belief into Christ means that it can become and will increasingly become the real.

It may be as well in conclusion to leave out of view those ultimate reaches of the Divine requirement, never forgetting them wholly, and begin in the presence of His Christ set forth as God's righteousness, set forth as God's perfect Saviour for sinning and failing men. Let us believe into Him, trusting Him for absolution, trusting Him for power, and so looking into His face to-night in full abandonment, know that the Christ of God will perfect that which concerneth us. In order that it may be so here and now,

> Jesus, I will trust Thee,
>   Trust Thee with my soul:
> Guilty, lost, and helpless,
>   Thou canst make me whole.

As we believe into Him, we fulfil God's first requirement in order that at last we may fulfil His final requirement.

CHAPTER XIV

THE PROBLEMS OF THE RELIGIOUS LIFE: THE OPPOSING FORCES OF THE RELIGIOUS LIFE—THE WORLD

THE WORLD, THE FLESH AND THE DEVIL CONSTITUTE THE trinity of forces which oppose the religious life. These are distinct from each other, yet they act in perpetual concert, so that any two of them are powerless apart from the third. I say this at once in order that we may realize the folly of dealing with the world alone, or with the flesh by itself, or with the devil as unrelated to both. Given the world and the flesh, minus the devil, and there is no opposition to religion. There is nothing inherently evil in the world or in the flesh. The flesh and the devil apart from the world cannot successfully oppose the religious life. The devil needs the medium of the world to appeal to the flesh. The devil and the world apart from the flesh cannot make any appeal to the spiritual essence of man. The world can appeal only to flesh. The world plus the flesh, plus the devil, equals conflict. In dealing with the world as an opposing force to the religious life we shall consider, first, the world in itself; second, the world as opposed to religion; third, the world in relation to the flesh and the devil; and, finally, the victory over the world.

We begin, then, first with the subject of the world itself. There is a great deal of nonsense talked about the world and worldliness. A great many things are called worldly that are not worldly, and a great many things are never called worldly that are of the very essence of worldliness. We need to be very careful to understand what is the real meaning of the term "the world" in the New Testament when it is used in such sense as to warn us against it. "God so loved the world that He gave His only begotten Son." "Love not the world, neither the things that are in the world. If any man love the world, the love of the Father is not in him." Such an apparent contradiction should at once compel careful investigation of the sense in which the world is a peril and an opposing force. Perhaps one suggestive illustration may be worth a great deal of argument at this point. I know men who denounce others for worldliness because these others play cards, and go to the theater, and dance. I am not now asking whether these things are worldly or not, but rather insisting that men who do none of these things may be as worldly as men who do them all. Worldliness does not necessarily consist in these things. I repeat, therefore, there is necessity for great care as we approach this subject.

I begin with the world in itself. Of course, you understand I am speaking strictly within the limits of the use made of that word in the New Testament. The word has become almost part of our everyday speech. The word "cosmos" originally meant simply order. It was then used to describe the whole of the universe because of its orderliness and its beauty. So that the world itself does not at all suggest evil. It does not hint at disorder but announces order. It has in it no suspicion of ugliness, but breathes the very spirit of beauty. That in itself is enough to make us pause and consider what is meant by the world, and how the world becomes an opposing force. When a child speaks of the world it thinks of the earth on which we live, and up to a certain point, quite accurately so thinks. May we not say that the word stands for the facts and forces of which man is conscious in his everyday life. That is not a perfect definition, because there are multitudes of men and women who are conscious of facts and forces in everyday life which lie beyond the material. The world means the facts and forces of which material man is conscious, the facts and forces of which material man is a part, the facts and forces of which material man is or may be master. In childhood some of us were taught that the earth and the things therein were divided into three kingdoms, mineral, vegetable, animal. These things have two qualities in common. They are all material, and temporal. Material, that is appreciable by the senses. Everything of form. Everything of sound. Everything of fragrance. Everything of color. Everything of flavor. Everything of tangibility. The things that can be seen and heard, and smelled and tasted and handled. All that the senses can know is the world. I hope you have imagination, then the vastness of this breaks upon you, for it is a great world.

These material things are also temporal, transient, passing; none of them abides. The form and the color change and fade and pass. Sound, though it be the most discordant or the most harmonious, ends. The fragrance passes away. The flavor dies. Nothing on which man has ever laid his hand is lasting. All the rocks are crumbling. Temporal, transient, passing.

The world, then, is the sum total of things material and temporal. I feel the utter inadequacy of the statement in certain ways. One might stay to speak of trees and plants and birds and beasts and men and cities. I leave all that to your imagination. All this is of God. This very material world in the midst of which we live is so marvelous that we are driven to the conclusion that it is easier to believe it to be the work of God than to believe that it originated in any other way. I take up my Bible and go back to the story at its commencement of the origins, and amid all the poetry and marvel of that ancient story I read this, "God saw everything that He had made, and, behold, *it was very good.*" That is true until that hour. If you think of the world in its most material sense, if you think of the world in the simplest sense, there is nothing inherently evil in it.

Then in what sense can it be said that the world is opposed to religion? Let me answer that inquiry by quotation of one passage written by Paul in his letter to the Romans, "They worshipped the creature rather than the Creator." That is worldliness. It is when a man does that that the world is an opposing force to religion. Let us think of that a little more closely. What is the rational process. Given an object—I do not care what object, sun or star, bird or animal, tree or man—given an object, say a tree for the sake of illustration, behind that tree is a thought. Nothing ever has been, so far as human observation has any right to declare, but that the deed, the act, the fact, was preceded by a conception, an intention, a thought. Begin with the simplest thing in the wide world. I take in my hand this glass—an object. Behind it is a thought. It was seen before it was made. It was intended before it was constructed. Or take the most splendid and matchless building that your eyes have ever seen—the whole thing was thought before it was erected. What is true there we believe to be true everywhere. Here is a tree, a flower, more wonderful than the most splendid cathedral that man ever raised, far more mysterious than the most magnificent piece of machinery that man ever constructed. We may call it argument from design. I know it is the fashion to declare that argument exploded. I say it has never been answered. The rational process, then, is this. Behind the object is a thought;

behind the thought is a thinker, for you cannot have a thought without a thinker, a mental mood without a mind, a conception without a conceiver. The rational process in the presence of the world is to pass through the object, sun, star, river, animal, to the thought behind it, and through the thought to the thinker, and in the presence of the thinker to bow in worship and service.

What, then, is the irrational process? To take the object, sun or star, animal or tree, and worship it, and serve it. That is the meaning of Paul's argument concerning the Gentile world. Instead of worshiping the Creator they worshiped and served the creature. They stayed in the realm of the things seen, and did not pass through them to the actuality of the unseen things. That is worldliness.

Let me put it in another way. Worldliness consists in dealing with the material, without recognizing the spiritual of which the material is an expression, dealing with the things that are temporal without recognition of the things that are eternal, living in the midst of the transient without having commerce with the abiding. When a man begins the religious life he still feels the pull of the world, the temptation to deal with finite things, without placing upon them the measurement of the infinite, without weighing them in the balances of eternity.

Let me attempt to illustrate this in a yet more immediate and practical way. There may be worldliness in religion, in education, in commerce, in pleasure. I take these only as illustrative. The fact may doubtless be illustrated in many other ways.

There are two manifestations of worldliness in religion. One is ritualism, the other rationalism. A man may be a ritualist, and not be worldly. I want to grant that at once. It is high time we were beginning to learn the lesson of being perfectly fair to men from whom we most profoundly differ. A man may be a ritualist and not be worldly. I have known men who through form and ceremony and splendor of ritual have commerce with God. But when a man observes so many days, so many ceremonies, and the observance being over, he turns back again to all the things that are contrary to the will of God, that is worldliness in religion. Worldliness in religion is the idea that things that are of the world, beauty of form and color, and the fine fragrance of incense, constitute religion.

Worldliness may manifest itself in religion as rationalism. By rationalism I mean contentment with present conditions. When religion deals simply with the present conditions of men and women it is worldly in the extreme. Sometimes this type of religion charges those of us who believe in God and heaven and hell with being other-worldly, by which it makes unconscious confession that it is worldly. It is of the dust. It begins and ends there. Anything that attempts to deal with men simply on the level of this world, the betterment of human conditions, pure humanitarianism, is worldliness in religion. Hear me again. If a man have commerce with God and the eternities, he cannot be indifferent to the condition of his brother men in the slum. Let there be no misunderstanding of my position. In proportion as a man really lives the spiritual life, and has dealings with God Himself, he is hot and angry in the presence of all human limitation; but when a man attempts in the name of religion to deal simply with these conditions, and forgets the infinite and eternal, his religion has become utterly worldly. Worldliness in religion begins and ends in things that are material and sensual and passing.

Then there may be, as there is, worldliness in education. Education which deals simply with knowledge of the material and temporal, and never puts on these things the measurement of the infinite and eternal, is worldly education.

There may be worldliness in commerce. Someone says, That goes without saying. I pray you, then, remember that there may be the spiritual in commerce also. What is worldliness in commerce? Commerce that is based on a passion for possession of goods to the neglect of God. Jesus Christ has given us an accurate picture of it. It is not a flattering picture; but you can hang it up in London to-day, and thousands of men, if they are honest, will see their own portrait. The rich fool, the man who says, My lands are increased, my wealth is increased, what shall I do? "And he said, This will I do: I will pull down my barns and build greater; and there will I bestow all my corn and my goods. And I will say to my soul, Soul, thou hast much goods laid up for many years; take thine ease, eat, drink, be merry." He fed his soul on goods! That is worldliness in commerce, and ultimately it means selfishness, greed, oppression. There is worldliness in pleasure. That needs no argument. Pleasure in itself is not wrong. God made no half measures in His universe. When He made a fish and gave it fins it was that it might swim. When He made a bird and gave it wings it was that it might fly. When he gave me a laughing apparatus it was that I might laugh. I have not said a more religious thing than that to-night. God made man for pleasure. The ultimate intention of God for man is pleasure. When Jesus began that great Manifesto of His Kingdom which scorches and burns, He used the word "happy." I read in my Bible that "God shall wipe away all tears from their eyes," but I never read that He will stop laughter, pleasure. Worldly pleasure is abuse of the senses by forgetfulness of the spiritual.

These are rapid and almost haphazard illustrations of

what the world really means. Though you never go to the theater, you may be a very worldly man. Though you sit regularly—I will speak of no other place than this—in Westminster Chapel, and sing the songs, and give to the collection, you may be an absolutely worldly man. What is a worldly man? I ask once more. A worldly man is one who lives as though this were the only world. He may think about another. He may tell you in conversation that he believes in another. He may recite the creed on Sabbath, beginning with the august and stately measure, "I believe in God the Father almighty, Maker of heaven and earth," but Monday, Tuesday, Wednesday, Thursday, Friday, Saturday, in business, at home, in pleasure, he lives as though there were no God in the universe. That is worldliness, though he recite the creed regularly and sings all the songs of the sanctuary. It is not the singing of songs, or the recitation on the creed that disproves worldliness. Worldliness is life lived in the dust to the forgetfulness of Deity, life that has no sense of the infinite and eternal, that does not bring the measurements of eternity and lay them on every half-hour.

Now I see how the world is an opposing force to religion. When it so engrosses my thought and attention as to make me unmindful of spiritual things, when it so obtrudes itself on my attention as to capture all my thinking and make me forget God, then it opposes religion. We have to face the fact that it is a very real force in opposition. "I see the sights that dazzle"—how often we have sung it, and how awfully and appallingly true it is!

For a moment we must stay here to notice the connection between the world, the flesh and the devil, because only by so doing can we understand how it comes to pass that the world opposes religious life. It ought to be the most natural thing in all material things to discover the presence of the spiritual. It seems as though it was impossible for the Man of Nazareth to touch anything of the earth but that somehow it flamed with the glory of the heavens. Yet He was quite natural. We hardly like to use these words about Him, yet you will understand me. A more artless and unaffected man never lived than Jesus of Nazareth. He loved the flowers, the gorgeous lilies of His own land. He looked at their beauty, and what did He say? Your Father clothes them, and "even Solomon in all his glory was not arrayed like one of these." Children, how He loved them! Yes, but what did He see when He saw a child? The angel beholding the face of God. So you may pass through all His life and you will find a Man with feet firmly planted on the earth, of the earth, belonging to it, and yet different from the earth, Master of it, King of it. Whenever He touched it He revealed by His touch its relationship to the boundless spaciousness of eternity, in which forevermore He was at home. He stood on the plains of Judæa, and talked to men, and He used their own language. Their eyes looked at him. Their hands handled Him. There He was, and yet He spoke of Himself as the Son "in the bosom of the Father." That is the utter, absolute opposite to worldliness.

Now I ask this question. How comes it that the world which ought everywhere to reveal the heights, the world which ought to suggest God, makes me forget Him? Man's attitude in the presence of the world is determined by his conception of himself. To live in the flesh is to be imprisoned by the material and temporal, never to see through the garments of God in the green sward to the God Who wears them, but to see only the grass. A self-centered and self-contained life seeks its satisfaction *in*, rather than *through*, the material world. What is a self-governed life? It is a devil-governed life. A worldly, self-centered life always results from the dethronement of God, and the dethronement of God is always the result of listening to a lie from without. When you track back the forces that oppose religion, you find the devil behind them all. This world, all the fair and beautiful handiwork of God through which I ought always to find Him, hinders the essential spirit within me. Why? Because an enemy has come between my soul and God, and persuaded me to dethrone Him and enthrone self, and has blinded me so that I have lost the true perspective, and proportion of things, and the sense that discovers God everywhere. These are the themes of future discussion. They are stated now only that the intimate connection between the opposing forces may be recognized.

Finally, is there victory over the world? I read my New Testament statement, "This is the victory that hath overcome the world, even our faith." I go back to that passage, and I find that the object of the faith that overcomes the world is Jesus Christ, the Son of God. The soul believing is begotten of God. The eye is opened, the ear is unstopped, the lost sense is restored. That is the final Christian evidence. You cannot make it known to any other man. It must be personal and immediate. No man need waste time trying to persuade me there is no God. I know. No argument you can adduce in proof of the existence of God will convince me. No argument you can adduce as against the existence of God will convince me. I know. As one man said in the presence of a material sign long ago, so say I in the presence of heaven and earth, on oath, "One thing I know, whereas I was blind, now I see."

Mark the issues of faith. Life becomes God-governed.

That is the devil's defeat. Self is found at last, realized within itself. Flesh is made subservient to spirit. Then "all things are yours; whether Paul, or Apollos, or Cephas, or *the world*." Mark that well. I have not lost the world. I have found it. I have found it in that I have discovered that the material and the spiritual are related, that on every blade of grass shines the grace of God, and in all the prismatic colors of the rainbow is revealed His beauty. I have not lost the world. I have found it. Only the temporal is now seen in its relation to the eternal, and change and decay are no longer destruction, but the perpetual process of that which abides. The man who has faith has not lost his world, but he is no longer worldly.

What, then, is the final word of injunction in the presence of these opposing forces? Again I quote from the New Testament and from Paul. "Use the world as not abusing it: for the fashion of this world passeth away." That is to say, use the world, but never imagine that it is all; and never use it save in its relation to that larger whole of the spiritual and eternal. Deal with the things of dust, but touch them with the force of Deity. Enter into all that the senses can reveal to you of the life in which you live, but know that for all these things God will bring you to judgment, not to punishment but to judgment, the finding of a verdict, and the passing of a sentence, the creating of a destiny. All the things of the world are mine, but I am not to live in them as though they were the whole. I am to understand that they are things of dust and I am to treat them as such.

To go back again to that word of John, "Love not the world, neither the things that are in the world. If any man love the world, the love of the Father is not in him." Dr. Chalmers' great sermon on that text is entitled, "The expulsive power of a new affection." What is the new affection?

The true affection, love of God. What does it do for a man? Puts out of his heart that love of the world which makes him forget God, and puts into his heart a new love of the world because he sees it to be the handiwork of his Father. I remember as though it were yesterday something that happened in my own life at least thirty-seven years ago. I was a boy, and there came to my father's house a young man who had been brought to Christ in some meetings my father had been conducting in the Welsh hills. This young man was out in our garden talking to me about all sorts of things. I remember how he interested me, and how I loved him. Suddenly he stooped and picked a leaf from a nasturtium plant. He held it in his hand and said to me, "Did you ever see anything so beautiful." As a boy I looked at it, saw all the veins and the exquisite beauty. Then he said this, and I never forgot it. "I never saw how beautiful that leaf was until six months ago, when I gave myself to Christ." How true I know that to be now in my own experience. The worldly man loses his world. The godly man finds it. Where are you going for your summer holiday? I strongly advise you to get right with God before you go, and if you will, you will have such a holiday as you have never had. When a man crossing the ocean sits on deck and refuses to look at the sea because it is worldly, he is the most worldly man on board ship. He is self-centered and even though he is spiritually proud, he is godless and worldly. The love of the Father, let that fill your heart, and then what? Then all the things He made are exquisite with beauty. You will listen to the music of the thunder at night, and thank God that you are a child of the Thunderer. You will look at all the wonders in creation, and rejoice more than ever that you are the heir of the God Who made them, and that consequently they belong to you. I have lost neither poetry nor art nor music because I am His, in answer to the call of His grace. I have found them because I no longer believe that they are all. When you look on a painting and tell me it will fade, I tell you not half so soon as the pictures He paints. He is so great an artist that He flings a picture on the sky, and as you look it is gone, but in ten minutes there is another. All the things of beauty in the world are mine because I am His and He is mine. When you lose your vision of God you lose your sense of the eternal, and live wholly in the things of His beautiful world. Then you have imprisoned your own soul. May God deliver us from all worldliness by bringing us into such unity with Himself that we shall look nowhere without seeing Him, touch nothing without feeling Him, be in the midst of no circumstances without being conscious of Him.

CHAPTER XV

THE PROBLEMS OF THE RELIGIOUS LIFE: THE OPPOSING FORCES OF THE RELIGIOUS LIFE—THE FLESH

BECAUSE OF THE NEAR PERSONAL RELATION OF THE FLESH TO every human being, this subject is at once supremely interesting and vitally important. The flesh is part of the ego, part of myself, not all of myself, but part, and an essential part so far as the present life is concerned. The world is outside me. The devil is other than I am, a distinct personality. But the flesh is of my very self. I cannot escape it. It goes where I go, it abides where I abide; it is with me in my thinking, in my loving, in my willing. I have to take account of the flesh. I may be able to escape, in some measure, from the world in cloistered seclusions, and within stone walls. I cannot so escape from the flesh. I may be able to escape from the devil in certain surroundings, and certain atmospheres. I can never escape from the flesh. Consequently, I say we are dealing with a subject which is supremely interesting and vitally important.

Now I propose to follow the same line of examination as when I considered the world as an opposing force. First, the flesh in itself; second, the flesh as opposed to religion; third, the flesh in relation to the world and the devil; and, finally, the victory over the flesh.

We are greatly aided in this study by the Incarnation. Therein we see human nature according to the pattern, true to the ideal. We have no real understanding of what was in the heart of God when He said, "Let Us make man," until we know Jesus Christ. We may have studied human nature; we may have studied human history, we may have a large and varied circle of acquaintances and friends, but we never know man until we know Jesus Christ. It is graciously and wonderfully true that He is the Revelation of God. It is equally and as graciously true that He is the Revelation of man. I know the meaning of this life of mine only when I know Jesus. Through all the ages, so far as I may glance at them through the windows of history, secular and sacred, I see man after man, some rising above their fellows, conspicuous heights among the mountains, but I never know what man is according to the Divine pattern until my eyes rest on the one Man of Nazareth. In Him we are able to understand, as we never could apart from that revelation, the failure of all other men. Had there been no Jesus Christ in the world, and no record of Him, no image of Him stamped on the human consciousness, I can conceive that men might be very well satisfied with themselves. But no man who has honestly studied the portrait of Jesus which the gospels present, who has stood face to face with the Man of Nazareth and allowed Him to put the measurement of Himself upon life, has escaped the conviction that he ought to say, Lo, I have sinned!

I know the kinship between Jesus and myself; but, my brethren, it is when I am most conscious of the kinship that I discover the immeasurable, appalling, and awful distance between Him and myself. The distance would not appall me if there were not kinship, but it is when I know He is flesh of my flesh, bone of my bone, blood of my blood, and then see Him rising into the infinite heights, towering above me in the sublime simplicities of His fulfilment of the ideal, in the simple sublimity of His realization of purpose, that I know how low I have fallen.

Now, in that light of that revelation we turn to our consideration. The first necessity is that we should understand the meaning of the term, "the flesh." There are two brief passages which I am going to quote in order that their light may fall on the subject. The first is to be found in the opening chapter of John's Gospel. "The Word was made flesh." The second is to be found in the first letter of the same writer, in the fourth chapter, "Jesus Christ is come in the flesh." Then it is certain that flesh in the first and simplest condition is not sinful. There is nothing inherently sinful in flesh. There is another passage in Romans, but notice very carefully what it really says. He was made *"in the likeness of* sinful flesh." He was not made sinful flesh, but in the likeness of it. He was made flesh, but not sinful flesh; and when you bring together these two words, sinful and flesh, you are recognizing the presence of something in the flesh, you are recognizing the presence of something in the flesh that does not belong to it, that ought not to be there. I lay my hand on this hand of mine, I touch this body of mine, and I handle and touch sinful flesh. But when the disciples in the olden days laid their hand on the actual flesh of the Man of Nazareth they laid their hand on actual flesh, but not on sinful flesh. And so I look at this Man—this ideal Man, this actual Man, this sinless Man, this Man Who challenged any to convince Him of sin, this Man Who claimed absolute holiness—and as I look I know that the flesh in its first and simplest condition is not sinful, that there can be flesh without sin.

What, then, according to that first Divine intention as revealed in Jesus, is the flesh? The idea is the instrument of the spirit, perfectly adjusted to the material under-world and to the spirit over-world. Man who is not a body, but who is a spirit inhabiting a body, is able to touch all the material through the medium of his flesh. When the psalmist, referring to the flesh, to the body, said, "We are fearfully and wonderfully made," he uttered a tremendous truth. Through the medium of the flesh man has been able to examine and discover, and manipulate, to exercise the dominion for which he was created. The body is the perfect instrument of the spirit, subservient to it, answering it; the medium through which the spirit touches all lower creation, and the medium through which all lower creation comes into living touch with the spiritual that lies beyond it. There is no inherent evil in flesh according to the original purpose and intention of God.

So that when you speak of the body of a man in terms of disapprobation be very careful lest you be found to blaspheme against God. For remember this body of mine is as much a work of God as is the spirit that indwells it, and it is a work of God made to fit the spirit, to be the dwelling place of the spirit, the temple of the spirit. Infinitely more sacred than any temple, or cathedral, or church that was ever erected is every human body. Made to be the instrument of the spirit, fearfully and wonderfully made, delicate in its organism, tough and tremendous in its strength, is the flesh.

How, then, can flesh be an opposing force to the religious life? Let me again cite three scriptures, and, at first, there may seem to be very little connection between them, and not much bearing on our subject. The first quotation is from the gospel according to Matthew, and the account which the evangelist there gives of words spoken by our Lord in the garden of Gethsemane to three of His disciples, who when they ought to have been watching were asleep. It is a word having a local setting and coloring, but revealing a great, and shall I say, an appalling truth. Jesus said to these men, "The spirit indeed is willing, but the flesh is weak."

The second quotation is from the Galatian letter, "The flesh lusteth against the Spirit, and the Spirit against the flesh." The Greek word, *epithumia*, may be translated "desireth." Let me use that word here. "The flesh desireth against the Spirit, and the Spirit against the flesh." In the Revised Version the word "Spirit" is spelled with a capital letter, and quite accurately. The whole context shows that the apostle was referring to the Spirit of God. In the first quotation I made, the quotation from our Lord, the word should be written with a small *s*, for the reference is not to the Spirit of God but to the spirit of man. The third quotation is from the first letter of Peter, "All flesh is grass."

Now, what are the facts which these Scriptures suggest to us? First, "the spirit indeed is willing, but the flesh is weak." In that word Jesus revealed the fact of internecine strife in human life, that is, mutually destructive strife. In these very disciples there was strife between the aspiration of the spirit and the ability of the flesh. The spirit willing, conscious of the beauty of the religious ideal, having seen the glory of the Christ, and having earnestly desired to follow Him; and the flesh going to sleep. Peter had said but a little while before, "Although all shall be offended, yet will not I." That is the willing spirit. That is the essential man, the deepest man in Peter, desiring to be true to his Lord, declaring that he can die for Him. In the garden Jesus said, "Simon, sleepest thou? couldest thou not watch one hour?"

The spirit is willing, but the flesh is weak. That is the trouble. Over and over again you find in the case of the man who has never yielded to Christ the spirit indeed is willing, but the flesh is weak. I know it is said that there can be no admiration of the good and true on the part of unregenerate man. That is not true. There are thousands of unregenerate men who know the beauty of holiness, but they cannot be holy. But now I am far more anxious to deal with the flesh as an opposing force in the lives of those who have yielded themselves to Christ, who see the ideal revealed in Christ, all the things high and excellent and beautiful. In such the spirit indeed is willing, but the flesh is weak. I ought to watch, but I go to sleep. I ought to win, but I fail. Jesus Christ could not have said that of Himself, The spirit indeed is willing, but the flesh is weak. In His case the spirit was willing, and the flesh was equal to the demands. There was never any failure. There was never any internecine strife between the spirit of Jesus and His flesh. His flesh was forevermore the instrument of His spirit, obeying it, answering it, serving it, helping it. Not so with other men. Not so with me.

Notice the second of these two quotations. "The flesh lusteth against the Spirit; and the Spirit lusteth against the flesh." That is to say, there is not only internecine strife, but in human life there is antagonism to the purpose of God in the realm of the flesh. The spirit of God is leading me toward the heights and calling me to the spiritual outlook and conception, and the flesh is dragging me to the depths and suggesting that I live the life of the animal. That word sounds hard and uncouth. Are you in rebellion against that definition? Are you saying, "Not the life of the animal; you cannot speak of the cultured life of to-day as the life of the animal"? Absolutely, if the sum total of life may be thus expressed, "What shall I eat, what shall I drink, and wherewithal shall I be clothed?" That is animal life. It means food and warmth and animal comfort. The flesh is drawing every one of us to that. That is the temptation of it. That is the suggestion of it.

The Spirit of God is calling me to the life of spirituality, the life that takes in eternity in its outlook, and has dealings with God in all its transactions. The flesh says, Just for to-day, what shall I eat and what shall I drink?

Once again, "All flesh is grass." That is to say, the flesh has on it the stupor of death, and always asks for ease instead of effort, for licence rather than liberty, and the issue is riot instead of realization. All these things are things of death.

In this way the flesh is an opposing force to the Christian life. I am not entering to-night on the question of how this happened. I am simply dealing with the fact. You can have your own theory about how it happened. I have my Bible and I still believe that man has fallen, and the humanity which I share, and which I meet in the city and in the village, on land and on sea, both rich and poor, both bond and free, is one humanity, fallen humanity; not humanity climbing up, but humanity helplessly and irrevocably down, so that it never can rise, except by a miracle of Divine power lifting it out of the dust. I am dealing with the fact. The moment a man sees the spiritual, and answers it by following Christ, he becomes conscious of conflict with the flesh. The conflict of the child of God with the flesh is the conflict of the subjugation of a recovered empire. Before you were a Christian you lived in the flesh. Now that you are a Christian you live in the spirit. Your own spirit is enthroned. You had it in the prison and starved it and neglected it, and sometimes even said that you did not possess it. In the moment in which you gave yourself to Christ He put that spirit, your spirit, back on the throne of your personality, and He put it there in partnership with His own Spirit, in order to realize your whole life; and the first thing is that the flesh become subservient to it. But the flesh does not become subservient immediately. The flesh which so long was degraded by the fact that you allowed it to have its own way by answering its lust, and dwelling wholly within it, when put in its right place, under the spirit, rebels. Regeneration does not mean a sudden convulsion, of such a nature that all the fibers of my flesh cease to make their own demands. The fight is long and strenuous, and sometimes almost to blood. I want every young Christian here, every young man and every young woman who is fighting this fight, to remember that he or she is subjugating a recovered empire. You have set up the throne, but you have to win and cultivate and restore the whole territory. A man can be cleansed in a moment by the Spirit of God, but there is then the whole campaign of subjugation to go forward. What I do plead for is that you shall be patient. That very thought comes out in the words, "Let us not be weary in well doing; for in due season we shall reap, if we faint not." That is a recognition of the fact that the flesh which has been rampant and masterful for years, when you take the throne in the fear and fellowship of the Holy Spirit of God, is not immediately subjugated, the long habits of years are not immediately broken.

Now, remember the relation of the flesh to the world and to the devil. As last time, I indicate this in very brief sentences, yet the three must always be taken in connection with each other. The degraded man is the man who degrades the world. The degraded world hinders the remade man. For the interpretation of the meaning of that I must refer you to the things I said when speaking of the world. The degraded man, the man who has lost true balance and proportion of things, and instead of being spirit with a body subservient, has become spirit imprisoned by flesh; he degrades the world. Then the world so degraded hinders the man in the moment in which he is remade. The old appeals and allurements of the world make their appeal to the flesh which has not yet come into the absolute consciousness of the mastery of the spirit.

The devil appeals to the degraded man through the degraded world, and he appeals to the remade man through the same medium of a degraded world, and thus fights against all the purposes of God in the man and in the world; for no man will ever be able to take hold of the world and use it as God intended he should use it and bring it to ultimate perfection unless he is a spiritual man. God's purpose for him is defeated, and God's purpose for the world is defeated so long as he is degraded. When man has found his right relationship to God, and the flesh is what it ought to be, what it was in the Christ, then "the wilderness and the solitary place shall be glad; and the desert shall rejoice, and blossom as the rose. . . . In the wilderness shall waters break out, and streams in the desert." The earth will come to its ultimate fulness and realization when man has found his true relation to God, and to prevent that the devil presents the degraded world to man and attempts to lure him back to the things of the dust only, forbidding him to take into consciousness the things of the eternities.

Finally, can I have victory over this flesh life? Do I mean to say by the things already said that all the while and always I must be defeated? Assuredly not! I have said, and I believe, that the conflict is long and continuous, but defeat is not a synonymous term with conflict. I need not be defeated. There can be victory over the flesh. Hear these words of Paul in the letter to the Romans, the eighth chapter and ninth verse, "Ye are not in the flesh, but in the spirit, if so be that the Spirit of God dwelleth in you." Take that whole passage, and be patient with me if I ask you to read it in the Revised Version, and notice particularly the spelling of the word spirit. You will find it written with a capital letter in certain places and with a small letter in others. After the most careful examination I am able to make, I am convinced our revisers have spelled the word correctly. "Ye are not in the flesh, but in the spirit," that is, your own spirit. If the Spirit of God dwells in a man that man is living on the spiritual side of his own nature, not on the fleshly side. I can live in the flesh or in the spirit. The difference between life high and noble and life low and ignoble is the difference between life in the spirit and life in the flesh. Life in the spirit means the spirit of man enthroned. Then is the flesh bruised and battered? Certainly not! What, then? The flesh is in its proper place, properly nourished, and forever more the servant of the spirit and never the master of the man. That is true life. Man can live in the flesh, answering every cry of his mouth and every appeal of his eye, and every itch of his hand, and every passion of his dusty nature. Where in such life is the spirit? Imprisoned, choked, starved, neglected. Where are you living? "Ye are not in the flesh, but in the spirit, if so be that the Spirit of God dwelleth in you. If any man hath not the Spirit of Christ, he is none of His." If you have the Spirit of God, then you are living in the spirit and not in the flesh.

Then I turn to the Galatian letter, and find these words in the fifth chapter, "I say, Walk by the Spirit, and ye shall not fulfil the lust of the flesh. For the flesh lusteth against the Spirit, and the Spirit against the flesh; for these are contrary the one to the other; that ye may not do the things that ye would." That is the statement of a principle. The flesh desires against the Spirit in order that you may not do the things that you would when you are following the Spirit. The Spirit desires against the flesh in order that you may not do the things you would if you are following the flesh. In the presence of the lust, the desire, the temptation of the flesh, what am I to do? "Walk by the Spirit." The only way of victory over the flesh is that of the reception of the Spirit and obedience to His direction. If we fight the flesh in the power of the flesh we shall be beaten by the flesh. If we have received this Spirit of God, Who takes our spiritual nature and puts it back on the throne, He says to us, Now, follow Me, walk by My rule, do the thing I suggest, obey Me, and you shall not fulfil the lust of the flesh.

You say to me, Now you are becoming mystical. No, I never was more practical in all my life. The way of the Spirit is revealed in the simplest things of life and in the simplest way possible. When did you yield to the flesh last? I ask for no public answer, no answer made to me in language. I ask for answer in your own heart. The moment you admit that you yielded you recognize the fact of allurement, temptation; and temptation and allurement recognize the fact that the voice of the Spirit was telling you the way, but you yielded to the flesh and obeyed it, and did not obey the voice of the Spirit. The Spirit said to you, Not that way home, but two miles round to be out of temptation! But you went that way home, and went down. Do not say that Christ cannot save you, and that the Spirit cannot keep you. It is a lie. If you will not obey Him He cannot. Of course, if you have never yet given yourself to Christ you do not know what it is to have the indwelling Spirit. The first thing necessary is the yielding of the life to Christ. Yield to Him. From the moment that is done, the Spirit is there the Mentor and Watcher, and infinitely more. Not the Mentor merely, but the Might you need. Not the Watcher only but the Worker able to deliver you. There is no man or woman here belonging to Christ who has fallen into known sin by yielding to the clamant cry of the flesh, but that if you are quite honest you will have to confess you did it wilfully and in disobedience to the call of the Spirit.

"The Spirit . . . shall quicken also your mortal body." That is not a reference to the resurrection. It is a present thing. The quickening of the mortal body means bringing the flesh into such subjection to the Spirit that the Spirit does master it. He breathes through the pulses of desire His coolness and His balm. He breaks the power of canceled sin and sets the prisoner free.

What I have desired to do supremely to-night—I know not whether I have succeeded—is to help every young Christian struggling in the presence of the pull of the flesh to understand that this fight is in the economy of your salvation, and that you are subjugating a recovered empire; and I want you to see that the only way in which you can have victory is that of obedience to the Spirit of God, Who interprets to your spirit the will of God. I want you to see, moreover, that if that be the only way it is a sure way; and so surely as we follow the leading and guidance and call of the Spirit of God resolutely we shall have victory not only over the world but over the flesh, and the flesh will become again an instrument of the Spirit. Our members yielded to Him, He will make use of them; the eyes of this poor earthly tabernacle may flash with the light of His love; the hands which have been ministers of iniquity may become ministers of His mercy to others; and the feet which have taken us into the highways and by-ways of evil may carry us, under the bidding of His love, on errands of mercy and loving kindness and help to the sons of men. "Know ye not that your body is the temple of the Holy Ghost? Yield yourselves, therefore, and your members as instruments of righteousness." So comes the victory, and more than victory, the redemption of the flesh and the realization in it of all the purpose of God.

CHAPTER XVI

THE PROBLEMS OF THE RELIGIOUS LIFE: THE OPPOSING FORCES OF THE RELIGIOUS LIFE—THE DEVIL

IN THIS STUDY, AS IN THE PREVIOUS ONES, OUR APPEAL IS MADE wholly to the Scriptures of truth. It is impossible to make such appeal and at the same time to deny the personality of Satan.

To deny the personality of Satan as revealed in the Scriptures is to have to believe that all the evil things with which we are familiar today, and all the dark and dastardly crimes of the centuries, have come out of human nature. This the Bible does not teach. There are two chapters at the commencement of the Bible and two at the end in which we have glimpses of this world unaffected by the devil. In the two first chapters he is not seen. In the last two chapters he is banished. Through the rest he is recognized and referred to as an actual personality of evil, and that to me is a most hopeful doctrine. If humanity is a part of God, then all murders and lies are part of the activity of God, and that is impossible of belief. I know it is not quite fashionable to talk about the devil today.

> Men don't believe in a devil now,
>   As their fathers used to do;
> They reject one creed because it's old
>   For another because it's new.
>
> There's not a print of his cloven foot,
>   Nor a fiery dart from his bow,

> To be found in the earth or air today!
>   At least—they declare it is so!
>
> But who is it mixes the fatal draught
>   That palsies heart and brain
> And loads the bier of each passing year
>   With its hundred thousand slain?
>
> But who blights the bloom of the land today
>   With the fiery breath of hell?
> If it isn't the devil that does the work,
>   Who does? Won't somebody tell?
>
> Who dogs the steps of the toiling saint?
>   Who spreads the net for his feet?
> Who sows the tares in the world's broad field
>   Where the Saviour sows His wheat?
>
> If the devil is voted not to be,
>   Is the verdict therefore true?
> Someone is surely doing the work
>   The devil was thought to do.
>
> They may say the devil has never lived,
>   They may say the devil is gone;
> But simple people would like to know
>   Who carries the business on.

I shall follow exactly the same method as I have followed in the previous two lectures, speaking first of the devil as he is revealed to us in Scripture; second, of the devil as opposed to religion; third, of the relation between the world, the flesh, and the devil; and, last, of the way of victory over the devil.

The personality of Satan is revealed as distinctly in the New Testament as is the personality of Jesus Christ. To deny the one is to deny the other. In casting out demons Christ perpetually addressed Himself to them as to definite personalities, possessing men, and all through that New Testament story it is quite evident that the personality of the devil was believed in.

But now what does the Bible teach concerning this personality? First of all, the Bible never suggests that Satan is self-existent; and if not self-existent, therefore created; and if created, created by God. God creates everything good, and nothing evil. "Do not I, the Lord, create evil?" is a distinct declaration of Scripture, but read the context, and it is at once seen that the word "evil" there means calamity, judgment on a guilty city. Therefore it is perfectly evident that, according to Bible teaching, Satan being not self-existent, but created, and that by God, was therefore created good. And if today he is evil, he has fallen from his original estate.

There was a time when the disciples came back to Jesus, and said, "Even the devils are subject to us," and there fell from the lips of the Master these very remarkable words, "I beheld Satan fallen as lightning from heaven." There a whole history is condensed into a flash; and a great unveiling of truth comes almost with a blinding glare. The disciples said, Even the demons are subject to us, and Christ's answer in effect was this, You need not be surprised that demons are subject unto you in My name. Satan, himself, the prince of the hosts of wickedness, the lord of the whole empire of sin, is not enthroned, he is fallen from heaven. It is testimony borne by the lips of Christ to a primal fall; to the fact that Satan is one of the principalities, one of the powers, an angel, but an angel fallen as lightning from heaven.

There is very little doubt that Peter heard that word of Jesus, and when I turn to his epistles I find in the course of an argument he declared, "God spared not angels when they sinned, but cast them down to hell, and committed them to pits of darkness, to be reserved unto judgment." That is an inspired declaration of the fact that God spared not angels when they sinned, but cast them down, committed them to pits of darkness. Jude, in his brief epistle, gives us a still more detailed and remarkable account of the primal fall of angels. Hear these words, "Angels which kept not their own principality, but left their proper habitation." The Authorized Version reads "their first estate." Which is the better translation I cannot tell. I should be inclined to change them both and read, "Angels which kept not true to first principles, left their proper habitation or residence, or sphere, or orbit, He hath kept in everlasting bonds under darkness unto the judgment of the great day." There is nothing detailed in all this, but there is quite sufficient to reveal all that it is necessary for us to know. It is the story of a fall of angels led by one. Jesus named the one in the forefront, the leader, "I beheld *Satan* as lightning fallen from heaven." Peter writes in the plural, "God spared not angels when they sinned, but cast them down to hell, and committed them to pits of darkness." Jude went a little more carefully into the matter and declared that they "kept not their own principality." They were not true to the principle of their own life, they left their proper orbit, habitation, residence, sphere, but they did not escape from Divine government when they so fell. He kept them "in everlasting bonds under darkness unto the judgment of the great day."

What was the sin? Who shall dare to say? In Milton's "Paradise Lost" we have splendid speculation as to what the sin was; and in all probability more than speculation.

Satan is never spoken of as having any independent existence. He is never spoken of as having sovereign dominion. The Bible never suggests that he has successfully cast off the government of God: He is in rebellion against it, but still held by it. That is the meaning of the petition in the Lord's prayer, "Bring us not into temptation, but deliver us from the evil." It is a recognition of the fact that the very forces of evil in the spiritual realm are still under the government of God. To imagine that the Bible teaches that Satan is a personality in the universe in rebellion against God successfully, is to contradict entirely what the Bible perpetually teaches.

Now notice what this means. The devil is not omnipotent. The devil is not omniscient. The devil is not omnipresent. Let me begin with the last first. The Bible never suggests the omnipresence of the devil. Someone says, The devil is here. How do you know? You have no proof of it. It is impossible for the devil to be in London and in New York at the same moment. To admit the creation of angels is to admit limitation and location. Whether you think of angels fallen or unfallen, I pray you remember none of them are omnipresent. They come, they go. They guard and watch the saints, for "Are they not all ministering spirits, sent forth to do service for the sake of them that shall inherit salvation." So also with Satan and all the fallen angels, none of them are omnipresent. The number of them is so great that in every assembly, and over every man, some of them watch in order to destroy. But Satan himself, marshaling, guiding, commanding the hosts of spiritual wickedness, can never be in two places at once. Swifter than the lightning's flash, quicker than the thought of man can travel, he may encircle the globe, but he is not omnipresent. He is personal only in the measure in which any angel is personal. He is personal only in the measure in which man is personal.

Neither is he omniscient, knowing everything, seeing the end from the beginning, as God is able to do. Far more subtle in his wisdom, far more keen in his intuitions, far cleverer than man has ever been, but certainly not seeing all the ultimate issue from the commencement. And assuredly he is not omnipotent, not having all power. Go to the book of Job, and put all that wonderful story into brief words in this respect. The devil, full of subtlety, and malice, and determination to spoil the work of God in a human soul, could nevertheless not touch a single hair upon the back of a single camel belonging to Job until he had asked God's leave.

The protest against dualism is out of place when you are thinking of the devil, according to Scripture teaching. The protest may be a very excellent one according to much misinterpretation of Scripture teaching which has possessed or obsessed the minds of men. If you once deny the existence of the devil in the universe because God is all and in all, that is to postulate a doctrine of the universe which is unscriptural. That doctrine must equally deny the existence of man. Is man a personality? If you admit that he is, then you may also admit the possibility of a personality in the universe other than God, created by God, who in some way is out of harmony with God, is indeed in antagonism against God, and yet who is not coequal with God in power, or in knowledge, or in presence.

Now, for a moment take the other side of this matter, and think of his power as revealed in the scriptures of truth. Do not forget that he is spiritual in essence. All the angels are spirits, flames of fire, and Satan, one of the hierarchy of heaven, fallen, is a spirit. If it be true, as Tennyson says, that "Spirit with spirit can meet," referring to man's possibility of approaching God, it is equally true that the devil as spirit and man as spirit can meet, and in that fact lies the tremendous power of Satan, and of all those hosts that he commands, the army of fallen angels that are spiritual in essence.

Then also he is subtle in method. "Subtle" seems a weak

word to use in connection with the devil. Paul describes the devil as an "angel of light." Peter describes the devil as a "roaring lion." Jesus refers to him as the "prince of this world." Each description suggests a different method, adopted according to the occasion, and according to the purpose—transforming himself into an angel of light to deceive if it be possible the very elect, appearing in awful ferocity and fierceness as a roaring lion to overwhelm the timid and afraid; the prince of the world offering to man all the kingdoms for a moment's homage, coming to men according to the method necessary to entrap them and spoil them, and harm them. This is awful sublety.

Then, again, he is revealed in Scripture as being strenuous in enterprise and stupendous in execution. He is the leader of vast hosts. "Our wrestling is not against flesh and blood, but against the principalities, against the powers, against the world-rulers of this darkness, against the spiritual hosts of wickedness in heavenly places." That is a graphic description of this army of spiritual forces fighting against everything that is in harmony with the will of God. Those of us who accept the teaching of Scripture as final, recognize the place of angels fallen and unfallen. At the head of fallen angels, marshaling all, is the great head and center, the mightiest of them, the wisest of them, the most wonderful of them, his might, his wisdom, and his wonder prostituted in the universe of God to the purpose of fighting against God and yet forevermore held in check and never allowed to pass the limit of the government of God.

Now consider what is taught in Scripture concerning the devil as opposed to religion. All I have attempted to say concerning him to-night as revealed in Scripture makes it patent that he must be and is the enemy of religion. Let us again appeal to Scripture for his character in relation to man. Jesus said concerning him, "He was a murderer from the beginning, and stood not in the truth because there is no truth in him. When he speaketh a lie, he speaketh of his own: for he is a liar, and the father thereof." A lie is essential evil. Jesus said, "I am the Truth," that is, essential good. A lie is the direct opposite. The original lie in human history was a denial of the creature's relation to God, and a suggestion in the heart of man that God was hard, unkind, capricious, prompting man to rebellion against Him. If I come to the writings of the Apostle John I read that he thus describes Satan, "The evil one." That is a term that describes him absolutely. He is the very embodiment of sin. Let me take you to three other descriptive words in order that we may see how he is opposed to religion. He is described as "the god of this world," as "the prince of the world," as "the prince of the power of the air, of the spirit that now worketh in the sons of disobedience." Put these three descriptions together and you will see that in this wonderful personality of evil, mastering the hosts of evil, there is the exact anthithesis of all we know of God—One, "God the Father"; the other, "the god of this world"; one, "God the Son"; the other, "the prince of the world"; one, "God the Holy Ghost"; the other, "the prince of the power of the air, of the spirit that now worketh in the sons of disobedience." Thus in this personality there reside all the things that are opposed to the things in God. In God the Father there is essential government, in "the god of this world" there is disorder, evil. In God the Son there is grace, and in the devil there is everything opposed to grace. In God the Holy Spirit there is guidance for the sons of men and for the world: the devil is forevermore leading men away from the true path out into the desert and out into darkness.

He is not coequal with God, but in the measure of his personality he is antagonistic to God, to His government, to His grace, to His guidance, forevermore trying to lead men astray.

"The god of this world." The world is devil-governed until this hour. Go to the homes of darkness in the far distant places of the world, and you will see that the fact is awfully patent. Is London governed by our God? Is love the master principle of human life? If not, then what? This. It is each for himself, and the devil take the hindmost. Men are under the government of Satan. Through all that great and remarkable antithesis the devil is seen, not coequal with God, not omnipotent, omniscient, or omnipresent, but a fallen seraph, far more wondrous in wisdom than any son of man, with more subtle and marvelous power than man has ever yet possessed, marshaling the great hosts of fallen angels, and fighting against all the things that are in the will of God.

It becomes evident that he is the active and awful enemy of any man who begins to live the religious life in the true sense of the word. God loves man, and therefore the devil hates man because the devil is against God. God loves Christ in man, and therefore the devil hates Christ in man, and will prevent, if he can, the outworking of the Christ life in human character. Christ's mission was "to destroy the works of the devil." The devil's mission is to prevent that, and to destroy the works of Christ. If I am beginning to live the life that is obedient to God's rule, the life of loyalty to Christ, the life in which the purposes of Christ and the plans of Christ and the power of Christ are present, then immediately I become one against whom the devil, either in actual person or through those who serve under him, is at war. The young Christian asks, How is it I am being tempted as I was never tempted before? There is the answer. Because the moment in which you turned your life back again toward God you became one against whom the devil is at war. That is the declared fact in the passage to which I have made so many references, "Our wrestling is not against flesh and blood, but against the principalities, against the powers." This is the terrible fact, and the man who does not face the fact is a fool. Our enemy patiently waits for the moment of weakness and is utterly merciless. It was a terrific word written in the book of Job, "Hast thou considered My servant Job?" There is a whole revelation of the devil's method in that word *"considered"*—watching for the opportunity of weakness and the place where to break in. The chain is only as strong as its weakest link, and the castle is only as strong as its least guarded door, and the devil is watching for the weak link, and for the least guarded door. There are men he will never tempt with a glass of wine, because a glass of wine is no temptation to them. Your least guarded door, your weakest link, pride, or passion, or lust, the intellectual, the emotional, the volitional, he is watching, mark the awfulness of the figure, *watching*. "Hast thou *considered* My servant Job."

It is against this enemy that we have to fight. That leads me to a brief word on the devil in relation to the world and the flesh. These are the media through which he acts, and in which he hides. You can find only one great occasion in all human history when the devil came out into the open. That was when in the wilderness he met Jesus Christ. He was not in the open in the Garden of Eden. He did not for a moment suggest that man should fall down and worship him there. What he said was, Please yourself! He suggested that man should leave the first principles of his life as the devil had left his, and depart from his proper habitation as the devil had departed from his. Is not that the primal sin? Is not that the sin of Lucifer, the son of the morning? Is not that the heart and center of all evil, self-pleasing? The devil hid himself. So he does to-day. In the middle ages the devil was portrayed by artists as with horns and hoofs. If you paint him so to-day no one will know him. Marie Corelli, in her *Sorrows of Satan*, gives her last picture of the devil going into the House of Commons. If he ever makes any appearance in London that is far nearer the truth than the horns and hoofs. That is part of his strategy, part of his subtlety. He is hiding to-day in half our theology and in half our new-fangled philosophies. We are told to-day that man has to fight against the beast in him, that there are angel and beast in him, and that if the angel in him will fight hard enough he will trample the beast under his feet. There is an element of truth in all that. But what has turned man into a beast? Lurking behind the flesh, making it the medium of his suggestion, is the devil. Once I say he was dragged into the open, and advisedly I say *dragged*. If the devil could have escaped that ordeal he would have. Jesus was driven of the Spirit into the wilderness to be tempted of the devil, led of the Spirit in the wilderness while being tempted of the devil. God dragged the devil out into the open. It is an appalling picture of the subtlety and power of the devil, but it also reveals the fact that all the artifice and subtlety of the devil is helpless when a man stands square on the will of God, and makes it the master passion of his life. Take that story of the temptation and consider it carefully, and you will see the limitation of the devil. He has only three avenues along which he can ever approach the citadel of man's soul, and they are all revealed there. The real enemy that we have to fight is not the beast in us, but the devil behind the beast. It is not the flesh and the world but the devil's misrepresentation of the world: "The god of this world hath blinded their eyes." The arch enemy, the master enemy, the one real foe of their religious life, is the devil and all the hosts that he commands.

Are we to be defeated by this foe? The apostle in the passage I read to you recognizes the conflict, "*our wrestling*." It is very definite conflict. We are to put on the whole panoply of God, we are to stand, to withstand, and having done all to stand. So that victory is possible according to the apostle's outlook. If you ask me the way of victory I take you back again to a passage which puts the whole truth into simplest form. James said, "Submit to God; resist the devil, and he will flee from you." Submit! There is deep reason for this. It gets down to the root of the whole matter. The devil's sin was rebellion, and his method with man is to propose rebellion, and the moment a man submits to God he crosses the devil's plan and purpose. The idea is that of a soldier. Submission is the first law of success in warfare. There can be no ultimate victory save under discipline and submission.

What next, "Resist." After you have submitted to God there will be conflict, but the conflict will be under orders, under the command of One Who knows every method of the enemy, Who holds in His own hand the reins of ultimate government. So that the conflict will no longer be in unexpected places. We sang about the devil being ambushed, but God knows where he is ambushed. The man who is really submitted to God starts out to real difficult conflict, strenuous fight, but he is under the command of One Who is never caught unawares, Who knows the whole field, the whole plan of the foe, Who never lost a battle, and Who never will, Whose soldier never will, so long as he obeys, and so long as he follows. Mark James's confident assertion, "Submit to God; resist the devil, and he will flee from you." That is the way of victory. I cannot add anything to it. Indeed, I am inclined to think that in any attempt to add I am in great danger of subtracting from the force and power of the simple statement. Submit and resist. Some man says, but I fail and fall. I hear the voice and I yield, I sin; why do I sin? Because you have not obeyed this method, Submit, and resist. I have known men who have submitted seriously, earnestly, sincerely, but they have fallen. Why? They did not add to submission resistance. I have known other men who have resisted, who are resisting, and they say, How is it I am beaten? I have put up this fight against the devil, and I am down again. You did not begin your resistance by submitting. If a man submits and never fights, God will not, cannot, lead him to victory. If a man fights without having submitted, he has not put himself under discipline, under orders, and he will be beaten. Or you submitted but never fought. The word of the writer of the letter to the Hebrews is very striking, "You have not yet resisted unto blood, striving against sin." You submitted but there was no resistance, you did not burn your bridges behind you. You locked the whisky up in a cupboard in case you should need it some day, and you were drunk in a month. There was no fight. You kept the impure picture in your own private cupboard and you were back in your devilish licentiousness within a week. You have got to put up a fight. Put yourself under control, act under the Captain's orders. Submit now, and resist the moment the devil meets you. That way lies victory. The old quaint hymn which we never sing now is nevertheless true if it be rightly interpreted:

> Satan trembles when he sees
> The weakest saint upon his knees.

I said, when it is rightly interpreted. If you get on your knees and do not fight, Satan is not at all afraid of you. If you know what it is to get to your knees and gather strength, and then fight, all the forces of the fallen intelligences are not wise enough, and all their might is not strong enough, to overcome you. Submit, resist. Let the two words abide with us as we part.

CHAPTER XVII

THE PROBLEMS OF THE RELIGIOUS LIFE: IS THE RELIGIOUS LIFE POSSIBLE?

THIS IS THE QUESTION OF ONE WHO DESIRES TO LIVE THE RE-ligious life, but who is afraid. I do not think that a man who sees nothing attractive in the religious ideal will ever ask that question. It is rather the question of one who considers that the teachings of Jesus constitute, to borrow the great Roman Catholic phrase, counsels of perfection.

The question is the result of conviction: first, of the ideal requirement of God, that what God requires of a man is the perfecting of his life; and, second, of the strength of the forces that oppose. Such a man, standing between the ideal and the opposing forces, asks, Is it possible to be what God would have me be in the presence of these forces that are against me?

The question is not only the result of a conviction, it is the result of doubt. It is the result of doubt as to the power of Christ. I am not saying that such doubt is sin. It is honest, sincere, but it is doubt of the power of Christ when a man says: There is the ideal, here are the forces of the world, the flesh, and the devil; you, Christian preacher and Christian people, tell me that Christ is able; well, honestly I am not sure! It is doubt of the power of Christ.

Sometimes the doubt, while being of the same nature, is of another accent. It is doubt of the salvability of man. That is an awkward word, an old theological word. We can do very well without it, but we cannot do without the idea that it suggests. Doubt as to whether it is ever possible for a man such as the inquirer feels himself to be to reach the height of the Divine purpose and plan. Can I ever be what God wants me to be? Is it possible for such as I am? I say it in order to touch a sympathetic chord in the heart of those who are asking the question, there are hours in my life to-day when that doubt comes to me. I can believe for other men more easily than I can believe for myself. Sometimes it seems far more possible for God to deal with other men than to deal with me. There are hours of heart-searching and examination, when I ask myself, Is it possible that I shall ever be what God wants me to be?

Our answer to the inquiry is, first, that the Bible teaches that the religious life is possible, and also that human experience agrees with this teaching of the Bible.

Let us take that general statement and deal with it from two standpoints. I first affirm the possibility of living the religious life by declaring that in the economy of God it is made possible. Second, I affirm that because it is made possible in the economy of God it is possible in the experience of man.

The religious life is possible in the economy of God because of the nature of man, and because of the nature of God. In a previous address we came to the conclusion that man has something to do with God because God has everything to do with man. In other words, that man is in nature such as to make possible the religious life, that God is in nature such as to make possible the religious life on the part of man.

When I speak now of the nature of man I am not referring to it as I find it to-day. I am speaking rather of essential human nature, human nature according to the Divine creation. Such human nature we know only as we know Jesus of

Nazareth, "Let us make man in Our image, after Our likeness," was the Divine word, according to the Genesis story. Where is this being? I cannot find him in London. I cannot find him the world over. I cannot find him in human history, read it where I will. Yes, I find him, but not as God made him, not as God meant him to be, not according to the pattern. Once and once only I meet Him in the process of the centuries. In lonely, superlative, imperial splendor, one figure rises above all the rest, the archetypal Man, that which was in the heart of God when He said, "Let Us make man." I am kin of that Man. My humanity is His humanity. I prefer to put it that way than to say His humanity is my humanity. My humanity is His humanity. In Him I see most clearly that man has essential capacity for the religious life. Man is capable of knowing God. Man is capable of loving God. Man is capable of obeying God. Let me examine these matters a little more carefully.

Man is capable of knowing God. There is in every man the capacity for the knowledge of God. If you question that, let me begin upon a very low plane. I will come to the very lowest of all. The consciousness of the supernatural is in every human being, the consciousness of that which is over the natural, above the natural, beyond the natural. That consciousness expresses itself in some of the races of men as we know them to-day in the strangest ways, in ways that we may look upon with contempt. Here is a man in the heart of Africa who has traveled hundreds of miles driving cattle before him to trade with a white trader, and suddenly in consternation he refuses to trade. Why? Because he finds out he has left behind him what we call his fetish, a little piece of stick, a bit of leather, an absolutely worthless thing, but it is that man's symbol of the supernatural, of that which lies beyond the material. That poor African says, I cannot trade with you, I must go back; and he will tramp back, hundreds of miles, in order to obtain his fetish. And we laugh at him! I would that people who believe in God had always the same honesty of conviction. The trouble is that a great many professing Christian people will trade cattle without God when the African will not trade cattle without his fetish. That is a low level of consciousness of the supernatural, ignorant and foolish, and the cultured man laughs at it, pities it, holds it in contempt; but it is evidence of an instinct which goes far out beyond the base, and beyond the material. Let me put the same thought in other words: every man knows the infinite! You deny me that at once. You say, No, that is what no man knows. Finite man cannot know the infinite. What is the infinite? Your answer is that the infinite is that which has no boundaries, no limitations. In that answer you reveal the fact that you have thought it; and in your thinking of it you know it. No dog knows the infinite. The moment in which you have grasped the conception of that which is limitless, boundless, as to time or place, your mind has encompassed that which you can never understand, fully and finally, but you know it. Listen to the word of the old writer, "God hath set eternity in their heart." That is the capacity for knowing God Himself. Jesus said, "This is the life of eternity, that they should know Thee, the only true God, and Him Whom Thou didst send, even Jesus Christ." I am not suggesting for a single moment that all men know God. I am affirming that in every man there is capacity for knowing God. Man can talk to God and hear Him speak, hold communion with Him and know in the deepest of his inmost soul the fact of His being. Man is made for God. That is the light that lighteth every man. It is the strange, mystic, inward capacity for God which is of the very nature of God.

So far I have only spoken of the lowest evidences of light. What is the highest? "Our fellowship is with the Father." The man of the world is just as ready to smile at the fetish of the African; but his smiling does not alter the absolute fact that in this house there are men and women who know experimentally the meaning of that word, "Our fellowship is with the Father," men and women who still, to use the figurative language of the ancient writing, talk to God face to face as a man speaketh with his friend. Although you deny the assertion, you cannot deny the light that sometimes lingers on the face, the light that never was on sea or land, the light that made the face of your mother gloriously beautiful in spite of all your cynical skepticism. Men and women hold fellowship with God. I am not describing that fellowship, but only affirming that the capacity for it exists.

There is also capacity for love. The lowest form of that capacity in religious application is selfish love of safety, the thing that makes a man say, "What shall I do to be saved?" That is the lowest form of love. The highest is the selfless love of sacrifice. Here is the lowest form of love to God, "He loved me and gave Himself for *me*." You say, That is very high. It is indeed infinitely higher than any other love we know of, but it is yet selfish love, quite proper, perfectly right, but self-centered. God generates it in the heart by dying for men, therefore it is worth generating, but it is the lowest form. If you want to know the highest form of that love here it is, "I could wish that I myself were anathema from Christ for my brethren's sake." That is the ultimate form of love for God. Every man is capable of this love, of this going out of the soul in adoration. Give any promiscuous audience to-day one hymn to sing—whether North, South, East, or West; in city, or village, on land or sea, I care not—you will find that hymn will touch a responsive chord in the heart, even though it be forgotten a moment afterwards;

> Jesu, Lover of my soul,
> Let me to Thy bosom fly.

I never hear that hymn sung by a great crowd of men, women and children—hundreds of whom sing it without understanding it—but that I am conscious for the moment they are singing it on wings uplifted. Without their knowing it, they are giving supreme evidence by that emotion of man's ability to love God. There is capacity in man for love of God.

Then there is capacity in every human being for obedience. The lowest manifestation of it is duty, and the highest is delight. I say the lowest is duty. Duty is high, noble, beautiful, but it is the lowest relationship that the soul bears to God. We have been told often, and rightly, of the nobility of duty; but after all is said and done, we have never entered into the highest heights of spiritual experience until we have canceled the word "duty" and substituted the word "delight." "I delight to do Thy will, O my God"—that is infinitely more than duty. Duty, yes, but duty transfigured on the holy mount until it becomes delight, the delight of doing the will of another. The capacity for that is in every human being.

Thus to see man in the essential fact of his nature, capable of knowing God, of loving Him, and of obeying Him, is to be convinced that it is possible for man to live the religious life.

That, however, is finally demonstrated by a consideration of the nature of God. What is the nature of God? You may express the whole fact in one word, and I choose so to do, and then to take two thoughts in elaboration thereof.

"God is love." That sounds very commonplace because we have said it so often. It has become so familiar that no preacher can say it and hope to move an audience by the declaration of it, unless as the poor sounding words fall from his lips they are baptized into power by the presence of the Holy Ghost. "God is love." Love is not attribute. Love is essence. Love is to everything else in God what character in a man is to the characteristics of a man. Do you ever write a character for a man? Some man has left your employ, and you say you will give him his character. You cannot write his character. You do not know his character. You can write two or three characteristics, you cannot write his character. You may have a very accurate estimate of a man's character. That estimate is formed by the observation of his characteristics, the different expressions of his essential nature. As are the characteristics of a man to his character so are the attributes of Deity to His essence. Mercy, beneficence, holiness, righteousness, are all expressions of love.

The religious life is the life that is bound to God, the life that is obedient to God. Is it possible? It is possible because He, being Love, seeks on the part of man for such action and attitude as is for the best and highest for man himself. What is the chief end of man? To glorify God and enjoy Him forever. My dear old friend, Margaret Bottome, the founder of the order of King's Daughters, told me of a child who was asked that question and answered it accurately, and then the teacher said, I wonder if you can tell me what the chief end of God is! To glorify man and enjoy him forever, answered the child. Rarely have theologians come so near the truth! What glorifies God in me? All the best that can ever come to me. It is when I reach the highest in my own life, when my intellect takes in the widest sweep and most accurately knows the details; when my emotional nature is under the sway of the mightiest love; when my volitional nature is most full of authority because most perfectly under control; that God is glorified in me, because He is Love. He never forgives in man anything that harms the man. What is that which you have to give up to be a Christian? Something which is spoiling you. God is as fierce as lightning against it. Why? Because it harms you. At the back of the thunder are the tears. Behind the awful fire is the tremendous love. If only we can get to know God we shall see the possibility of the religious life, because we shall find that He is Love and is set upon our well-being.

Take out of that great essential and final fact these two matters. First, because God is Love He is patient; and if you want to understand that, think of the relationship between father and child. Second, because God is Love He is reasonable; and if you want to understand that, think of the ideal relationship between the perfect king and the subject of such a king. Patient. A father is interested in the development of his child, and therefore is patient with the feeblest effort of the child toward the ultimate perfecting; and is gentle in his method. The feeblest little child in your home is the one who interests you most. You are interested in it as you see it growing up, developing, and, oh, the delight of your heart at the strange, mysterious sounds that it makes when it tries to talk. Mothers can always understand the baby language. I will tell you something if you will not tell the mothers. I do not believe babies say half the things mothers say they say! But that is a man's ignorance. If I have got some of you back home, face to face with your youngest child, that is what I wanted. Do you know that what you feel toward that child is in kind what God feels toward us? There is nothing elegant in the walk of a child before it can walk; but is it not the most beautiful thing in the whole world? I have been watching a wee bit lassie trying to walk on my lawns at Mundesley. There was nothing elegant in it, but there was poetry in it, music in it. All that I feel about my bairn is a dim shadow of what God feels about me. There is nothing elegant in my walk as a Christian man. It is clumsy, awkward, bungling in the sight of heaven, but "like as a father pitieth his children, so the Lord pitieth them that fear Him." Patience with the feeblest effort issues in gentleness in method. That was a great word of the psalmist, "Thy gentleness hath made me great." What is gentleness? George Matheson once wrote a little article in one of the religious periodicals. I cut it out and still have it somewhere. I cannot remember the exquisite, poetic wording of it, but the thought of it is with me now. Said George Matheson, we speak of gentleness and often do not understand it. We speak of the gentleness of the brook as it ripples through the summer fields. There is no gentleness in the brook. It is going as hard as it can, and all the strength it has it is exerting to make the pebbles rattle. You may speak of gentleness when you stand beside the mighty sea on a summer day, and when in its mighty strength you see it kiss the shore and bathe the feet of the child who is paddling. Gentleness is strength held in reserve. God's gentleness makes men great. Think what He could do and think what He does. Think how He lays His hand upon us in our feverishness as tenderly as the sunbeam falls on the face of a sick child. The sun could blast to a cinder, but it kisses to health. "Thy gentleness hath made me great." That is God.

Then there is the reasonableness of God. He has perfect knowledge of every one of us and He demands only that we fulfil the real purpose of our own life. He never asks anything that we are unable to give Him. The trouble is that we set up false standards and imagine they are God's standards. The first great word of the prophet to the sinning people of old was, "Come now and let us *reason* together, saith the Lord." He never makes demands upon man that man is not equal to answering.

By the nature of man who is capable of knowing God, of loving God, and of obeying God; and by the nature of God Who is love, and has patience, and is reasonable, I submit to you that it is possible to live the religious life.

In conclusion, let us mark the conditions. Look at man as he is. His nature is perverted. He does not know God. He does not love God. He does not obey God. You say, Ah, now you are coming to the real difficulties. These are the real sources of the question, Is the religious life possible? Very well, let us face them. Man does not know God. The carnal mind does not know Him, neither can it. Man does not love God. He is afraid of Him, hates to hear His name, escapes from the man who talks about Him, avoids the places of His worship, and taboos the subject of religion at his dinner table. Man does not obey God. He does not take God into account when he goes into business.

Yet to such men there come voices of truth concerning God, visions of the ideal concerning themselves. Then they find not only that their nature is perverted, but that it is paralyzed, and each exclaims, "When I would do good evil is present with me." Is the religious life possible to a man like that?

The answer to the inquiry now is the answer of the Christian evangel. First of all, how does God answer that inquiry? I go back to one of our earlier subjects. Can a just God forgive sins? Without going again over the arguments, I repeat the affirmation that He can. He can be just and the Justifier of him who believes in Jesus. If that once be accepted I want you to see what it leads to. God can pardon sin. What does that mean? The pardon of sin means a new vision of God. "Blessed are the pure in heart, for they shall see God." In the moment in which a man's sins are forgiven and he knows his sins forgiven he sees God as he never saw Him before. You can listen to me if you like quite theoretically, but I make this affirmation on the basis of experience and testimony. There has fallen asleep this week a man whom I loved with my whole heart, a man who has been an inspiration to me in this chapel over and over again as I have preached. Ned Wright, as you know full well, forty years ago was a prize-fighter and a burglar, and, as he himself would have admitted, just about as low down as it was possible for a man to get. I cannot tell you all I am thinking about him. I have seen him sit over yonder on Wednesday afternoons, and in the Institute Hall, as I have lectured on John's Gospel, and on no face has there been a more glorious light; and when one came to speak of God, and the love of God, and the ways of God, his face shone with the brightness of an angel. When did all that begin? Forty years ago, when he knew his sins forgiven. Up to that moment he had feared God and hated God's people, and kept away from them; but with the forgiveness of sins came a vision of God and he came to love Him. Have you had that vision of God? It was that vision which made Scheffler write:

> O God, of good the unfathomed sea,
> Who would not give his heart to Thee?

That is where the religious life begins. The forgiveness of sins always means a new vision of God. You have thought of God as a King, a Potentate, mighty, awful, terrible, exacting; but He says in your deepest soul, when you have put your trust in Him, "Thy sins are forgiven thee," and you find He is tender, gracious, loving. Out of that knowledge comes the religious life.

Pardon not only means a new vision, it also means as a result of it, love. To see God is to love Him. Then it means desire to obey Him, for to love God is to desire to please Him. Mark the order and see how everything comes out of that first fact of forgiveness. Man knows his sins. The forgiving word is spoken in the innermost recesses of his soul as he submits himself to Christ. He sees that God is love and he loves. Then he desires to serve and obey. That is the passion of the religious life.

The answer of God is not merely pardon. It is power immediate and progressive. The moment in which a man yields himself to Jesus Christ and receives pardon of sin power is at his disposal. It does not work mechanically, however; it must be appropriated. Whereas there is all power at my disposal, it is only at my disposal as I make adjustment. God puts power at the disposal of the soul that trusts in Him, but we have to make contact, to obey, to put ourselves in line with His condition.

That leads me to the last word I want to say. What are the conditions on which the religious life is possible, in view of the pardon God gives, and in view of the power He provides? First, an act of abandonment to Jesus Christ. Then an attitude of abiding in Christ. There must be a moment in which I take my life and hand it over to Christ, God's Son and my Saviour, sent forth from the Father for the doing of this work. After that I must abide in that attitude of abandonment. I am not saved to-day because I believed twenty years ago. I am saved now because I believe now. There must be not merely the act by which the life begins, but the abiding by which the life continues.

The religious life to-day in the midst of present limitation is the life which has found its true center, and which is adjusting the circumference to that center. There is a great deal to be done, a great deal to be learned, many disciplines to be passed through, a great deal to be accomplished ere the work is done. There are tenses in the Christian life. It is perfectly accurate to say we were saved then, pointing to a date, an hour, a place. It is perfectly accurate to say, We are being saved, the continuous process. It is quite accurate to say "Now is our salvation nearer than when we believed." The final stage is yet ahead.

In the presence of limitation, the life religious is the life which has found its center in God, and which through struggles, through strain and conflict and stress, is adjusting the circumference to that one center.

The psalmist said, "My soul followeth hard after Thee: Thy right hand upholdeth me." I sometimes think, in some senses, that is the most wonderful verse in the Bible. "Followeth hard" is one word in the Hebrew. It quite literally means, impinges upon Thee, clings, adheres, abides fast, clings! It is the strongest of words, indicating tremendous effort. Now listen, "Thy right hand upholdeth me." The

Hebrew word "upholdeth" means sustains, holds fast. I can take these two Hebrew words and translate with perfect accuracy, "My soul *clings fast* to Thee: Thy right hand *clings fast* to me." No violence is thereby done to the text. That is the real thought. That is the religious life. The soul clingeth fast—conscious of perils, the world, the flesh and the devil, all the forces that are against it—clinging fast to God; and all the while this great assurance, "Thy right hand upholdeth me." Remember the religious life is life centered in God, and occupied earnestly, definitely, about the business of putting the circumference into true harmony with the center. That is not done in half an hour. It will never be complete until in the rapture of the morning of the second advent He will fashion anew even the body of our humiliation that it may be conformed to the body of His glory. I cannot yet be perfect at the circumference, but I can be right at the center.

CHAPTER XVIII

THE PROBLEMS OF THE RELIGIOUS LIFE: IS THE RELIGIOUS LIFE NECESSARY?

I CONFESS TO A GREAT SENSE OF DIFFICULTY IN APPROACHING this subject, resulting from the obviousness of the reply from my standpoint. To me the question is as though one should inquire into the physical realm, Is it necessary to breathe, to eat, to act? Nevertheless, the question is asked, and if we are to deal with it we need to get at the viewpoint of the man who asks it. We must understand his attitude of mind. The question moves on a much lower plane than the one we discussed last week. In that there was recognition of the beauty of the ideal, and the only question was one of fear whether it were indeed possible to live that life. In the inquiry that we are taking to-night the ultimate perfection of the religious life is not so much in sight as the conditions upon which that ultimate perfection can be realized. I think if a man says, Well, after all, is it necessary? he is not referring to that highest ideal of the religious life, that ultimate requirement of God that man should be perfect in his own being. He is rather standing face to face with the conditions which are imposed when a man is asked to give himself to Christ and to begin the truly religious life.

If a man is to live the religious life he must submit to authority, the one true final authority of the will of God. He must renounce all the things which he knows to be out of harmony with the will of God. It is necessary for him to cultivate the habits of the religious life; he must give himself to prayer, to the study of the Word, to perpetual watchfulness, and to service on behalf of others, without which the religious life is never possible. There must be discipline and diligence. When a man faces these conditions he asks, Is the religious life necessary? I think what he means is, "Suppose I decline, what will happen?" As I understand it, that is the question that we have to face. Such inquiry involves the necessity for restatement of the positive values of the religious life. The positive is the revelation of the negative. In proportion as we see what these values are we shall see what is the result of living the irreligious life.

I propose to confine our consideration to the individual. Taking a human life, and believing it to be spiritual in essence, I want to think of it in its continuity, but recognize the line of division at death. So in two parts I shall ask this question. Is the religious life necessary for the life that now is? Is the religious life necessary for the life that is to come?

That is a very old-fashioned method of dealing with this thing, but I know of no other possible. I put the dividing line there simply because it is there. The fact of death must be admitted and taken into account. It is sometimes affirmed that we have no right to appeal to the fear of man by preaching about death. The fear of man? I do not appeal to the fear of man when I speak about death. Are you afraid of death? Why? No man ought to be afraid of death. Why do you not like to hear about death? I will tell you, in the words of inspiration, "The sting of death is sin." That is why you do not like to hear about death. So I keep that dividing line which is quite a simple and natural one, and one that we all have to admit.

What are the values of religion in the life that now is? First of all, let me speak of the principle of the life of religion, then of its method, and so lead to the results of the religious life.

First, then, as to the principle. What is the principle of the religious life? The mastery of the will of God. There are very many things I am not proposing to deal with which nevertheless must be taken for granted, all those necessary matters which cannot be neglected if men would come into proper relationship to that will, "Ye must be born again," "Repent and believe." All these are simple terms that indicate how man is to readjust life, when it is out of harmony with God. The ultimate principle is that of the recognition of the sovereignty of God, and the beneficence of His will, followed by the abandonment of all other mastery, and the acceptance of that will as the perpetual, unceasing, and ever applicable law of the life.

The method of the religious life is that of obedience to that will discovered and accepted. What does obedience mean? Inquiry, consent, activity. Perhaps that is not quite clear. Let me pause with my words for a moment. First there must ever be inquiry. For a man to say that he accepts the will of God as the master principle of his life, and then having said so in the sanctuary or in conversation, to go out and take up his business, or to make a friendship, or to decide on where to spend his holiday, or to select a house, without ever seeking to know the will of God, is the utterest nonsense, and indeed is blasphemy. There must be inquiry. The religious life in its method asks what is God's will for me here and now, to-day and in this matter? I said here recently that the blasphemy of the man who prays, "Thy Kingdom come," and never seeks the Kingdom, never submits to it, is more perilous than the blasphemy of the profane swearer in the slum. Someone has written questioning that. I stand by the declaration. The man in the slum was born in the atmosphere of swearing, has always sworn, does not know he is swearing. I have heard some such men in the early days of their Christianity swear in prayer, but there was no blasphemy in it. For any man to say, "Thy Kingdom come," or to recite the creed, "I believe in God the Father Almighty," and then to refuse to submit his life to Him, for six days in the week, is blasphemy of the worst kind. The religious life inquires, waits for the voice, seeks to know. When the light comes the will consents to it and inspires actual obedience. Until the consciousness is borne in upon the soul, that this or that is the will of God, the religious man never moves hand or foot.

What are the results of such principle and method? What are the issues of making the will of God the master principle, of following the method, of making inquiry after the will, consenting to it, and rendering it active obedience? In such life there is, first of all, realization of fellowship with God. The man, woman, yea, or little child, who, not able to state the thing, not able to formulate perfectly the principle of life, nevertheless is submitted to God—that man, woman, little child, knows what fellowship with God means. The day is not gone when God speaks in the deepest soul of man, woman, or child if they will but listen. The consciousness of fellowship is the first result.

That fellowship means the appropriation of all forces. I believe that word of Paul in his Roman letter, "To them that love God all things work together for good," means not merely that God is laying His hand on all things and taking the keen edge off them and blunting that which would hurt, and making everything come right at last. The statement is not that all things will be *compelled*, but that all

IS THE RELIGIOUS LIFE NECESSARY? 241

things *work* together for good. All forces are at the disposal of the man who is living in harmony with God. All the forces of life are at the disposal of the man who is living in harmony with God, so that the very things which harm one man help to make the man whose life is homed and centered in God. This means in its final statement, that the religious life is life more abundant. Life more abundant means not that there is superadded to your human life a life of another nature, but that your own human life comes to its fulfilment and realization. When a man is living the religious life whatever is in him by nature is glorified, fulfilled. He comes into possession of what he is. There is no more significant word, and yet no word that we more lightly consider, than this word of Jesus, "Whosoever shall lose his life shall find it," not another life, not an angel's life, not the life of some other person, but his own life. It is when a man is living the life of right relationship to God, and, consequently, is living the life in which all the forces under the government of God minister to his making, that he comes to fulfilment of his own life. What is in you? Someone went into the studio of David Cox—or one of the artists, I have heard the story told of several—and, looking at one of his pictures, said to him, I never saw anything like that in nature. The artist answered, No, you only wish you could. Have you that vision, the artist's vision? Can you stand by the sea, and, looking out over the waters, see glories which I cannot see? Is your life homed in God, responsive to His volition? Then that vision is not dimmed. You will see, as you never saw, that the light of God in your inmost soul illumines all your outlook on nature. What is in you—music? I love to hear music, but I am no musician. I always come to decision as to whether a piece of music is classical or not by the blackness of the page! That is not your outlook on music. You hear symphonies. If you are right with God you will be more keen in your appreciation of music than you ever were in your life. I am not talking in figurative language. I am talking about actual music. The touch of a godly man on a harp will bring out finer music than any other touch. A human life is lifted, ennobled, glorified, brought to its own when it is life lived in relation to God.

Reminding you that the positive reveals the negative, take the life irreligious, the life that has no vision of God, that never waits for His voice, has no sense of the eternal, no commerce with the spiritual, no traffic with the unseen, the life which Peter describes when he says, "seeing only the things that are near." Was there ever more graphic description of the irreligious life than that? "Seeing only the things that are near." What is the principle of that life? Self is enthroned! The exclusion of God, which means the exclusion of perfect knowledge and the exclusion of all-sufficient power. What is the method of that life? Self-served. That is obedience to unintelligent desire, strife after experience without ability to realize. What is that? Friction, fret, fever. What is the result? Self lost. Hunger without bread. Thirst without water. Desire without ability. The illustrations of what I am trying to say in brief words are to be found everywhere. They are to be found in the East End of London. They are to be found in the West End. The East and the West are still far apart, but they are tremendously near together. The East and the West talk two languages, but out of one humanity. Give me a man of the East End who is living a godless life—he lives for himself. He was born in the very atmosphere of blasphemy. He is away down in the depths. When we begin to deal with statistics and political economy we speak of the submerged tenth and of the upper ten. Both are submerged so far as their humanity is concerned. Take the man in the East end, hot restless life, unable to find quietness, satisfaction, peace. Bruised, bitter, rebellious, angry! The word that you use to describe that man's condition is *despair*. I cross over from the East to the West, and here I find culture. Mark me very carefully, I am not undervaluing culture and education. Let no man charge me with such unutterable folly. I find culture and refinement. I find something in the West that it has taken centuries to produce. There I hear another word. It is not an English word this time but a French word, as though by the use of a French word you could heal a wound. I hear the word *ennui*. Do you imagine when you hear someone say *ennui* that it is a small thing? It is hell! Culture, refinement, things that are quite beautiful, admirable in most ways, but in the heart, no rest, no peace. I know the things whereof I speak. I know them better to-night than I did four years ago. I have had to listen to story after story, and to share agony after agony, and to come into definite touch with this thing. The godless life is anchorless, rudderless—no peace, no quiet—fever, friction. All the finest things absent in spite of the culture and refinement that the schools can give and the process of the centuries can give. The light of the infinite morning is never on the brow. The breath of the eternal hills never brings recreation. No grasp of God and therefore no grasp of life. I submit to you that if you simply take the life that now is, godless life has lost its own key and secret, and does not possess the power to realize itself. The godly life is the life that holds the key to all the treasure house and admits into the richest and best, even of the present life.

I bring you now to the dividing line, and speak of

the life to come. Take the positive again. Let us see what the religious life is. How does the life to come begin? It begins with death. What is death? Transition. The laying aside of a tent. The entry on the consciousness of vaster environment. That is death. The tent is laid down and the occupant passes on. Of course, I am taking for granted the authority of this Book and the whole testimony of the Catholic Church [church universal]. I am not going to argue these things. I simply state them. The great Lord and Master of us all uttered words once full of light on this subject. I have often quoted them in other connections; let us see them in this connection. He said, "Be not afraid of them which kill the body, and after that have no more that they can do." What is the concept of life that lies behind that? Do you see what the thought of Jesus about human life is? Let us express His thought in His own words, "A man's life consisteth not in the abundance of things which he possesseth." Or again, "What shall a man be profited, if he shall gain the whole world, and forfeit his life?"—What is this conception of life? That the individual is spiritual in essence. That is the Christian conception of individuality. What, then, is death? Simply the moment when a person passes on to another plane, on to another level. You remember the exquisite, marvelous line in the course of the slave's dream in which the author describes the passing out of the slave into liberty through death, and speaks of the body of the slave as a worn-out fetter which the soul had broken and cast away. That is the Christian conception of death. I want to take again a side issue for a minute. I do not want anyone to imagine I am callous in the presence of death. I am not. I know its bitterness to those who are left. I hate the idea that no tears are to be shed in the presence of it, that we are to steel our hearts against emotion. I am looking at death from the standpoint, not of those who are left, but of those who go. This is death. The earthly tabernacle, the tent, dissolved; then a building, a house not made with hands, eternal in the heavens. The earthly tabernacle dissolved. I remember Moody saying to a group of friends, "Some day you will see in the newspaper that Moody is dead. Don't you believe it. The day you read that in the newspaper, Moody will be more alive than ever he has been." That is the Christian outlook, triumph over death.

What is the relation of that life to this life? When you begin to see that death is simply the laying aside of a tent and the going on of the same person, what is the relation between the life that now is and that which is to come? It is necessarily most intimate. There is continuity. The set of the life is the same five minutes after as five minutes before death. The direction, the conception, the character, the trend is not changed in the hour of death. A great many things are changed. Environment is changed. It is a new plane, a new level, a new world, but the direction is the same. I think there are some people who imagine that when they cross over in their essential life they are absolutely changed by the passing. Not so. There is no warrant for such teaching in the New Testament. You are exactly the same. There will be a great deal to learn on the other side for most of us, and I think we shall not know it all immediately, but the direction will be the same. What is to be the principle of that life? Exactly the same as the principle of life here, the mastery of the will of God. What is to be its method? Exactly the same as that of the life here, obedience to the will of God. What is to be the result? The result of the life here I said was life more abundant. The result of the life there is life *most* abundant. Christian people for a long time have been praying for dying grace. Such prayer is a waste of time. What we need is living grace. "Enoch walked with God: and he was not; for God took him." The statement "he was not," does not merely refer to the method by which he was taken, but to the method of all his life for three hundred years before he went. *He* was not, God took him into fellowship. He went with Him along the way of earth through those centuries and then Enoch was not, the earth had lost him but God had gained him into fellowship a little closer, but in the same direction. Death is not going to do anything for me that Christ has not done, or cannot do, save bring me to a larger outlook, and leave me more free for development along the very lines on which I have been progressing, if I am a child of God, from the moment I received the Christ life.

If these are the positive aspects, mark well the negative. What is the beginning of the life to come for the man who is irreligious? Death. What is death for that man? Exactly what it is for the other, transition, the laying aside of a tent, the entry upon a vaster environment. What, then, is the difference? Let me answer that question, by asking another. Is there still a point of identity? Yes, there is. As in the life of the saint the word that marks the relation of this life to the life that is to come is continuity, so also is it in the life of the godless man. The set of the life here is the set of the life hereafter. The direction of the life here is the direction of the life hereafter. When a man lays aside the tent he enters upon a larger, more mysterious, wonderful existence. What is he there? What he is here. You ask me about a second probation. The word of God has nothing to say about a second probation, and I have nothing to say about it. I do know of the present probation, and I know that the probation of to-day is to every man in the world, and I know that the basis of the present probation is the light a man has, and not the light he lacks. As a man passes out of this life into the next the matter of supreme importance is not what he believes about Jesus, for there are thousands who have never heard His name. What is the matter of supreme importance? The set of the life, the direction of the life. The matter of supreme importance to me as I pass out of this world is not the actual influence of the moment, but the direction, the master passion of the life, the thing that drives and impels and inspires, for that is the central thing after all. "As he reckoneth within himself so is he." What is your thinking? That is the deepest of you! Is it passionate desire to do the will of God? That is the set of your life and death does not change it. Is the deepest thing in your life desire to please yourself? That is the set of your life and death does not change it. You go out into the vaster environment in which vaster environment you discover more terribly and awfully your inability to satisfy the deepest cry of your own life. Hunger without bread. Thirst without water. Desire without answer.

I pray you consider his question. If life is one and indivisible; if I have now begun the life that runs on, and if continuity is the word that tells the story of that which is to come in its relation to that which now is, then I ask you to carefully consider the question: "Is the religious life necessary?" You must decide whether or not you are prepared for the continuity of the life you are now living. Strip yourself of the habit of saying your life is this, or that, or the other. These are the methods by which you are attempting to satisfy the deepest thing in your soul. Do not measure your life by the method but by the purpose in your deepest heart. That is a difficult thing to get men to do. Take that round of pleasure, of strenuous work amassing wealth, and has a moment come in your life when you have said, "My soul, in this pleasure, in this wealth, thou hast found thy resting place"? Have you really found it? It is not the fact that for the moment pleasure is pleasure, that wealth is a delightful possession and gives you power that matters. The inquiry is, "Have I in my inner heart and life found rest in these things?" For, remember, the life that is to come is a continuity of the life that is, only all the present things, the transient things, will have passed away and the soul will go out in its nakedness, in its loneliness, and if it have not found satisfaction it will lack it forever. In the life religious the soul goes out in its loneliness, but if it have satisfaction in fellowship with God, it is satisfied forever.

The religious life is the life of obedience to light. The discussion of the problem of the heathen in Africa or in London is irrelevant, I am not dealing with it. What is *your* light? Put yourself into contrast, some of you, with the people in the West end. Some of them have had no more chance of vital godly life than the worst man in the East end slum. Put yourself into contrast, and remember this, you are not going to be judged by their standards nor they by yours, but each by the standard of the light possessed. Your light is not a rushlight that you yourselves light in a room which you have darkened by pulling down all the blinds. The light by which you will be judged is the light of the Christian revelation, as you have been brought up in its very presence and atmosphere. The religious life is the life that obeys the light. God as revealed in Christ. Man as revealed in Christ. That is the light. The religious life is obedient to it. Are you obedient to that light? Here is the almost overwhelming difficulty of the hour. These lectures have provoked letters, the majority of them kindly, courteous, but terrible in their revelation of the fact of how men will fritter away their time and strength and intellect on the fringes of things, and refuse to come to the central purpose. As to whether verse thirty-nine in chapter thirteen, is in harmony with verse forty-one in chapter twenty-two, a man is going to risk his eternal welfare on that. Suppose they do contradict themselves utterly, take out of your Bible that one imperial lonely splendor of Christ and walk in the light. That is the religious life. Is it necessary? Again I say, I leave you to decide. For me it is necessary, in order that I may live the life that now is at its highest, best. Necessary, entirely, absolutely necessary in order that when the fetter is broken and thrown away I may find home, and refuge, and rest, and fulfilment of my being. For I lack rest forevermore, if I have deliberately chosen in this life to disobey the light.

CHAPTER XIX

THE PROBLEMS OF THE RELIGIOUS LIFE: IS THE RELIGIOUS LIFE WORTH WHILE?

IN THIS QUESTION THE EMPHASIS IS CHANGED ONCE MORE. In the first question, whether the religious life is possible, the beauty of the ideal is not for a moment questioned, but the possibility of realization is doubted. We attempted to answer that inquiry by declaring the religious life possible because of the nature of man, because of the nature of God, and, finally, because of the plenteous redemption that God has provided, even for the man who has failed.

The second question moves on a lower plane than the first. The man who asks it does not question the beauty of the ideal, neither does he doubt the possibility of realization; but in view of the conditions he inquires, Is it absolutely necessary? We attempted to answer that inquiry by declaring that the religious life is necessary for the life which now is, and for the life which is to come, in order that life may be fulfilled. The life that now is is less than life, unless it be the life religious; and the life that is to come and this life are one, death makes no change in a man's character. He passes over the boundary line and the set and direction are the same on the other side as on this side. Consequently, to admit the necessity for the religious life here in order that life may be fulfilled, is to be compelled to admit its necessity for the life to come.

The man who asks the third question admits the beauty of the ideal, admits the possibility of realization, admits the

IS THE RELIGIOUS LIFE WORTH WHILE?

necessity for the religious life, if life is to be fulfilled; but, in view of the cost, suggests that perhaps after all it is hardly worth while, and inquires, Why not be content with something less than the best? Is it worth while?

I said, I think in the first of these last three addresses, that there is a descending scale in these questions. The man who asks, Is it possible? is asking a question on a higher level than the man who asks, Is it necessary? And the man who asks, Is it necessary? is on a higher level than the man who asks, Is it worth while? I have known cases in which these three questions have been asked and always in this sequence. In fear and trembling, a man confronted with the beauty of the ideal of the religious life asks, Is it possible? He is brought to conviction that it is possible, and then he asks the second question, Is it necessary? He is brought to conviction that in order to reach perfection of life it is necessary, and then he asks this lowest question of all, Is it worth while?

The first question is a question of desire mingled with doubt. Is it possible? The moment there comes to a man the conviction that it is possible a new peril is created, that of attempting, somehow, to find an excuse for not yielding to the truth. Then follows the next question, which is a mixture of conviction and compromise. When this is answered and a man knows that it is necessary to the perfecting of life, again a new peril presents itself, and the third question is a mixture of rebellion and risk. It is with that question we now have to deal.

In order to answer that question there are two things we must consider. First, the cost of the religious life; and, second, the value of the religious life.

The man who says, Is it worth while? is thinking of the cost, and of the values, and he is trying to strike a balance. Is it worth while? Let us see clearly, if we can, both the cost and the value.

I begin with the cost, and I want to say in your hearing as clearly as I know how that the religious life is costly. Whatever others may say, Jesus was perfectly clear in His teaching about this fact, and I do most solemnly say, especially to young men and women, be very suspicious of the preacher or teacher who tells you that the religious life is simple and easy. I dare any man to make that affirmation on the basis of what Christ taught. There is nothing more remarkable in the ministry of Jesus Christ than the fact that He forevermore repelled men by the severity of His terms. Oh, there was a wooing winsomeness about our blessed Master, and men crowded after Him wherever He went; it was only to look at Him to want to go with Him, only to listen to Him to be captured, and men said and said truly, "Never man so spake." But as the multitudes thronged and pressed Him, He turned upon them and uttered things so severe as to scatter them like chaff before the wind. All the way, from the beginning to the end of His ministry, Jesus Christ insisted on the fact that the religious life is costly. I make my appeal to-night wholly to His own words.

Let us see what Christ thinks about the cost of the religious life. In chapter fourteen of Luke's gospel, it is recorded that thrice over He said, "cannot be My disciple." Hear the connecting words: "If any man cometh unto Me, and hateth not his own father, and mother, and wife, and children, and brethren, and sisters, yea, and his own life also, he cannot be My disciple." "Whosoever doth not bear his own cross, and come after Me, he cannot be My disciple." "Whosoever he be of you that renounceth not all that he hath, he cannot be My disciple." If we had never read those words before, and had not been so busy trying to lower the standard of Jesus in order to accommodate it to our own ideas, they would startle us so that we hardly dare sleep to-night. Look at them: except a man hate all the nearest and dearest, *he cannot be My disciple.* Except a man take up his own cross, *he cannot be My disciple.* Except a man renounce all that he hath, *he cannot be My disciple.* I pray you notice carefully what is involved in this threefold word of Jesus on the cost of the religious life. The first word indicates that if a man is to live the religious life he must submit himself to the absolute mastership of Jesus. "If any man cometh unto Me and hateth not his own father, and mother, and wife, and children, and brethren, and sister, yea, and his own life also, he cannot be My disciple." By all of which He meant that if a man is to follow Him he must put Him absolutely first, so that if the love of father or mother or wife or children, of brethren or sisters, or of his own life, shall at any moment or in any circumstances, for any reason, conflict with loyalty to Him, that love must be crucified. That is the supreme and most appalling claim ever set up on the soul of a human being. That is where Christ begins. I know the difficulty of the word "hate" in this passage, but we must remember that in this Eastern language there was little light and shade. It was positive or negative. Love and hate stood opposite to each other. What Christ demanded that men should do for Him, He did for men. On another occasion He said, "He that loveth father or mother more than Me is not worthy of Me." One day they came to Him and said, "Behold, Thy mother and Thy brethren stand without, seeking to speak to Thee," and He replied, "Who is My mother? and who are My brethren? . . . Whosoever shall do the will of My Father which is in heaven, he is My brother, and sister, and mother." By which He meant to say, there is an affinity far higher than that of blood relationship, that of the spiritual relationship of those who do the will of God. That is the principle underlying this word of Jesus. A man must make his relationship to Christ as revealing God, and so his relationship to God, his attitude toward religion, the supreme thing in his life. If he allows the love of father, mother, wife, children, brother, sister, or of his own life, to conflict with his loyalty to Christ and to God, then he cannot be a disciple. There are many of us here who do not know how costly a thing that may become. I confess there is a sense in which I do not know the costliness of that requirement. I was born of Christian parents and my love for them never conflicted with my loyalty to my Lord; but no farther back than last Saturday night I talked with one person after our meeting who was face to face with that old word, actually, positively, at the present moment. Love of father and love of Christ were in conflict. I need go no further with the story. There it is. Christ says, If it causes a conflict like that, you cannot be My disciple unless you put Me first. That is the cost.

He said a second thing, "Whosoever doth not bear his own cross, and come after Me, he cannot be My disciple." Some time ago I attempted to deal with that word of Jesus and His illustration of it in Luke. I want in a hurried manner now to repeat what I said then. What did Christ mean when He spoke about building a tower and going out to fight a battle? The popular interpretation has been that Jesus meant to say if a man is coming after Him he had better count the cost. He meant nothing of the kind. What He meant was this. You are not to count the cost. It is I Who must count the cost. After the stern words to which I have made reference in which He demanded that a man should love Him before father, mother, wife, children, brethren, sister, and his own life, He began to explain the severity of His own terms. "Which of *you* desiring to build a tower, doth not first sit down and count the cost? . . . Or *what king*, as he goeth to encounter another king, doth not sit down first and take counsel whether he is able with ten thousand to meet him that cometh against him with twenty thousand? . . . *Therefore* whosoever he be of you that renounceth not all that he hath, he cannot be my disciple." He said, in effect, You ask Me why My terms are so severe. I will tell you. I am come into the world for building and for battle, and I cannot commit My enterprises to any save those I know I can depend upon. It is He that builds the tower, not I. He is the King conducting the warfare, not I. Because He is here to build, and here for battle, His terms are severe. I must, He says, have men and women coming after Me who will take up their own crosses and follow Me as I take up My cross: men and women who will not faint or grow weary when the battle thickens, or until the building work is done.

First, the devotion of the disciple must be so supreme that all other loves are put into abeyance. Second, the one ambition of the disciple must be for the enterprises of Jesus, for His building and His battle. He must take up his own cross, that is to say, there must be crucifixion of any thought in the life of the disciple of place or power. So long as I am seeking place for myself or power for myself, I cannot be His disciple and I cannot help Him in His building and battle. In order to be a Christian man, in order to be a disciple of Christ, in order to live the religious life, there first must be devotion, absolute loyalty; and, second, there must be such abnegation of self that there shall be no seeking for place or power, but, the enterprises of Christ possessing the soul, willingness to take up the cross daily and follow Him.

Once more, "Whosoever he be of you that renounceth not all that he hath, he cannot be My disciple." First, devotion, then ambition, now possession. If a man is to live the religious life he must lay all his treasure at the feet of his Lord, and recognize not only that what he *is* he is for Christ, and what he *does* he does for Christ, and that what he *has* he holds for Christ. Renunciation of what a man has does not mean flinging it away, but placing it at the feet of the Lord and recognizing that the man of vast possessions is a steward for the Master. I am weary to death of people who are telling us that we ought to give a tenth of our income to God. I believe the whole movement is wrong. Not one single farthing of yours belongs to you if you are a Christian. All that a man has is to be renounced. You are to spend this in dress for the glory of God, and that in food for the glory of your Lord, and that in recreation for the glory of your King; but over the superscription of King Edward there is the superscription of the Cross of Christ and the Kingdom of God. All that he has is to be renounced, so that the disciple no longer says that anything he has is his own, it belongs to his Lord and to his Lord's enterprises and to his Lord's work. We are a long way off from it yet, but these are the terms of discipleship according to Christ. I repeat, it is costly. If you want to know why there has been decrease —and I feel more able to speak about it this week because the Congregational statistics have been published and there is decrease there also. I hate these statistics. The hunt for increase is part of the reason of the decrease at the present hour. Be that as it may, if you tell me there is decrease not merely in numbers but in spiritual intensity and fervor, I ask why? It is because we have lowered the standard of discipleship and talked to men as though it were easy. We have to get back to the ideal of Christ which presents the religious life as strenuous, severe, costly. When we get back there we shall increase. I admit the cost, and if you stand outside and say, Is it worth while? your question is justified so far. It is a costly business to be a Christian. You can call yourself a Christian and sing hymns and give to collections and drift through the world and never do anything for God or humanity. But if we are going to be Christians indeed, Christ men and women, religious men and women in the profound meaning of the great word, there is blood in the business, there is cost in the business. Go back for one brief moment to the ninth chapter of this Gospel of Luke and see the illustration. One man said, "I will follow Thee whithersoever Thou goest." To another man Jesus said, "Follow Me." The third said, "I will follow Thee, Lord; but first suffer me to bid farewell to them that are at my house." That passage is remarkable if you keep it in its setting. "It came to pass, when the days were well-nigh come that He should be received up, He stedfastly set His face to go to Jerusalem." Nothing more significant than that was ever written. Jerusalem was hostile to Him and He knew it, but He stedfastly set His face to go. Jerusalem was doomed and He knew it; but He stedfastly set His face to go. Jerusalem was to be rebuilt, not immediately; but after long processes and centuries and millenniums there should be a Jerusalem from on high, and He stedfastly set His face to go. On His way, with His face stedfastly set to go to Jerusalem, a man came to Him and said, "I will follow Thee whithersoever Thou goest." Jesus answered, "The foxes have holes, and the birds of the heaven have nests; but the Son of man hath not where to lay His head," which was an explanation to the man not merely of what the man would have to do but of what Jesus was doing. He said to another man, "Follow me," and the man said, "Lord, suffer me first to go and bury my father." I never understood that until I was talking to Dr. George Adam Smith about it, and he told me this story. He was traveling in Syria, and desiring to get into a part of the country where no ordinary guide ever takes the traveler, he went to a young Arab sheikh—whose father was still living—and told him that he wished to go to this out-of-the-way part, and wanted him to accompany him as guide. The Arab sheikh said it was impossible for him to do so. Dr. Smith pressed him, and, at last, with a salaam, the sheikh said, Suffer me first to go and bury my father, which did not mean that his father was dead, for his father was sitting by him as he spoke. It is the Eastern method of saying, I have family ties and affections that I cannot break away from. Christ said, "Leave the dead to bury their own dead; but go thou and publish abroad the Kingdom of God." His face was toward Jerusalem, and that was the attitude of His soul, passion for the Kingdom of God overcoming all lower instincts.

Once again, "No man, having put his hand to the plow, and looking back, is fit for the Kingdom of God." Put that into close contrast with "He stedfastly set His face to go to Jerusalem." "No man, having put his hand to the plow, and looking back, is fit for the Kingdom of God." There is illustration of the religious life. Jesus of Nazareth was religious. He had not where to lay His head. He had no possessions, nothing which could prevent His progress toward the ultimate goal. His passion for the Kingdom of God overcame all lower instincts, and He never gave a backward look, but plowed His furrow straight to the ultimate victory. Now, remember that if He said these things when His own face was set toward Jerusalem, He said them to men on the subject of their following Him, and they are illustrations of the great principles revealed in the fourteenth chapter. That is the cost of the religious life. Is it worth while? That is the question.

What is the value, if that is the cost? The cost is the denial of self, therefore the value can never be stated as what I gain, but what others gain. I wonder if you take me at that point. Is it worth while? How am I going to answer it? By telling you what you will gain by being religious? No. You will gain. Jesus put the personal equation into these tremendous words, only He put it the other way, "What shall a man be profited, if he shall gain the whole world, and forfeit his life?" If you want the personal equation there it is. You ask, Is the religious life worth while? Christ asks, Is the irreligious life worth while? I am not going to deal with that equation. I want to show you the value, not in the gain that comes to you personally, but in the gain to others. The gain to Christ if you will be a religious man, the gain to the world if you will be a religious man.

The gain to Christ. I take three words because they are all His words, and I am going to put them in the singular as though I were talking to one man only. If you will give yourself to Christ and begin the religious life, Christ will gain a friend. Christ will gain a witness. Christ will gain a servant. Christ will gain a friend. What does that mean? Identity of interest. Unity of purpose. Harmony of method. If you will give yourself to Christ, Christ will have a friend where you live, where you work. He will have a man in that store whose interests are His interests, whose purposes are His purposes, whose methods are His methods. Christ will gain a witness, that is, one who is a sample. How is London going to find out what Christ can do? Not by preaching, unless the preaching makes samples. A witness is not necessarily one who talks, but one who reveals. Christ will gain a witness, a man of whom other men will say, That is what Christ means. Christ will gain a servant, that is, someone whose one business will be the preparation of His Kingdom, someone through whom there will be the operation of His power. Christ's gain, if I may but lay that upon you to-night, is it worth while? Yes, for the sake of Christ and God it is worth while that you should be good, and religious, a Christian. I am coming more and more to think that is the final reason and the final impulse. The man who led my father to Christ still lives, Richard Roberts, in the Wesleyan ministry. I have at home a little book written years ago by Richard Wrench, being a pen-and-ink sketch of Richard Roberts. He says of Richard Roberts that his highest ambition was to place another gem in the Redeemer's diadem, to weave another garland wherewith to deck His brow. I believe that. I believe that is the highest ambition of all. Never mind whether you gain anything or not, Christ will gain immeasurably if you are a Christian.

If so, it follows that there will be gain to the world. What will be the gain to the world? Let me state three things. First, the maintenance of a testimony to the reality of the spiritual and eternal. To live the religious life really, truthfully, the life that has commerce with God, the life that counts with God and on God, daring even in this unbelieving age to season the speech with salt and to say, "If the Lord will," I will do this or that, is to live so that the world gains one man at least who lives as though there were a God and as though there were eternity. It is a great gain in this age. There is so much life that seems to shut Him out. But the world will gain more than that if you are religious. It will gain this, that in you there will be perpetual antagonism to all the things that are contrary to the will of God and which therefore destroy man. You will become a fighting man. Some of you are quite astonished at that. It is quite true, only you will fight the right thing. You cannot be a Christian man and be wholly a man of peace. Dr. Dale was once asked if he believed in peace at any price, and he said, Yes, even at the price of war. I am not discussing the Peace Congress. That is not in my mind. I think that all war as between man and man with weapons that are carnal, and where there is bloodshed, is begotten in hell. "The weapons of our warfare are not carnal," but we have a real warfare. If you become a religious man, a Christian man, you are going to fight everything that spoils your brother, because the thing that spoils your brother wounds the heart of your Father. The world will gain another man fighting the wrong for the establishment of the right. The world will gain in you if you are a religious man, one full of sympathy for all who are scattered, distressed, wounded, and one who out of that sympathy will work in order to uplift and to bless. Is this worth while?

When Moses wanted Hobab to accompany him, he said to him, "Come thou with us, and we will do thee good." What was the result? Hobab did not go. He was one of those independent men who said, No, thank you, I do not care for you to do me good. I will go my own way. Then Moses said, Come with us "and thou shalt be to us instead of eyes," and he went. "Come with us, and we will do thee good." No. Perhaps he ought to have gone. It is quite true that Moses could do him good and the company of the people of God could do him good. There are thousands of men to-day to whom that invitation does not appeal. I have resolutely to-night not said to you that it will do you good to be religious, but you can be eyes to somebody else if you are. You can do somebody else good if you are religious. If you are not careful you ought to be careful about the perfecting of your own life, but if not, then for the sake of Christ and for the sake of the world you ought to be good, you ought to be religious. It is only by submission to this one Lord Christ that I can ever hope to be able to help to bring in the Kingdom of love and truth and purity, and to bring in that Kingdom it is worth while.

My appeal to you, then, in answer to this question is on the highest ground. I affirm the costliness of being a Christian, but I declare the value issuing far outweighs the cost. If only you and I will give ourselves to this same Lord Christ—I say nothing to-night of the effect on our own life—what I say is this, it is worth while to do anything for Him, and it is worth while to do something for the world.

> One Lord there is, all lords above;
> His name is Truth, His name is Love,
> His name is Beauty, it is Light,
> His will is Everlasting Right.
>
> But, ah! to Wrong, what is His name?
> This Lord is a consuming flame
> To every wrong beneath the sun:
> He is one Lord, the Holy One.
>
> Lord of the Everlasting Name,
> Truth, Beauty, Light, Consuming Flame!
> Shall I not lift my heart to Thee,
> And ask Thee, Lord, to rule in me?

> If I be ruled in other wise,
> My lot is cast with all that dies;
> With things that harm, and things that hate
> And roam by night, and miss the gate—
>
> The happy gate, which leads to where
> Love is like sunshine in the air,
> And Love and Law are both the same,
> Named with an Everlasting Name.

Because I want to help to bring in that order, it is worth while.

CHAPTER XX

THE PROBLEMS OF THE RELIGIOUS LIFE: THE ALL-SUFFICIENT SOLUTION

Christ Jesus—Mighty To Save and To Keep

IN LOOKING BACK OVER THE SUBJECTS WE HAVE CONSIDERED together I am quite conscious that I have laid myself open to the charge of having approached these inquiries prejudiced in favor of Christianity. I at once admit the fact. To me religion and Christianity are synonymous terms. Do not misunderstand that. I recognize as fully as any man that there is much sincere religion in the world which does not call itself Christian, but of all other religions I would say,

> They are but broken lights of Thee,
> And Thou, O Lord, art more than they.

Consequently, if I speak of religion I speak of Christianity. In this final address I want, as I am able, to give my reasons for that prejudice. Broadly stated, they are that Christ answers my first questions satisfactorily, masters my enemies completely, disposes of my difficulties perfectly. Or more briefly, as indicated in the title, He is the all-sufficient Solution. This conviction is the result of knowledge of Him, which, in turn, results from experience of salvation. My prejudice in favor of Jesus Christ is not due to any theory I hold concerning Him, it is due to what He has done, and is still doing for me.

I shall ask you to follow two lines of consideration.

First, Christ the all-sufficient Solution; and, second, Christ the all-sufficient Saviour.

First, Christ as the all-sufficient Solution. The first questions of the religious life are: Has man anything to do with God? Can a just God forgive sins? What does God require of man? Has man anything to do with God? What is Christ's answer to that inquiry? The New Testament introduces me to a Man Who in actual life presents a perfect ideal. I do not think I need stay to argue that. I am inclined to think that it will be granted not merely by those who stand within the center of the Christian Church, but by all competent judges outside the Christian Church. It is a remarkable fact, and it is well that we should be reminded of it sometimes, that the most scholarly and brilliant critics of Jesus Christ have always ended by putting some wreath upon His brow. Every man who has come to the study of Christ presented by the gospels, while perhaps denying certain things which the gospels say concerning Him, does nevertheless admit the perfection of the ideal He presents. I start with that fact in answering this inquiry. I then ask what does this Man say in answer to the inquiry, Has man anything to do with God? The whole of His life and the whole of His teaching attest the fact that man must have to do with God, because God has everything to do with man. Think for one moment of the teaching of Jesus. His teaching concerning God was teaching which declared God's knowledge of man, God's love of man, God's government of man. You may gather up into one brief sentence His whole message to man about his relationship to God: "Seek ye first His Kingdom, and His righteousness." First, before what? What are the things that lie around the text in the great manifesto? Not luxuries, but the necessities of life. "What shall we eat? What shall we drink? or Wherewithal shall we be clothed?" Christ says of them all—recognizing the necessity for them by a word full of tenderness and beauty, "Your heavenly Father knoweth that ye have need of all these things"—that they are not first. "Seek ye first His Kingdom, and His righteousness." That is the word of a Man, admitted by foes and friends alike, to be the most perfect man ever presented to the vision of humanity. When I look at Him, I say Thou art the Man of all men I would rather be like. If Thy Manhood is the explanation of my humanity then I long to realize my own life. If it may ever be like that life in which there was the combination of strength and sweetness, that life in which there was mingled the thunder of fierce denunciation and the tears of infinite pity, then I want to be like that. When I would learn the secret of that life, He says, "Seek ye first His Kingdom." "I do always the things that are pleasing to Him . . . the things which I heard from Him these I speak. . . . I do nothing of Myself." "I must work the works of Him that sent Me." The master passion of His life was the will of God. The whole of His life was a life that had commerce with heaven, traffic with God. When I look at the ideal humanity of Jesus and ask its secret I discover that its secret is His profound, intense, personal conviction that He had to do with God, and that His whole life was a life or relationship to Him. His first recorded words are these, "I must be about My Father's business." His last recorded words are these, "Father, into Thy hands I commend My spirit." That answers my first inquiry. I have to do with God. I must find God and obey God.

I take the second of these inquiries. Can a just God forgive sins? How does Christ answer that question? I know that here we touch the realm of mystery because our finite mind cannot appreciate perfectly the infinite mind and the infinite power. Let me state the case thus. First He exercised the prerogative, He claimed to be able to forgive sins. He distinctly said, "Thy sins are forgiven thee." But He revealed the method also. By the mystery of His Cross He unveiled God's attitude toward sin, and God's activity in the presence of sin. In the hour of the Cross He did not try to persuade God to change His mind; but working together with God He unveiled before the astonished gaze of man that passion of God whereby He is able, Himself bearing human iniquity, to forgive it, to cancel it, to set the prisoner free. You say that is all theory? Follow me yet further. He told men they were forgiven. He has been telling men they are forgiven ever since, and men have entered into the consciousness of the forgiveness of sins. They have professed to know sin forgiven. You say that is only human profession, and I reply that men have exemplified the truth of their profession in the new lives which they have lived. I hold that the last and ultimate proof of the absolute Deity of the Man of Nazareth is the consciousness in the soul that sin is forgiven by what He is and what He did. The demonstration that sins are forgiven is to be found in the fact that a man whose sins are forgiven mourns the sins forgiven to the end of his life and fights against them, and rises on the basis of that deep and inner consciousness to life that is pure and strong and holy. That is the supreme miracle of Christianity. When you are next theorizing about the atonement, and the forgiveness of sins, spend an hour in the slums, in a Salvation Army barracks, and look into the faces of some of the men; find out what they say, what they are, and hear from their lips the repetition of the apostolic word, "We are His witnesses." In the Cross He drew the veil a little way aside, and I see God in Christ, suffering, and so setting me free from sin. I cannot believe in the possibility of the forgiveness of sins by a just God until I come face to face with the Christ. Then, whatever the theory may be, I know, and so my second inquiry is answered.

Take the third of these inquiries. What does God require of man? The answer is Jesus Himself as the Revelation of God's actual requirement. He requires of every man that he shall be like Christ. Christ is the pattern. I pause there because it is a most alarming thing to say, or it ought to be. Before Mr. Gladstone died he said one of the greatest weaknesses of the age was the weakened sense of sin. I believe that with all my heart. I am sometimes told to-day that men are not convinced of sin as they were in the days when our fathers preached. How are you to account for it? That is an inquiry that would take me more time to deal with than I have, but let me say this briefly. We are not preaching the perfections of Jesus as we ought. If we were, and men measured themselves by Him, there would be a profound and awful conviction of sin. Whenever I come into the presence of Christ I tremble. When I put what I am by the side of what He is, and then, when I discover that He is the Revelation of what was in the heart of God when He said, "Let Us make man in Our image," I know my sin. So, when I ask, What does God require of man? that is Christ's first answer. If that were all, I should be of all men the most miserable and the most helpless. The Man upon Whom I look is infinitely more than the perfect ideal. He is also the One Who comes down to me in my ruined condition and communicates to me a new life. Christ is not merely pattern, He is power. He is not merely a vision, He is virtue in the old root sense of the word.

> Strength into strengthless souls He speaks,
> And life into the dead.

When I ask what God requires of man He first shows me the pattern, and then teaches me that God requires of the man who cannot attain unto it that he shall submit himself to Christ, Who will perfect that which concerneth him, and at last in spite of all the paralysis make him what God wants him to be. What does God require of man? To be like Christ. What, then, does God require of me? That I shall give myself to Christ and trust Him. If I do, what then? Presently He will present me faultless before the presence of His glory. I am not afraid any longer to know what God requires of me, for I hide me in that rock, I follow that King, and through processes it may be, of discipline, pain and suffering, He will make me all that God wants me to be.

Then I turn to the opposing forces, the world, the flesh and the devil. I prefer now to take them in another order, because, as I have said in dealing with them separately, it is the devil we have to deal with finally. The world and the flesh are all right if only we can get hold of the devil and deal with him. The world is God's world, fair and beautiful. The flesh in itself, essentially, primarily, according to Divine intention, is not evil. "An enemy hath done this," I say whenever I see tares in the field.

What did Jesus do with regard to Satan? He first dragged him into the light. God led Jesus into the wilderness in order to make the devil stand out in the light. He was led of the Spirit in the wilderness. He was driven by the Spirit into the wilderness. With what result? A Man standing quietly within His own Manhood and obeying the law of God masters the devil at every point. He puts Himself in the will of God and stands squarely there, and the devil is defeated. In His life He mastered the forces that harm and spoil humanity. Paul, in one of the most daring phrases of his writings, tells us what He did with Satan in death. Speaking of the principalities and powers, the subtle forces of spiritual antagonism that thronged around the dying Christ, Paul says, "He made a show of them openly, triumphing over them in it." So whenever I meet the devil now I meet a vanquished foe. The woman's seed has bruised the serpent's head. In Christ humanity has won its Armageddon as against all the spiritual hosts of wickedness. There is a good deal of administrative warfare going on, I still have to fight, but I fight under a victorious Lord against a vanquished foe.

What about the flesh? He took flesh, and sanctified it by taking it. He was made in the likeness of sinful flesh. The apostle is very careful to show that His flesh was not sinful, but in "the *likeness* of sinful flesh." The purely flesh life of Jesus was as holy as His spiritual life. The flesh was subservient to the spirit, the body was the instrument of the Spirit. The eye was the window of the spirit, and was never allowed to gaze on that which might harm it. His body was the temple of His spirit. His spirit reigned over His body, and so the very flesh-life of Jesus was pure and spotless and beautiful. And mark this well, He did not bruise His flesh. He never scourged Himself. He left His brutal enemies to that work. He did not produce holiness of spirit by bruising and battering the flesh. That idea was born in hell. His life was a perfectly natural life, so natural that His critics said He was a gluttonous man and a winebibber, the friend of publicans and sinners. He loved flowers and children, went to the wedding feast, as well as to the house of mourning. His life was perfectly human, and because of the mastery of the spirit it was perfectly holy. Then through that mystery of death, which we must ever reverence and never can fathom, He set free His own life; and by regeneration He gives His life to other men, so that in the power of it they also begin to live the life of holiness, cleansing themselves from the filthiness of flesh and spirit in the power of His indwelling life.

What of the world? He entered it, and He redeemed it by entering it. He entered into its joys and its sorrows, never for one single moment so living that men could think of Him as ascetic. He entered into the world and loved its mountains, its seas, its children, its flowers, and all wonders. May I borrow a word of Paul and apply it to Him? He *used* the world as not abusing it. Then by the suffering of His death He introduced into broken creation healing forces that shall never cease their working until the whole creation which to-day groans and travails in pain shall be remade, and shall sing the song of redemption. He entered into the world and redeemed it, as He redeemed man. By redeeming man He put him back on his lost throne, over the things of the cosmos, in order that at last the desert should blossom as the rose, and the sin-scarred earth become what God meant it to be, a veritable paradise for the dwelling of man. So this great Christ masters the enemy, and by so doing restores all the physical and material to its proper place of subservience, thus making possible a fulfilment of the Divine ideal.

I turn to the last group of questions. The first, Is it possible? is answered at once by the things I have already said. If man sees the beauty of the ideal of the religious life and asks, Is it possible? Christ says, Yes, it is possible if you will admit Me and crown Me. "I can do all things through Christ which strengtheneth me." The religious life was quite impossible to scores of people in this building until they admitted Christ, and crowned Him and trusted Him. From the moment in which they did so they have found it possible.

Is it necessary? He answers that inquiry by His revelation of what life ought to be. He gave us some glimpses of the far-flung splendor of the ages to come, showing us the value of one human life, as He held in His own hand the balances. "What shall a man be profited, if he shall gain the whole world, and forfeit his life."

Finally, Is it worth while? You will remember in dealing with that inquiry our answer was that it is worth while, not simply because of what it means to us, but for Christ's sake, and for the sake of the world. Christ inspired that heroism in the heart of every man who feels it. He is the File-leader of faithful souls, the first of the hosts; and everything heroic, everything done for the sake of those who are suffering, all toil endured for the sake of others, all this is due to the inspiration of that one supernal life by which Christ says to men, It is worth while to be right with God in order to lift other men.

Finally, Christ is the all-sufficient Saviour. Here I take one brief and all-inclusive declaration of the writer of the letter to the Hebrews, "He is able to save to the uttermost them that draw near unto God through Him, seeing He ever liveth to make intercession for them." Let me take a minute or two with the terms of that declaration. "To save," what does this mean? The word here translated save simply means to render safe. I was very interested in looking this up to find the Greek word translated in different ways. Here are some of them. "To heal"; "preserve"; "do well"; "be whole." These translations are interesting, because all the thoughts suggested by them lie in this great word, "He is able *to save* to the uttermost." He is able to heal. That is the initial thing. That is the first thing I want. I cannot live the religious life because I am spiritually diseased. But He heals me. Then He is able to preserve. I would like to be a Christian, but if I start I am afraid I cannot. On this side of the Atlantic, North, South, East, and West, I have heard the same phrase, I am afraid I cannot *keep it*. On the other side I have heard the phrase, I cannot *hold out*. The answer is, He is able to preserve. Both these expressions show that men have a wrong idea of salvation. I am afraid if I am a Christian I shall not be able to keep it. Keep what? You have nothing to keep, you have to be kept. I am afraid I shall not hold out. You have not to hold out. You have to be held. There is responsibility. The responsibility is that of maintaining always the attitude of repentance and faith, the back turned on sin, and the face turned to the Christ. These conditions being fulfilled, He is able to preserve.

"To save" is a great and gracious word. Do not drop it out of your vocabulary, and do not drop it out of your experience. "He is able to save." It begins just where our need begins, with healing. It continues with the continuity of that need, with preservation. He is able to do all this. I love the word because it is a word that man needs to hear. Man cannot do the thing he supremely wants to do. He knows the beauty of holiness, but cannot live it. "He is able to save." Christ gives virtue where man lacks. He touches paralysis with power.

Take the next term, "to the uttermost." That is a great word that occurs only twice in the New Testament. It signifies the fullest measure, the furthest extent. It occurs in that wonderful story of the woman who was bent so that she could not stretch herself up. She walked doubled up, with infirmity, and could not straighten herself, to the uttermost. "He is able to save to the uttermost." You say, Spiritually I am decrepit, I cannot stand straight, or go straight. He is able to make you straight as He made that woman straight. That is the first application of it. He is able to save to the fullest extent, that is, the whole of your life, volitional, emotional, intellectual. It is one of the greatest words in the New Testament.

Tarry a moment longer with the terms, for the terms are everything in this declaration. "He is able." The Greek word from which we have derived our word "dynamic" is here. In the case of the woman who touched the hem of His garment Jesus said, "Virtue hath gone out of Me"; that is dynamite. He is *able* to save. You say you cannot be saved. God help you to fix your eye upon this Saviour. It is not what you are able to do. It is what He is able to do, to heal, to preserve, to set right all that is wrong in your nature, to preserve you against all the forces that oppose you, and to present you faultless at last.

What are the conditions upon which He saves men. "He is able to save to the uttermost *them that draw near unto God through Him.*" The goal, God. The way, through Him. How, then, can I live the religious life? By turning back to God. How am I to find my way back to God? Through Him. There is mercy, there is pardon, there is power through Him. So that to-night if you are perplexed with problems, the place in which to begin the work of solving them is Christ. If a man shall give himself to Christ I do not mean that all his intellectual problems will be solved at once. By no means. Again suffer words of experience. My intellectual problems are by no means all solved. Sometimes men come to me and say, You believe that Bible from cover to cover?

By all means, but I do not perfectly understand it. I do not understand the problem of evil. I do not understand how God wrought in the mystery of His own Being in order to atone. I do not understand all the Bible teaches about the ages that lie beyond, either concerning the wicked or the good. Some men do, or think they do! I am content to postpone many things. The one sure and certain thing is, that we can be good if we trust Him. I like that word "good." That is why I used it.

> There was no other *good* enough
> To pay the price of sin.
> He only could unlock the gate
> Of heaven and let us in.

How does He do it?

> He died that we might be forgiven,
> He died to make *us good*.

I do not ask you to shut your mind to your intellectual difficulties, to say that these things do not matter; but to get right at the spiritual center of your life, and then to correct the circumference therefrom.

CHAPTER XXI

HOLINESS: DEFINITION

To grant unto us that we being delivered out of the hand of our enemies should serve Him without fear, in holiness and righteousness before Him all our days.
                                    LUKE 1:74, 75.

THE GOSPEL ACCORDING TO LUKE IS THAT OF THE UNIversal Saviour. In it, Jesus is seen as Man, and His work is dealt with in its widest application. The true ideal of God's ancient people Israel is recognized. Messiah is revealed as of the stock of Abraham, and yet as the Saviour of all men. The song of Mary, the prophecy of Zacharias, the chanting of the angels, and the speech of Simeon, all sacred and beautiful utterances peculiar to the Gospel, recognize Jesus both as the Messiah of the ancient people according to their prophecies; and as the Saviour of all such as put their trust in Him, without regard to nationality. The benefits accruing to the chosen people are recognized, but they are ever seen flowing through them to all peoples. In the song of Zacharias, in which our text is found, Jehovah the God of Israel is declared as visiting, redeeming, and raising up a horn of salvation in the house of David; but the purpose of this visitation of His ancient people is that the light may shine on them that sit in darkness, and in the shadow of death.

In order to perform this wider mission, the Messiah brings to His own people "salvation from our enemies and from the hand of all that hate us, to show mercy toward our fathers and to remember His holy covenant, the oath which He should swear to Abraham our father, to grant unto us that we being delivered out of the hand of our enemies should serve Him without fear, in holiness and righteousness before Him all our days."

These two words, *holiness* and *righteousness*, mark two aspects of one condition. Holiness has to do with character; righteousness with conduct. They cannot possibly be separated from each other. They are as intimately related as are root and fruit. There can be no fruit unless there be a root. If there be living root it must issue in fruit. There can be no righteousness unless there is holiness; holiness must issue in righteousness. Holiness describes being; righteousness describes doing.

The particular word translated *holiness* in this verse occurs twice only in the New Testament; in this passage, and in the letter to the Ephesians, in which the apostle urges those to whom he writes to "put on the new man, which after God hath been created in righteousness and *holiness* of truth." In each case it is linked with the word *righteousness*. Thus in each of these passages the root principle out of which righteousness grows is recognized.

"In holiness and righteousness." The essential meaning of *holiness* is *right* but it is right in intrinsic character. The essential meaning of *righteousness* is *right*, but it is right in actual conduct.

In the son of Zacharias holiness and righteousness are declared to be the condition of life resulting from the salvation which the Messiah and Saviour should bring to men. In the Ephesian letter righteousness and holiness are declared to be the result of the new man created after God. Thus whether we take the passage from the song of Zacharias, which recognizes the right and privilege and responsibility of Israel, and all the Divine intention to bless the peoples through Israel; or whether we take the specific writing of the New Testament apostle, it is perfectly evident that the work of Christ was directed toward righteousness of life, issuing from holiness of character.

Let us, then, consider this subject of holiness according to New Testament teaching. It is a very remarkable fact that thousands of the saints of God are a little afraid of the word "holiness." I believe a great many Christian people keep away from all sorts of conventions and conferences because of this fear. It is not very long since a very dear friend of mine, a Christian man, said to me, You know, I don't believe in holiness. I told him how very sorry I was to hear it, because the Bible says that without holiness no man can see the Lord. Of course, he did not mean quite what he said. I have quoted it only to indicate the attitude toward this great word, and this great subject, which is alarmingly prevalent in the Christian Church. I recognize the reason of this fear. A great many unholy things have been said and done by those who perhaps have been loudest in their attempt to explain, and in their claim to the experience of holiness.

Yet is it quite fair that we should turn away from a great word, and a great thought, and a great intention of the Christian religion, because the word itself has been prostituted to base uses, and an interpretation of its meaning not warranted by the Scripture has become widespread and popular? It is well that we should understand what the New Testament teaches, for this much is evident, whatever God means by holiness, whatever the intention of the Holy Spirit is by the use of the term, whatever the New Testament writers meant when they used the word, that for holiness Christ came into the world; that the real intention of His coming was that men being delivered from their enemies might be able to serve Him in holiness and righteousness before Him all their days; that the ultimate charge of Paul in this great crowning letter of his whole system of teaching is that Christians should put off the old man, and put on the new, which is created after God in holiness and in righteousness.

Therefore, with the utmost simplicity of statement of which I am capable, I want, first of all, to speak by way of definition. What is holiness? In the first place, let me repeat in one brief sentence the sum and substance of that already said in introduction. Holiness is rightness or rectitude of character, inspiring righteousness, which is rightness or rectitude of conduct. There is no motive for right conduct sufficiently strong to maintain it in all places, and under all conditions, other than holiness of character. Any other motive breaks down sooner or later. Men do right things from self-respect for a very long while, but sooner or later, under stress of temptation, swift and sudden and subtle, or in the presence of some alluring advantage, they will turn to the thing that is mean and low and dastardly and ignoble. A high sense of duty is not enough at all times and under all circumstances to compel righteousness of conduct; and it is perfectly certain that if men are right only from policy they will break down. There is an old maxim I remember writing when I was a boy in my copybooks, Honesty is the best policy. I think it is true, but it is a pernicious thing to give a child to write, because you thereby inculcate an entirely wrong view of honesty. Honesty is the best policy. Is that the reason why I am to be honest? Then I shall become a rogue before many years pass over my head. The man who is honest only because it is the best policy is a rogue at heart.

No, policy is not enough to compel righteousness. To do right at all times and under all circumstances is only possible to the man who is right in the deepest of him. There is no other motive sufficiently strong to impel and compel righteousness of conduct than that of holiness of character. Now the thought suggested by the word holiness, as the thought suggested by the word righteousness, is that of a standard. What is the standard of holiness? If holiness be rectitude of character, what is rectitude of character? The only answer possible to such an inquiry, at least to the mind of the Christian believer, is that the standard of holiness of character is the character of God. I know how hard that sounds, and yet what other can I say? Holiness is not an idea, formulated in experience, by which we measure God. It is an idea in human experience derived from the revelation which God has made of Himself to humanity. And whether men to-day are worshiping our God after our fashion or not, every true ideal of holiness obtaining in our common life is derived from revelation, and God remains forevermore the ultimate standard both of holiness and of righteousness. Holiness in man therefore is approximation to the character of God. Righteousness in man is partnership in the activity of God. So that holiness and righteousness alike, in the experience of man, result from fellowship with God.

And yet so far that is but to define a method of discovery rather than to state the discovery. I once again ask, and I know the difficulty of my inquiry, what is the holiness of God? Will you allow me to say, talking quite freely and familiarly to you, I have sat down quite alone in the presence of that inquiry and attempted to discover the answer, and all the while I have seemed to know the meaning, and yet have been unable to define it. The only definition, therefore, that I shall venture to make is by quotation of words occurring in the New Testament descriptive of Jesus. For, after all, is not that the only way to know God? Must I not find my way to a knowledge of God through Him? If you take Him away, then I am in the midst of an infinite and incomprehensible and overwhelming Wisdom and Might, which I cannot know. But when I come into the presence of Jesus I know God. I read this wonderful thing written of Him by the seer of blue Galilee, John the mystic: "The law was given by Moses; *grace and truth* came by Jesus Christ." And to my inquiring heart, in thinking of this subject, and asking what is the holiness of God, that is the only answer that came, from which I could not escape. What is holiness? Grace and truth. I may speak of the love of God, and declare that at the center of love is holiness, and yet is that quite accurate as definition? Is not holiness rather the combination of these two things, grace and truth? Take that word "grace," in its more original intention, not so much as descriptive of the great river of tender compassion and mercy and mighty salvation which, flowing through the ages, heals men. Oh, that is grace, and some of us still like, with our friends of the Salvation Army, to sing

> Grace is flowing like a river.

Yes, but what is the nature of the river? Grace is love in action. That is, grace and truth. Love is grace, and its action is truth. We cannot possibly divide these things. Jesus Christ, describing the devil on one occasion, said two things concerning him: "He was a murderer from the beginning." "He is a liar, and the father thereof." Those are the superlative opposites of grace and truth. What is the opposite of grace? Murder, the ultimate of hate. What is the opposite of truth? A lie.

Holiness in God is the combination, or unity of grace and truth. We cannot speak of cause and effect when we speak of these in action. Everything God does is inspired of love, and governed by truth. That is holiness in God; and in the universe, and in all human history, that is the standard of holiness. The holiness of God is the standard of holiness in man. Holiness in man means approximation to the character of God.

I am not now dealing with the methods by which this is made possible, with the earlier statements of this song of Zacharias, that He came to deliver us out of the hand of our enemies, but rather with the result of that great deliverance, "that we . . . should serve Him without fear, in holiness and righteousness." Holiness in man is right relation to God, resulting in participation in the very character of God. I go back to the very beginning of the story of man as told in the Bible, and I read that man was made in the Divine image, and after the Divine likeness. The enemy entered with temptation at the base of which was the infinite blasphemy that he proposed to present the initial purpose as an ultimate goal. You shall be like gods. Therein lay the subtlety of the temptation. It was suggested that man should realize the highest, be like God, but should do so by a wrong method. I have quoted the Genesis story only to lead on to the ultimate word of Jesus: "Ye, therefore, shall be perfect, as your heavenly Father is perfect"; and to another word in the Ephesian letter, "Be ye therefore imitators of God, as beloved children."

Holiness of character, then, is approximation to the

character of God, which is love and truth. If we were less conventional, and could now pass into absolute silence, in order to apply that test to our own lives, what a startling experience it would be for very many of us. How far am I in character a man of grace and of truth? I choose to ask the question personally, rather than of any other, for there are things the preacher cannot say to men, but must say with men. I shrink from the test, yet that is holiness, a life love-mastered, and true in its every activity. Moreover, it was in order that men should be holy that Jesus came. That is the meaning of the Christian religion. The Christian religion is not an arrangement by which a man can sin and escape the penalty. The Christian religion is great and glorious deliverance from enemies in order that in holiness and righteousness we may serve God. And to be satisfied with anything short of this character is to be satisfied with something short of the intention and purpose of the coming of our Lord into the world.

Righteousness, then, is conduct inspired by grace, and governed by truth. In business life, professional life, political life, how far are we righteous? We are righteous in the measure in which we are holy.

Thus, if we take these New Testament words, and interpret them in the light of New Testament teaching, we do not drag the idea of holiness to the dust. We are compelled rather, whether we will or not, to climb the mountain, and feel the rare and searching atmosphere above the snow line. Oh, my God, I am inclined to put my hand on my lips, and say I am a leper, unclean, unclean! By these standards the life of the past week is unhealthy, and the man who glibly declares that he has been holy for seven years has never seen the light, or climbed to the whiteness of the purity of God.

But if this thing is to search our hearts, and humble our spirits, it is nevertheless part of an evangel. He came to deliver us from our enemies in order that we might serve Him in holiness and righteousness all our days. And if we look back over the life of the past week, and over the whole period of our Christian experience, and know how little we have been love-mastered, and truth-governed, let us remember that it is because of the very enemies from whom He came to deliver us. If we have not yet been delivered our inquiry should be, not how are we to climb to that height of holiness, but how we can submit ourselves to the Christ that He may be able to lift us to the height of holiness? He came to deliver us, and if He has not delivered us it is because we have not put ourselves absolutely and utterly under His control.

Now, brethren, if that is holiness essentially and eternally in God and in man—because I would not for all my soul send away any child of God who is aspiring after the heights and earnestly desiring to attain thereto, discouraged or crushed or broken—let me spend a few moments in speaking of what holiness is experimentally and temporally. I am not going to lower the standard for a moment, but I do propose to declare the measure in which holiness of character is possible, and what the experience is, according to the teaching of the New Testament. And I will do that quite briefly in seven statements, which, in the first place, are negative, but each of which has its positive side.

Holiness is not freedom from all sin as imperfection: but it is freedom from the dominion of sin, and from wilful sinning. I say that holiness is not freedom from all sin as imperfection. Now let me in the simplest way explain that.

What is sin? I fall back upon the word most often translated sin in the New Testament, or the Hebrew word most often translated sin in the Old Testament, each of which has the one significance. "Sin," taking the word in its most general sense, is missing the mark, imperfection. Whether I can help it or not does not matter, does not enter into the thought of this particular word. The ideal is recognized, if I do not realize it, that is sin, missing the mark. In that sense holiness for to-day does not mean sinlessness. At best, we are unprofitable servants, and in the present life we never can come to the absolute perfection of consummation. In the sight of heaven, and according to the infinite standards of God, everything lower than the highest is sin.

But holiness does mean freedom from the dominion of sin. I need not be mastered by sin, and I never need sin wilfully. Surely, brethren, I need not argue that. I know how it has been argued, and yet think, and think quietly and simply and honestly, is there any need that I should wilfully sin? In the presence of a clear shining of light, when two paths are in front of me, and I am called to choose, there can be no necessity that I should walk in the wrong one. Perhaps there is no escape for a man who has never yet crowned the Christ. But He came to deliver me from my enemies, and He has made possible the freedom of the will. I can understand that somebody studying psychology says to me, What do you mean? I mean this, "To me who would do good evil is present." That is the language of the man who has never yet known perfectly the power of Christ. But the language of the man, that same man under the dominion of Christ, is this, "I can do all things in Him that strengtheneth me." I will the good, and do the evil, until I have surrendered myself to the Lord Christ. But when I have surrendered to Him, I will the good, and do it. Thus my will is free, for action follows its choice.

Imperfect still, at the close of every day I hasten back to the cleft Rock, to the shelter of the blood redemption; and yet all the way it is possible, in this life, in the power of the present Christ, not to sin wilfully.

But again: *Holiness is not freedom from mistakes in judgment; but it is freedom from the need to exercise judgment alone.* To the end of the chapter we may make mistakes in judgment, cut of absolute sincerity and loyalty to Christ; but at least remember this, we are not left alone to exercise our judgment if we are under the dominion of this One Who was manifested to deliver us from all our enemies. We can have government and light. You tell me God does not speak to men as He did to Abraham. Will you let me correct that statement? This is the truth, men are not listening as Abraham listened. Right in the depth of the soul, by a direct and definite revelation, He will speak to the man who wants to hear Him. I would to God there might be throughout all the churches of Jesus Christ a return to a recognition of the doctrine of the truth of the inner light. We can have guidance about the business we are to take up, the profession we are to follow, the house in which we are to live. Of course, the trouble is that we seek guidance so seldom.

Again: *Holiness is not freedom from temptation, but it is freedom from the paralysis which necessitates failure.* So far from being freedom from temptation, holiness means a new sense of temptation, a new attack of the forces of evil; but holiness means freedom from that paralysis, that necessitates failure under temptation. Tempted I shall be to the end, but defeated I need not be.

Holiness does not mean freedom from bodily infirmity, but it does mean freedom from all ailments which are the direct result of disobedience.

There is a vast amount of physical sickness in the Church of God that ought not to be there. And if there were real holiness of life there would be a great absence of very much which we suffer.

Holiness does not mean freedom from conflict, but it does mean freedom from defeat. I know at that point some of my friends do not agree. They say that the life of holiness means cessation of conflict. I do not believe it. I believe that to the end there will be conflict. Against principalities, against powers, the world rulers of this darkness, spiritual hosts of wickedness in the heavenly places, we have to fight our way through. But there need not be defeat. The great and gracious word of the apostle comes back to the mind, "Having done all to stand."

Holiness is not freedom from liability to fall, but it is freedom from the necessity of falling.

The freedom of the will remains as an essential part of redeemed human nature, and it is ever possible to choose to turn aside from the path of obedience; but the freedom of the will in the new sense, to which we have before referred, means that we can ever yield ourselves in hours of crisis to "Him that is able to guard us from stumbling."

And once again, and finally: *Holiness is not freedom from the possibility of advance, but it is freedom from the impossibility of advance.* Holiness does not mean that those who are living the life of present holiness have now arrived at a stage of Christian experience from which there can be no advance. It means rather a condition of life which makes it possible to advance. On a previous occasion I have spoken of health as being holiness, and of growth as being consequent thereupon. Such is the relationship of holiness to advancement. You gave yourself to Christ but recently, but a few days, or weeks, or months ago, therefore you are but a babe in Christ, you have but commenced the journey. You can be holy, and yet there is much for you to know, to learn; and ere the work be done in you there will be long years of advancement and growth and development. Holiness, I repeat, is not a condition from which it is not possible to advance. It is a condition in which it is possible to advance.

And now turning back again for conclusion to the actual word of this great song of Zacharias, I pray you remember that the Christ around Whose name and Whose presence we are gathered this morning came that we might be delivered out of the hands of our enemies, in order that we might "serve Him in holiness and righteousness all our days."

What there is in us therefore that is unlike grace and unlike truth is there because we have never allowed our Lord to win His victory, and have His way.

May He lead us into such close fellowship with Himself that in the measure possible to us at the moment the very purpose of His coming may be fulfilled as we begin the life that is inspired by holiness of character and expressed in righteousness of conduct.

CHAPTER XXII

HOLINESS: A PRESENT POSSIBILITY

That ye may be blameless and harmless, children of God without blemish in the midst of a crooked and perverse generation, among whom ye are seen as lights in the world.
PHILIPPIANS 2:15.

IN OUR FIRST STUDY WE ATTEMPTED TO UNDERSTAND THE meaning of the term "holiness," and its relation to righteousness. I may summarize that study by reminding you that holiness is rectitude of character, and righteousness rectitude of conduct. Apart from holiness there can be no righteousness. When there is holiness there must inevitably be righteousness. While righteousness is that after which we seek, and for which we pray, we must ever remember that it can be established in individual, social, national, or racial life only when there is holiness of character.

Now, somewhat narrowing our outlook, we are to inquire what the New Testament teaches concerning the possibility of holiness in the present life. Holiness of character, ideally, is attractive to every man in the deepest of him. There are very many devout and sincere expositors of Scripture who hold that the unregenerate man has no admiration for holiness. I differ entirely from that view. If you will allow the word stated as testimony rather than as theory —I have yet to meet the man who does not in the deepest of his thinking know that the life of holiness is the life of beauty.

The man who has never yet come into living relationship with the Lord of holiness and righteousness, the Lord Christ Himself, does most strenuously deny the possibility of living the holy life in this present world. He dismisses quite readily, and quite resolutely all contemplation of the ideal of holiness, because of his deep and profound consciousness of his inability himself to be holy. Of course, no person born of God denies the beauty of holiness, or the desirability of realizing the character of holiness. To have received the Spirit of God, the gift of life Divine, is to know a great desire after holiness of character. It is quite possible that we so stifle the desire, so resolutely refuse to submit to all the indications of method, as by and by, even though we still name the name of Christ, to lose that desire altogether. Then we shall speak of the ideal as a counsel of perfection. You will remember that this phrase, "counsel of perfection," has come to us from the Roman Church, and is used by its theologians in reference to the laws of life for such as give themselves to the vocation of saintship. It is declared by them that the life of holiness or saintship is not possible for the ordinary Christian man or the ordinary Christian woman, that it is reserved for a select few who have received some higher call, and abandon themselves thereto. Among those of us who are of the Protestant faith there is a great tendency to deny the possibility of holiness, using that very phrase, "counsel of perfection." All Christian people agree that in heaven we shall be holy in character. This admission is evidence that we think that death will be able to do something for us that the living Saviour cannot do. That statement in itself ought to be sufficient to make us inquire quite carefully whether this life of holiness expressing itself in a life of righteousness is possible here and now.

HOLINESS: A PRESENT POSSIBILITY

I think that the one verse I have read, not so much that I may deal with it in detail this morning, but as a key to a line of investigation, ought to answer forevermore the question whether the life of holiness is possible. "That ye may be blameless and harmless, children of God without blemish." Oh, yes, you say, that will be so in heaven! Let the apostle finish his sentence before you object, "*in the midst of a crooked and perverse generation.*" I do not think you will care to suggest that to be a description of heaven. It far more accurately describes London, or the place where you live. "In the midst of a crooked and perverse generation, among whom ye are as lights in the world." How? By the life that is "blameless and harmless," the life of "children of God without blemish."

Our inquiry ought not to be made of any system of theology, or of the experience of the Church. Thousands of people who have seen something of the glory of the life of holiness, and earnestly desire to attain thereto, turn from the great spiritual vision to inquire what man has to say concerning this. Without desiring to touch on things that are controversial, let me say that for many years in this country there have been two schools of interpreters of holiness, labeled, accurately or inaccurately, Keswick and Methodist. Happily they are becoming so merged that you can hardly tell which is which. Now if we want to know what the New Testament teaches about holiness we should turn to the New Testament itself.

A letter has reached me this week from a sincere seeker after truth, after knowledge of the law of this life of fulness of the Spirit. The writer, after a long letter, puts this as a question to me: "Will you tell me if you have met anyone living the Spirit-filled life?" I am not a judge. I have no right to judge. The Lord knoweth them that are His. I would warn everyone against attempting to decide as to the possibility of the holy life from the experience of saints. I will not, however, leave the inquiry at that point without another word. Yes, I have known saints, so far as I have a right to judge, in whom perfect love has cast out fear, in whom perfect love has become the law of life, gentle, tender, gracious, patient, wooing, winsome souls; strong, angry souls, protesting against all iniquity, holy men and women, and, therefore, righteous men and women. Yet I will not base anything on the experience, either the exceptional or average experience, of the saint. If it cannot be demonstrated that any man or woman has ever yet in nineteen centuries realized the ideal which the Bible presents, I yet decline to lower the ideal to the attainment of those who have failed. It is for me to strive after the highest if no other has. The teaching of Scripture is that the highest is possible. Therefore, I desire, taking this verse simply as a keynote, a starting point, to make my appeal to the teaching of the New Testament. The difficulty, in a brief summary of statement, must necessarily be that of selection. I propose, therefore, to make a sevenfold statement in answer to the inquiry whether holiness is a present possible experience, in each case selecting one principal declaration of the New Testament in interpretation of the general thought.

First of all, then, the New Testament declares that holiness of character is possible because it is the will of God for His people.

In the twenty-ninth verse of the eighth chapter of the letter to the Romans the apostle writes these words in the midst of a great argument concerning the life of spiritual fulness: "For whom He foreknew, He also foreordained to be conformed to the image of His Son, that He might be the firstborn among many brethren." Take that simple little passage out of the great paragraph, a paragraph full of mystery and yet full of revelation, a paragraph in which the apostle is showing the original thought and intention of God in the work of His Son, a passage in which occur the words that still fill us with fear as we attempt interpretation of them—the words "foreordained" and "elect." The foreordination is not to salvation but to character, "foreordained to be conformed to the image of His Son." That is the will of God. A great deal has been lost in our own Christian thinking and in our own Christian life by treating the initial things of Christian experience as though they were the final things, by not getting far enough back in our endeavor to understand the real purpose of God in the mission of Jesus and the work of Christ. Some time ago I passed through these writings of the New Testament, and made a catena of passages in which the purpose is declared, passages in which the word "that" occurs in the sense of "in order that." Take one illustration: "The grace of God hath appeared, bringing salvation to all men, instructing us, to the intent that, denying ungodliness and worldly lusts, we should live soberly and righteously and godly in the present world, looking for the blessed hope and appearing of the glory of our great God and Saviour Jesus Christ, Who gave Himself for us *that* He might redeem us from all iniquity, and purify unto Himself a people for His own possession, zealous of good works." Mark the purpose of the great and gracious work which originated in the councils of eternity, the work that operated in the stream of time, a work that includes within itself the marvelous mission of God in Christ—Who gave Himself for us in order that He might forgive our sins? No, but rather to "redeem us from all iniquity," and purify unto Himself a people for His own possession, zealous of good works. The will of God is our sanctification, that we should be "conformed to the image of His Son." In the days of our childhood we used to sing, "I want to be like Jesus." Have we ever ceased singing it? If so, why? It was a profound word. It was a word full of simplicity, so simple that the child sings it yet and loves it, and catches something of its meaning; yet it is a word as sublime as the eternal purpose of God for every child of His love. Nothing less than that can satisfy the heart of God. Nothing less than that ought to satisfy the heart of the child of God, that we should be "conformed to the image of His Son." That is fundamental; the New Testament declares holiness to be possible when it declares that it is the will of God for His people.

Second, the New Testament declares holiness of character to be possible because it clearly teaches us that for the creation of that character Christ came into the world.

Already in the minds of all of you who are at all familiar with the New Testament, passage after passage has been remembered. Take the first and simplest in the Gospel of Matthew, the word spoken to His mother by the angel in connection with the foretelling of His coming: "Thou shalt call His name Jesus; for it is He that shall save His people from their sins." Not He shall forgive sins; that is initial, preliminary, very true, but that is not the statement. "He shall save His people *from their sins*." His people, the Hebrew people, yea verily; only remember that by the coming of Jesus Christ the horizon was flung back and the Gentiles were brought to the rising of His light, and into all the values of His mission. The phrase "His people" includes all such as turn to Him, submit to Him, trust Him. It does not mean He will save from his sins the man who is still in rebellion. It is *His people* that He shall save from their sins. It is these first principles that we are in danger of forgetting. The word does not say that He shall save His people from the punishment of their sins, but from their sins, from the sins which are the outcome of sin; He saves them from sins by saving from the power of sin. Therefore it is possible that I should live the holy life, according to the purpose of God, and according to the work that Jesus Christ came to do.

Third, the New Testament declares holiness of character to be possible because of the administration of the Spirit of God in the life of the trusting soul.

"There is therefore now no condemnation to them that are in Christ Jesus. *For the law of the Spirit of life in Christ Jesus made me free from the law of sin and of death. For what the law could not do, in that it was weak* through the flesh, God, sending His own Son in the likeness of sinful flesh and as an offering for sin, condemned sin in the flesh." While this passage may be perfectly clear to the majority of you, be patient while I attempt to make it clear to the youngest. The term *law* in verse two has no reference to the Mosaic economy, neither has the phrase, "*the law of sin and of death*," any reference to the decalogue. In the third verse the term *law* has reference to the Mosaic economy. What, then, is meant by the term *law* in the second verse? Allow me to substitute a phrase for a word, and read: "For the *master principle* of the Spirit of life in Christ Jesus made me free from the *master principle* of sin and of death." That is a scientific statement of the work of the Spirit of life in the believer. What is it that the indwelling of the Spirit does in the life of a man? It sets in operation a new law which negatives the old one. Can this be? Surely we know it can be. Often the simplest illustration will help the seeking soul. At this moment, as I hold this book in my hand, one law is negativing another law. The law of gravitation is pulling the book toward the desk. The law of muscular contraction is holding it there, mastering the other. If for one single moment I withdraw the law of muscular contraction, the law of gravitation obtains, and the book falls. The law of the Spirit of life in Christ Jesus sets me free from the law of sin and of death. The law of sin and of death is in my members. "I see a different law in my members, warring against the law of my mind," paralyzing me, making it impossible for me to do the thing I would do, "to me who would do good evil is present." But, says the apostle, there is another law, the law of the Spirit of life in Christ Jesus, and that sets me free from the law of sin and of death, makes me master where I was mastered, or, better, makes the Spirit master where sin had been master. It is a unified statement, and the whole of that section of the Roman letter is needed to illuminate it. By the indwelling of the Spirit a new law is at work in the life of the man, contradicting, negativing, denying the law which had mastered him, "the law of sin and of death."

Fourth, the New Testament teaches that holiness of character is possible, because the spiritual forces that are against holiness of character are all defeated.

There is no greater passage in all the New Testament as revealing this than the one in the Colossian letter, in which Paul, in a few bold, black strokes, sets before us the work of Christ. He makes the Cross the final battleground between Jesus and the spiritual antagonisms which are against human life and human character. I am quite well aware that in these days one speaks in an atmosphere of unbelief in regard to these spiritual forces. "Our wrestling is not against flesh and blood but against the principalities, against the powers, against the world-rulers of this darkness, against the spiritual hosts of wickedness in heavenly places." All of the New Testament writers believed in the antagonism of spiritual personalities outside human life, in fallen angels, in demons marshaled and mastered by Lucifer, the son of the morning, fallen from heaven. There in the Cross is seen the last battle between Jesus and these forces. Again and again He came into open conflict with them. In the wilderness the prince of the power of the air was dragged into the light, and Jesus entering into conflict with him, mastered him by standing wholly within the will of God. The same voice spoke through Peter at Cæsarea Philippi; and in the Garden of Gethsemane its echo was heard in the very prayer that Jesus offered. All the way the forces of evil were against Him in His pathway of holiness and righteousness. The apostle declares that in the Cross He finally triumphed over them, making a show of them, mastering all the underworld of evil. Therefore, when we enter on the life of faith, and put our lives under subjection to the Lord Christ, we begin to fight against a defeated foe, and we serve under the Captain of Salvation Who already has met and vanquished the enemy. Not ultimately and finally in our experience yet is the victory won, but in the measure in which we follow Him Who never loses a battle we too are victorious.

Perhaps I may put all this into another form and say, if we will be quite honest about our failure in the Christian life, about the sins we committed yesterday even though we are children of God, about those hours in which we yielded to temptation and grieved the Holy Spirit, and smirched the spotless linen of our purity, and disgraced the name of our Lord, we all know that we failed because we did not fight under the orders of the King, but leaving our proper habitation of loyalty to Him, walked in the way of temptation, and attempted in our own strength to overcome, and thus were defeated.

I can yet sin, being allured and defeated by the foe. I need not sin for the foe is mastered by my King, Who has bruised the head of the serpent, and if I follow Him the serpent's head is bruised under my feet also by virtue of the victory my Lord has won.

Fifth, the New Testament declares holiness of character to be possible because it is already, in germ and potentiality, imparted to the believer. When Paul wrote his first letter to the Corinthians he did not write to Christian people who were living as they ought to have lived: "I, brethren, could not speak unto you as unto spiritual, but as unto carnal." They were divided among themselves, were careless of their Church discipline, were lending themselves to some of the unclean practices of the pagan world in the midst of which they lived. Yet to these people he said, "Ye were washed . . . sanctified . . . justified," by which he meant to say that in the hour in which they rested in Jesus Christ all the potentiality for the fulfilment of God's ideal was given to them. There is no man or woman who has really rested on Jesus, and received by the gift of the Spirit of God His life in the soul, but that in that reception has received all the forces needed for living this life. Everything that is necessary for holiness is mine in Christ.

Sixth, the New Testament declares holiness of character to be possible because the whole sanctified territory is possessed by the Spirit of God.

I go back again to that Corinthian letter, and I read these remarkable statements made to these very people. "Ye are a temple of the living God," not, Ye may become a temple of the living God. "The Spirit of God dwelleth in you," not, He will come and dwell in you if you pray long enough, and wait long enough. "If any man hath not the Spirit of Christ, he is none of His"! That is the clear, sharp, dividing line between the man of faith and the man of the world; the one is a man indwelt by the Spirit of God, while the other lacks that Indweller.

Are we really Christ's? Have we believed into His name, and received absolution? Then He calls us His own; then we are the temple of the Holy Spirit; then the Holy Spirit is at this moment dwelling within us. We may be locking up certain chambers of the temple from the administration and arbitration of the Spirit, but we are the temple of the Holy Spirit. Hear the great promise, "I will dwell in them," the resident God; "and walk in them," the active Deity; "and I will be their God," the governing One. These are the promises of God, and these things the apostle wrote, not to a company of men and women who were living on the highest height of Christian experience, but to a church of men and women who were sadly and awfully failing. When next, in the hour of stress and temptation, we are tempted to declare that it is not possible to live the holy life, let us remember this, "We are the temple of the living God." We must find some other reason for our failure, for there is no reason why we should fail if we are submitted to that Indweller.

Seventh, and finally, the New Testament declares holiness of character to be possible because of the limitless resources at the disposal of the believer.

In the Colossian letter we have Paul's great argument concerning the mystery of Christianity. He begins with the widest circle of the mystery, that of the Church. Then he passes to an inner mystery, that of the individual membership of the Church, "Christ in you." Finally, he comes to the ultimate mystery, that of Christ Himself. In the course of that argument he makes two statements: first, "In Him dwelleth all the fulness of the Godhead bodily"; second, "in Him ye are made full." If, then, I declare that the life of holiness is not possible I affirm that Christ is not able to make me holy, or that the statement that all He is, He is for me and in me, that all the resources of His wisdom and might are put at my disposal, is not true.

Such is the teaching of the New Testament. May we be constrained by the Spirit of God to bring our lives to its measurement and standard, and if the doing of it searches us, scorches us, shames us, so much the better for us and for the world, and for the Kingdom of God, if as response to such searching and scorching and shame we yield ourselves anew to Christ, that He may in us fulfil all the high purposes of His will.

In conclusion, let us return to the passage with which we commenced. "That ye may be *blameless*." There is a very great difference between that and "faultless." The New Testament never suggests that it is possible for the Christian man to be faultless in this life. At last, when the work is all done, when the Potter has perfectly molded the vessel to ultimate perfection, then we shall be faultless. He will present us faultless before the throne. But we can be blameless here and now. I do not think I can better illustrate the difference between faultless and blameless than by using an old illustration. I think it was first used by Mr. John McNeil, of Australia, in his little volume on the Spirit-filled life. I remember reading and being impressed by it; but it became vivid to me when it happened in my own experience. I will use the illustration from that experience. When in 1896 I first crossed the Atlantic there came to me the first letter from my first boy. He was then about six years old. The spelling was individualistic, the grammar original. Whenever he referred to himself he wrote the personal pronoun with a small letter. I did not correct that, for we all grow out of it quite soon enough. It was a very faulty letter, but I have it yet. I cherish it, for it was blameless. Love prompted it. Love did the best it could at six years of age. I had another letter from him last week. If I put them side by side the last is no more blameless than the first, but it is far less faulty.

"That ye may be blameless, and *harmless*." Harmlessness always grows out of blamelessness. In a beautiful phrase the two things are combined, "Children of God without blemish," that is, such children that the Father can say He is pleased with them. He will not announce it to your neighbor, and you will not announce it either. If you announce it we shall question it. It is a secret the Father whispers in the ear of His child, "without blemish." Have no anxiety about the opinion of your neighbor, but be very anxious about the opinion of your Father. "Blessed is the man," said the psalmist, "unto whom the Lord imputeth not iniquity." He did not say, Blessed is the man unto whom his neighbor imputeth not iniquity. It is infinitely easier to please God than any man or woman ever born. He is more tender, more gentle. "Children of God without blemish." I know the call is to a life, high, noble, pure, but I know the God Who calls. He is a God of patience; He judges the motive, the aspiration. If I am His child, though I tremble and fail, He in infinite love counts my life blameless when the master passion of the whole endeavor is the pleasing of His heart.

How can I live this blameless and harmless life? Go back to the words which immediately precede. "Work out your own salvation with fear and trembling; for it is God which worketh in you." I am to work out that which He by the power of the Spirit works in. I am to translate into manifestation all that He works in mind, and heart, and will, as I yield myself to Him. So holiness is not to be obtained by climbing to a height, it is to be lived by being a little child keeping close to the side of the Father, and following Christ by the guidance of the Spirit.

CHAPTER XXIII

HOLINESS: CONDITIONS

Having therefore these promises, beloved, let us cleanse ourselves from all defilement of flesh and spirit, perfecting holiness in the fear of God.
II CORINTHIANS 7:1.

IN THE FIRST STUDY IN THIS SERIES ON HOLINESS I attempted to answer the inquiry, Is holiness of character possible in the present life? declaring that the New Testament affirms its possibility. We now take one step further, and consider the teaching of the New Testament concerning the conditions on which we may live the life of holiness.

We already have insisted that according to New Testament teaching holiness is a condition of character. It is not necessarily the consummation of character. In other words, holiness is perfect health of soul rather than its ultimate perfection.

Starting with the great declaration made in the prophecy of Zechariah concerning the mission of the coming Messiah, that "He shall deliver us from our enemies, that we may serve Him in holiness and righteousness," we sought to discover both the difference and the relationship between holiness and righteousness. Holiness is rectitude of character. Righteousness is rectitude of conduct. Holiness as rectitude of character is the possible present experience of the children of God because it is the will of their Father that they should be holy; because in order to make them holy Christ came; and because the object of the Spirit's work in them is the realization of that good, and perfect, and acceptable will of God. At the close of last Sunday morning's service one of my deacons drew my attention to a very remarkable and beautiful definition of holiness from the pen of John Morley. I want to read it to you. It appears in the latest volume of *Miscellanies:*

> It is not the same as duty; still less is it the same as religious belief. It is a name for an inner grace of nature, an instinct of the soul, by which, though knowing of earthly appetites and worldly passions, the spirit, purifying itself of these, and independent of all reason, argument, and the fierce struggles of the will, dwells in living, patient, and confident communion with the unseen Good.

When you have written Good you have written God: when you have written God you have written Good. Mr. Morley writes Good where we would write God. I have no desire to discuss the attitude of Mr. Morley. Such writing as that bids me forevermore suspend my judgment. I do not believe we are so far apart as some imagine. That is the finest brief exposition of what holiness is that I have ever seen. Nevertheless, what is not told me in that exposition is what I supremely want to know. Is holiness an instinct of the soul in some, and therefore forevermore impossible to others? How can I get into such "living, patient, and confident communion with the unseen Good" as to enable me in the spirit to purify myself of earthly appetites and worldly passions, and so live in the power of that unseen grace? The description is a beautiful one. It is the description of a man who has seen; but there is no explanation of how a struggling, sin-sick soul like myself can find its way into that experience. I am not criticizing Mr. Morley. He made no attempt to unlock the secret. He described the grace. It is, however, at this point that Christianity delivers its central message, and it is here that I find the supreme and lonely splendor of the Christian religion. It comes to men who are in all respects unlike that description, and declares to them that they also can be made holy, and that not by effort of the will, not by struggling as within themselves. How, then? The answer to that inquiry is the theme of this meditation.

"Having therefore these promises, beloved, let us cleanse ourselves from all defilement of flesh and spirit, perfecting holiness in the fear of God." This verse stands as the first of the seventh chapter in our Bible; but it ought not to be the first verse of a new chapter; it is the completion of the previous chapter. Its central injunction is "let us cleanse ourselves from all defilement of flesh and spirit"; the basis of the apostolic appeal is, "Having therefore these promises"; the issue of the cleansing enjoined is, "perfecting holiness in the fear of God." Let us turn to the basis of appeal. It is that because by it we are driven to inquiry concerning the promises to which the writer makes reference.

"Having therefore these promises." What promises? We turn to the words at the close of the previous chapter. I take out quite bluntly and somewhat awkwardly the actual promises to which the apostle is making reference. "I will dwell in them. . . . I will walk in them. . . . I will be their God. . . . I will receive you . . . I will be to you a Father. . . . you shall be to Me sons and daughters." "Having therefore these promises, beloved, let us cleanse ourselves." These promises fall into two series. The first series reveals the secrets of strength. "I will dwell in them"; God's promise to be resident in His people. "I will walk in them"; the symbolic language that tells that the resident God is also active in His people. "I will be their God"; the final word in the first movement in the series of promises indicating that the God resident and active is governing as Sovereign, as absolute Lord. These are the promises. "I will dwell in them . . . I will walk in them . . . I will be their God."

Then the second series in the group indicates the method by which we enter into this experience, "I will receive you . . . I will be to you a Father." Remember that promise of Fatherhood is not a promise of philanthropy in our sense of the word merely. It is not a promise that God will open an orphanage and act as though He were our Father. That promise has in it all the deep, mysterious, fundamental values of evangelical Christianity. The word of the ancient economy was gracious and beautiful, "Like as a Father pitieth." But this is not that. This is more than that, "I will be a Father." I will give you of My very nature. You shall partake of it, be related to Me by that intimate bond which is the result of regeneration. And "you shall be to Me sons and daughters." "Having therefore these promises, beloved, let us cleanse ourselves from all defilement of flesh and spirit, perfecting holiness in the fear of God."

I am very conscious of how hurried and fragmentary a method that is in dealing with the promises. I have gone back to them only that we may remember them. I may summarize them, and make this declaration. In order to perfect holiness by fulfilling the personal responsibility of putting away all defilement of flesh and spirit, there must first be the immanent and indwelling God. Where that is so human responsibility begins in the matter of holiness. In other words, I have no right to speak to a man whose whole life is being lived away from, apart from, in rebellion against, God, and charge him to be holy. He has no responsibility concerning holiness. He cannot be holy. To the children of God the appeal may be made. To those who have been received, to those to whom He has become in the new and mystic and gracious and spacious sense of the New Testament a Father, to those who are in very deed His sons and daughters, partakers of His life, sharers of His nature, heirs of all that He is, to those there is responsibility—we must begin there. It seems to me that such a declaration is at once a word full of comfort, and a word that burns and searches and scorches like a fire. Have we struggled along after this ideal of holiness—whether we call it by that name or not matters very little? Have we seen something of the fair vision described in the paragraph I read to you from the pen of a man who honestly, sincerely, is not sure of the things which we do most surely believe? Have we seen the vision, have we struggled after it, but never attained to it? Then let us earnestly inquire whether we have ever begun at the right point by the reception of the life of God. On the other hand, are we indeed struggling after the ideal, knowing that we are children of God? Then let us take heart, "Having therefore these promises." Yet we must not forget that there is the process, "let us cleanse ourselves from all defilement of flesh and spirit, perfecting holiness in the fear of God." The first great necessity is personal, actual, definite relationship with God. The indwelling God is the secret of holiness in human character, and consequently also the energy of righteousness in human conduct.

These things being granted, let us now consider this injunction, "let us cleanse ourselves." What are the conditions upon which we may do this. They have often been enumerated. I do not propose to do any other than to take certain old words of which we have all made use for very many years. These are the conditions. Conviction, renunciation, surrender, and faith. The first is the reason of the rest. The last is the power in which the others are carried out.

Let us leave the central two, and take the first and last, conviction and faith. In certain senses they are identical. Still, the two words do indicate two phases of the one tremendous fact. Conviction is the first thing, and conviction is faith. Yet there may be conviction without that activity of faith which brings us into the realization of all that which our heart is seeking. Faith is conviction, but it is conviction active. The faith that saves, faith in the initial stages of the Christian life and all the process of discipline of Christian life is not conviction merely; but yielding to, obedience to, abandonment to conviction. Where conviction is answered by active obedience, there you have faith that brings into living contact with all the resources of power. There are certain things that one is compelled to repeat again and again in very many connections. The faith that saves is not faith *about*, but faith *into*. Those familiar with the Greek New Testament will remember how perpetually we have the use of the preposition *eis* with the accusative, which indicates motion into. Belief into is more than belief about. Belief about is conviction. Belief into is conviction compelling activity. Belief about is conviction of the light. Belief into is walking in the light. There must first be conviction if there is to be holiness. There must also be faith, that is, obedience to conviction.

Now the two words, "renunciation" and "surrender," are valuable because they indicate the activity of faith following upon conviction. Conviction is God's gift. It comes like a flash of lightning to the soul of man, unsought, unexpected, uncompelled by mental activity. The great conviction comes in the midst of a service, comes in the silence of our own home, comes when and where we least expect it. I recently had a conversation with one who told me she had been brought up in another faith, in a home that knows nothing of Christ and will not have anything to do with Him. She read, *The Wide, Wide World*, years ago, and there was born in her heart the conviction that it was desirable to be as good as Ellen. It was forbidden her to read or know anything about Christ, but some years after she read Emerson's essays. Again she saw this selfsame Christ, saw Him portrayed as perfect Man. Then said she, "I will read my New Testament on that basis. I will not think of Him as Christ but as a great man." So she read the New Testament. When she put it down she said, "He is not merely a man, but my Lord and my God." Conviction came when she read *The Wide, Wide World*. It was a strange way. I am not advising anyone to look for conviction in fiction. But God does avail Himself of many ways. Through that book there came the conviction of the beauty of holiness to this girl. That is the first thing. It comes in many ways, but it must come.

It is important that we should know what this conviction really means, and therefore we recall the words of Jesus. Speaking of the Spirit of Truth, He said, "He, when He is come, will *convict* the world in respect of sin, and of righteousness, and of judgment; of sin, because they believe not on Me; of righteousness, because I go to the Father, and ye behold Me no more: of judgment, because the prince of this world hath been judged." Mark in the briefest way the meaning of that great declaration. This is the threefold conviction that always precedes holiness. The conviction of sin is conviction as to what it really is, rejection of God. The conviction of righteousness is conviction of its possibility because the Man Jesus has overcome all enemies, and passed triumphantly to the presence of God. The conviction of judgment is conviction of victory. The prince of this world is judged, and therefore all our enemies are defeated. This is the preliminary conviction. I repeat that we cannot compel it. It comes in the darkness of some lonely night, in the midst of the great multitude, by the silent voice of Nature, in the thunder or in the lightning. Until there is that conviction there can be no holiness. I am bound once again to repeat that we cannot compel it. It is the gift of God. I pause resolutely, carefully at this point, for someone will say, For that conviction I am waiting! Are you quite sure? Will you be perfectly honest? Has it not already come? The moment we recognize that this conviction is the gift of God we are in danger of making that fact the way of escape from responsibility. We are in danger of saying that we cannot be holy because we have never had that conviction.

Let us be honest and sincere. In the hidden secret shrine of our inner spiritual life have we not already seen the sinfulness of sin? Has no profound conviction ever come to us of the exceeding beauty of holiness? It may be that as I read that brief extract from John Morley we said, Yes, in the deepest of our souls. If so, that was the hour of conviction, if it had never come before.

That conviction having come, there must be obedience to it. That is faith. Faith, in the presence of sin, expresses itself in renunciation and by surrender. We have read the great promises.

Side by side with the promises, there are injunctions and conditions. These injunctions and conditions teach what is meant by renunciation:

> Be not unequally yoked with unbelievers: for what fellowship have righteousness and iniquity? or what com-

munion hath light with darkness? And what concord hath Christ with Belial? or what portion hath a believer with an unbeliever? And what agreement hath a temple of God with idols? for we are a temple of the living God; even as God said, I will dwell in them, and walk in them; and I will be their God, and they shall be my people. Wherefore

> Come ye out from among them, and be ye
> separate, saith the Lord,
> And touch no unclean thing;
> And I will receive you,
> And I will be to you a Father,
> And ye shall be to me sons and daughters.

This is not my imagination. This is the word of inspiration.

It is an explanation of the meaning of renunciation, and is closely connected with the great promises. It is a call to renunciation of all known wrong. "Come ye out from among them, and be ye separate," that is, separate from sinning men and women; "touch no unclean thing," that is, renunciation of all known sin. If we would perfect holiness in the fear of God we are called to immediate and irrevocable renunciation of all that we know to be out of harmony with the mind and will of our Lord. Do not let us misplace the emphasis of this word of the apostle, for I think that by so doing we rob it of its strength. He does not say, If you will have no fellowship with evil things you shall become a temple of the living God. His declaration is rather, Have no fellowship with them, because you are the temple of the living God. To me the difference is almost overwhelming in intensity of appeal. If I am told that I am to perfect holiness, that I am to have no fellowship with sin and evil things, in order to become the temple of God, I am filled with fear because I am so weak and frail. That, however, is not the apostolic method. He reminds me, first, of the strength which is mine, and then urges me to Holiness. Because we are temples of God, we are not to desecrate the temple. God is in us. We are not to insult the Indweller by the retention of things that are unlike Him. This is the groundwork of appeal.

Because of these facts we are called on to put away all the things we know to be wrong, in our friendships, in our habits, in our inner thinking. These things must be put away or there can be no perfecting holiness. The threefold definition of sin is very familiar. Sin is transgression of the law. Sin is neglect to do right. The questionable thing is sin whether it have the appearance of good or evil. We are to decide by that threefold definition of sin what things need to be put away. The things we know to be wrong. The things we have neglected to do which are right. The things about which we are doubtful.

Of all these there must be renunciation. "Come ye out from among them, and be ye separate; and touch no unclean thing." There must be no excuse, no compromise, no delay. When we deal with sins God will deal with sin. When we resolutely determine to put away the things we know to be sinful He will purify the center and create in us that grace of holiness which expresses itself in graciousness and rectitude of character.

How are we to know the things that are to be put away? "Awake, thou that sleepest, and arise from the dead, and Christ shall shine upon thee." This is the testing promise. If we desire to know we must awake from our lethargy, sleep, carelessness; awake from the influence of opiates that have made us lack sensitiveness to the will of our God, awake and put ourselves honestly confronting Christ, and He will shine upon us, and in the shining luster of His glory we shall discover the things that are unlike Him, and those are the things that are to be put away.

No man imagines it is possible to live the holy life if he is resolutely keeping sin in his life, something in his habits, his home, or his business. We know that these things grieve the Lord. We excuse them, and holiness is never perfected, and we lack the grace and loveliness of character which ought to be the testimony to the power of our Lord because we have not yet begun to be determined to renounce the hidden things of darkness and to put out of our lives the things that are unlike our Master.

Beyond renunciation, there must be surrender. By that I mean the yielding of ourselves up to God. In the first letter to these Corinthian Christians the apostle uses these words, "Know ye not that your body is a temple of the Holy Ghost which is in you, which ye have from God? and ye are not your own; for ye were bought with a price: glorify God therefore in your body." In the letter to the Romans he says, "I beseech you, therefore, brethren, by the mercies of God, to present your bodies a living sacrifice, holy, acceptable to God, which is your spiritual worship." I deliberately adopt the marginal reading there. That is a wonderful *verse*. Study its psychology. "I beseech *you* . . . to present *your* bodies." Your body is not you. The apostle is not dealing with the body, he is dealing with the essential man. Or in the Corinthian epistle, "your body is a temple of the Holy Ghost which is in you . . . glorify God therefore in your body." You glorify God in it: you are not it: you indwell it. The body is the tabernacle, the tent of the man, not the man. I pray you mark the significance of this, and see the reason for laying emphasis on these two passages. What is surrender? To give myself over to the Lord. That is, all my spiritual life. How am I to do that, or demonstrate that I have done it? By presenting the body in which I dwell. That is spiritual worship. We thought spiritual worship consisted in singing hymns and praying. All these things are spiritual, or should be, but spiritual worship is the body dedicated to the Lord.

> Take my hands, and let them move
> At the impulse of Thy love;
> Take my feet and let them be
> Swift and beautiful for Thee.

That is surrender. That is not merely that my hands and feet are at His disposal, but that I am His, and that I indicate to Him and to the world my abandonment by putting the members of my body at His disposal and refusing to allow brain, or heart, or head, or hands, or feet to act save under His command and in His sacred service. The intellect, emotion, will surrendered, and consequently the whole body acting under His direction.

The putting away of the evil thing and surrender to the Lord of the body are the only conditions. Wherever these conditions are fulfilled the promises are fulfilled. "Having therefore these promises"—"I will dwell in them . . . I will walk in them . . . I will be their God . . . I will receive you . . . I will be to you a Father, and ye shall be to Me sons and daughters." Where the evil thing condemned is put away and the whole life is surrendered, God has His chance. That is what He wants.

Heart of mine, this is the trouble with thee, thou hast not given thy Master His chance. I have locked up some chamber in the temple. I have barred Him from entering into some activity of the mind. I have retained some place in my emotional nature for other than Himself. I have not given Him his chance.

Do we desire the holy life? Here are the conditions. Conviction He gives. That we are to respond to by the faith that renounces evil, puts away sin, abandons the life to Him. Holiness is not realized by my endeavor, but by His working in me, when I have given Him His chance.

May God lead every one of us not merely to conviction, but to the faith that renounces the things He disapproves, and surrenders to Him all that is His by the indwelling of His Spirit.

CHAPTER XXIV

HOLINESS: ITS FRUIT

Wherefore if any man is in Christ, he is *a new creature: the old things are passed away; behold, they are become new. But all things are of God.*
II CORINTHIANS 5:17, 18.

THE WORDS, *"he is,"* WHICH APPEAR IN OUR BIBLES ARE supplied, and do not exist in the actual text. Our revisers have suggested an alternative reading, *"there is* a new creation." I venture to adopt that partially, omitting the words *"there is,"* and reading the text thus, "Wherefore if any man is in Christ, a new creation, the old things have passed away; behold, they are become new. But all things are of God." The phrase "a new creation" is thus placed in apposition to the phrase "in Christ"; and is an exposition of it. If any man is *in Christ,* he is therefore *a new creation.*

What then is the difference between that new man, and the man he was before? It is expressed on the negative side in the words "The old things are passed away." The apostle is careful at this point not to create the possibility of a false impression. "The old things are passed away; behold *they,*" the same things, "are become new." What, then, is the difference on the positive side? "All things are of God." In his letter to the Romans, when dealing with man in his sin, by citation from the Psalms, the apostle describes the attitude of the sinner in the words, "There is no fear of God before

316

their eyes." Let us put the final sentences of that description into immediate opposition to my text.

Their feet are swift to shed blood;
Destruction and misery are in their ways;
And the ways of peace they have not known;
There is no fear of God before their eyes (Rom. 3:15-18).

If any man is in Christ a new creature; the old things are passed away; behold, they are become new. But all things are of God (II Cor. 5:17, 18).

The contrast is graphic. By bringing together these two passages we see exactly what the difference is, or ought to be, between the Christian man and the man who is not yet a Christian.

In this fourth study of our series on the subject of holiness we are to consider its fruit. In his Roman letter Paul charged his readers, "Have your fruit unto sanctification," that is, "Have your fruit unto holiness." What is that fruit? What are the manifestations of holiness of character?

Holiness results in the passing of all the distinctive excellencies of Christianity from the realm of theory into that of experience. The ideal which we have seen and admired will become the real in actual life, in the measure in which we are holy in character.

I am conscious that such a statement may make it appear as though holiness were the privilege of the few, rather than the possible experience of all who share the life of Christ. There are one or two simple things which therefore need to be clearly stated at this point. First there can be no holiness save by the work of the Holy Spirit in the life. Second, granted the work of the Spirit, the normal Christian life is holy life, and the measure in which we fail of holiness is the measure in which we fail of Christianity. Yet here again extreme care is necessary. I would not have that misinterpreted to the discouragement of any struggling soul. I do not deny your Christianity any more than I deny my own, because neither you nor I have yet realized the character of holiness in all its fulness; yet you will admit, if you think carefully, that the measure in which we lack holiness is the measure in which we lack the true normal Christian character. Holiness is not the preserve of an aristocracy in the family of God, in our ordinary sense of that word "aristocracy." The whole family of God is an aristocracy, or ought to be. Aristocracy, what does it mean? Forgive me if I am elementary enough to remind you that the root significance of the word is *best strength*. That is what an aristocracy ought to be, and the best strength of the world ought to be the Christian men and women of the world. Holiness as a blessing, second or otherwise, is not the privilege of a select or elect few. It is the normal life of the Christian, according to the purpose and power of God. Holiness is not ultimate perfection. Holiness is the condition which makes it possible for us to "grow up in all things into Him, which is the Head." Holiness is not perfection of consummation. It is simply health in the spiritual life.

Our text indicates a line and suggests a method by which we may understand the fruit of holiness. "If any man is in Christ, a new creation; the old things are passed away; behold, they are become new." He will still live in the same house, in the same city, with the same people; following the same profession, the same business, but everything will be changed. The old things are passed away, because he is himself a new creation. If the old things have been made new because the man in Christ is made new, and his vision is therefore new, what are the new things? The whole change is summarized in the words of the apostle, "All things are of God." Let us now inquire quite simply how that works out.

The first change is one of personal consciousness. In order that we may see the difference, let us consider a man who is not yet a Christian—and I do not propose taking that man on the lowest level, that is, measuring by the ordinary standards of observation; I desire rather to look at the man of the world, the man who is not a Christian, on the highest level attainable by him. What are the dominant notes in the consciousness of such a man? May I rapidly state them and then dwell on each for a moment or two. Love of self, admiration of the world, passion for ownership of goods, great love for kindred and friends, patriotism.

Now, "if any man is in Christ, a new creation; the old things are passed away; behold, they are become new. But all things"—these very things—"are of God."

Love of self. I begin there because that is the root principle of all godless life. If I talk of admiration of the world, passion for the ownership of goods, love for kindred and friends, patriotism, we are all ready to admit that all these things are admirable; but the most selfish man is ever ready to denounce selfishness in other people. I am increasingly impressed with the fact that selfishness is a hateful thing to the mind of humanity, unregenerate or regenerate, and yet it is the master passion of all life apart from Jesus Christ. It has many means of expression, self-indulgence, self-consideration, self-consciousness, but the man of the world is inevitably self-centered. All the circles are drawn around self; the home, society, the nation, the world.

Admiration of the world. That always means admiration of something in the world that is a little out of reach. The man in the slum gazes occasionally on the man who lives in the West End, and admires—however much he professes not to—his luxury, and would obtain it if he could, notwithstanding all he declares to the contrary. The man who is higher in the social scale looks still a little higher, and admires what he sees. There is an old proverb, which I quote, and leave you to think about when you are alone, "A nod from a lord is breakfast for a fool." There is a great deal of philosophy in it. Men look a little up, and a little further up; and will scheme and plan, and even put their wealth at the disposal of kings in order that it may be said that they are the companions of kings. Kings see the glory of the world and forevermore are seeking for that enlargement of empire that ministers to pride. Come with me back to the desolate wilderness, and look at one lone Man facing the great foe of the race, who showed Him all the kingdoms of the world and the glory of them, and offered to give Him all if only He would give him homage. That temptation in the wilderness was the dragging out into clear daylight of the perpetual methods of Satan. Men everywhere are admiring the world.

Passion for the ownership of goods. I need not in this particular age dwell on that. It is the driving force of this feverish age. The mere passion for possession has caused war. That is an ultimate statement, which I do not now stay to deal with more fully. No one denies that a man of the world desires power.

Love of kindred and friends. That is a gracious and beautiful thing, I freely admit; and it exists among men of the world quite apart from Christianity.

Patriotism. That is love of fatherland, love of one's own country, the love which calls forth the long letters about lost ideals and new ideals, and the necessity for teaching our children the fact that they must sacrifice themselves for the making of their country.

Now at once I may be challenged, by those who in astonishment inquire if I intend to affirm that holiness means that these things cease? Let us be perfectly clear about this. I mean only, but I mean certainly exactly, what the apostle says, "If any man is in Christ, a new creation; the old things are passed away; behold, they are become new; but all things are of God."

To begin at the center. The man in Christ Jesus is no longer self-centered, but God-centered. Let the writer of this letter tell us his own experience in language we have quoted so often, and never perhaps yet perfectly understood, "I have been crucified with Christ; yet *I live*." I have not lost my identity, but it is changed. My personality has not ceased to be, but it is remade. "I live" is the declaration of the positive immediately following the affirmation of the negative. Let us still be careful, for the apostle continues, "Yet no longer I, but Christ liveth in me." That is true of the normal Christian life. That is the central thing in holiness. In order to bring men to that the words of Jesus were perpetually severe. "If any man would come after Me, let him deny *himself*, and take up his cross daily, and follow Me." We quote that searching word and even sing it, but it does not bite, and burn, and break us as it ought to do. That word ought to put every one of us on the cross. "Let him deny himself." The Christian man is a man who at the center of his own being is no longer enthroned, having dominion over his own life, but a man who has put Christ on the throne. That is the fundamental difference.

Then as to the world this selfsame writer says, "the cross

of our Lord Jesus Christ, through which the world has been crucified unto me, and I unto the world." Does that for a single moment mean that he had lost interest in the world, and the affairs of the world? Nay verily, for this is the man who interprets for the Christian Church, and for all time, if we will but listen to it, the agony of the world, "The whole creation groaneth and travaileth in pain." Here, then, is the difference. Holiness of character means, first of all, the circumferencing of the life around the center, Christ, and then that the world is seen as it really is. Tinsel is known as tinsel, and the touch of decay is seen on all the glory that men admire. Nevertheless, behind the false the true glory is discovered. The Christian man is the man who has lost his admiration for the coronet because he is conscious of the aching brow on which it rests. The Christian man has no eyes for the purple, because the eyes of his heart see the broken heart underneath it. It was Henry Ward Beecher who said that Paul had no love for Greek art because he did not describe a Greek temple in any of his epistles. I do not believe that for a moment. I think he was a master of architecture. If you study his description of the building of the Christian Church it is the language of a man who knew a great deal about architecture. When Pausanius came to Athens he described the temples and buildings, and wrote of the culture and poetry; but only one brief, palpitating account is given by Luke of Paul in Athens, and this is it. "His spirit was in a paroxysm as he beheld the city full of idols." The Christian man does not withdraw himself from the world, has not lost his sense of beauty in the world; but he sees the world's agony, and is so busy attempting to deal with it that he has no admiration for the glitter and tinsel of the things wherewith the men of the world, hungry all the time for God, are attempting to satisfy themselves. His admiration for the world is over.

Ownership of goods. The Christian man believes that Christ knew exactly what He was talking about when He said to His disciples, "Lay not up for yourselves treasure upon the earth"—mark the fine satire of Jesus—"where moth and rust doth consume, and thieves break through and steal; but lay up for yourselves treasures in heaven." The Christian man has lost his passion to own goods for the sake of the power such possession gives him, because the possession of Christ gives him a new and beneficent power. The Christian man will no longer devote himself wholly, absolutely, utterly, to the work of amassing wealth simply to possess it. That does not mean for a single moment that the Christian man will not be a successful man of business; that he is to count himself somehow doing wrong if his enterprises succeed. It does mean that the Christian man will never deviate one hair's breadth from the line of rectitude in order to make wealth; and it does mean that when he has made it he says forevermore, This is the means by which I may lay up treasure in heaven. "Make to yourselves friends *by means of* the mammon of unrighteousness; that, when it"—the mammon—"shall fail, they"—the friends you have made—"may receive you into the eternal tabernacles." If you are wealthy men, and Christian men, your wealth is your opportunity to make a fortune, only the dividends are postponed to the other side. What are the dividends? Men and women you have helped. Souls that by the proper use of your wealth you have uplifted. Boys and girls you have delivered from that hell of time and eternity to which they were going but for your help. To put the whole case into a sentence, the man of the world amasses wealth until wealth holds him; the Christian man may be successful in business, but he forevermore holds his wealth in trust for his Lord. That is the difference.

Concerning the love of kindred and friends, many people are troubled by the words of Jesus, "He that loveth father or mother more than Me is not worthy of Me." "If any man cometh unto Me, and hateth not his own father, and mother, and wife, and children, and brethren, and sisters, yea and his own life also, he cannot be My disciple." Does this mean that the life of holiness is a life of hardness, a life out of which all human affection passes? To ask the question is at once to have a negative reply. Jesus Himself so loved the will of God that He said, "Who is My mother, and who are My brethren? . . . Whosoever shall do the will of My Father which is in heaven, he is My brother, and sister and mother." Yet, in His dying agony, with the awful passion of the world's redemption breaking His heart, He thought of His mother, and handed her over to John to love her and take care of her. He Who did that does not mean that we are to cease to love father or mother, wife or children, brothers or sisters. The man of the world for the love of the one whom he loves will in the hour of crisis often do the sinful thing; but the Christian man will not allow love of father or mother, wife or child, to make him disloyal to his Lord and to truth. That is the difference.

What of patriotism? Does the Christian man cease to be patriotic? By no means, but he has a new outlook on national life and national greatness. He insists that "righteousness exalteth a nation; but sin is a reproach to any people." The Christian man forevermore lives there. He does not care at all how big the empire may be, but he does care enormously whether it be pure. I am going a step further than that. The

Christian man in the fulness of Christian experience ceases to be particularly anxious about the national greatness of his own people in his passion for the national greatness of all peoples. When leaving His disciples, Jesus Christ said, "All authority hath been given unto Me in heaven and on earth. Go ye therefore, and disciple the nations." The Christian man recognizes the right of the other nations as well as that of his own. He cannot have any interest in anything that goes to the making of his own nation if by making that nation great some weaker people is harmed and hurt and downtrodden. "He made of one every nation of men." Jesus Christ to-day loves as devotedly, as passionately, as perfectly the nation lowest in the scale of civilization as the highest: the German as much as the Englishman, the Boer as much as the Briton. The measure in which we are Christian men is the measure in which we climb this height of the recognition of the oneness of humanity, and entertain a great love for it.

What has all this to do with holiness? Everything, because it has to do with righteousness. There will be no righteousness in our dealing with men unless there be this holiness of character, the tides of the Christ life surging through the life of His child, creating His consciousness in the presence of all these things. The old things are passed away. No longer self-centered but Christ-centered, therefore the master passion of the life not to please self but to please Him. The old things are passed away, therefore no longer admiration of that which is superficial in the glory of the world, but the recognition of the tremendous beauty and glory of the world that God has made, together with recognition of its pain and suffering; and an earnest desire to hold out a helping hand to those who need. No longer a passionate desire to amass a fortune; but diligence in business in order that there may be possession of wealth to use for the glory of God in the good of humanity. No longer that inordinate love of kindred and friends that will permit us to do the wrong thing; but a tender love of kindred and friends, the outcome of devotion to Jesus Christ, so strong that no wrong thing can be done even for father or mother, wife or child. No longer patriotism that sings songs of war and of the greatness of one nation, but the great world-interest that takes all men into its heart and seeks to make great its own nation in order that it may uplift and ennoble the nations of the world.

As I understand the teaching of the New Testament, this is holiness. It is that inward grace of character which is not weak, soft, anæmic, able only to sing songs of spiritual experience and to see visions of the heaven which is not yet. It is that inner refinement of heart and life and soul which comes from the indwelling Christ, and makes the life strong in its relationship to the world.

That leads me to my final word. Holiness is a life of usefulness. The unalterable and unchanging purpose of God is the accomplishment of His purposes through His people. That is rendered possible through holiness of character. Cleansed vessels are the vessels that Jehovah makes use of. "Be ye clean ye that bear the vessels of the Lord," was the word of the Hebrew prophet. "Come ye out from among them, and be ye separate, saith the Lord, And touch no unclean thing," is the word of the Christian apostle. It is through holiness of character that I become a vessel ready to the hand of God for the accomplishment of His will. Surrendered instruments are those which He employs. Not only is it true that clay cannot say to the potter, What formest thou? It is true that the instrument through which he will form and fashion the clay must be plastic in his hand even as the clay is. Believing souls He trusts. The measure of my confidence in Him is the measure of His confidence in me. Let me put that in this form. Are you a man that God can trust? You are if you are a man who can trust God. Trust, again let me remind you, is not merely singing the song that declares your confidence, but it is the life of obedience that relies on God. "He made known His ways unto Moses," gave him the program of events; "His acts unto the children of Israel"; they had to wait and walk step by step. "The secret of the Lord is with them that fear Him." Has God ever told you a secret, something in your inner life that has become a flaming, fiery passion? You spoke of it and the world crucified you for doing it. The men to whom God has whispered His secrets of ultimate purpose and present plan are men absolutely at His disposal, and they have had to suffer in the world, but by their suffering the Kingdom is coming. If I want to find a highway along which God is moving toward ultimate victory I shall follow the tracks where I discover the blood of martyrs. He can tell me His secret only as I trust Him wholly.

Holiness is the work of the Spirit. When I am willing, He baptizes me into union with the life of Christ. He seals me as the property of God. He anoints me for all service. The ultimate argument for the holy life is not the perfection of life, but the fact that life being rendered perfect, becomes God's instrument in the world. That, I think, is the final appeal. In the light of that appeal my heart says,

> Lord Jesus, I long to be perfectly whole,
> I want Thee forever to live in my soul;
> Break down every idol, cast out every foe:
> Now wash me, and I shall be whiter than snow.

That, not merely that I may be whiter than snow, but that through me may flow the river, and from me may flash the light, and by me may be exercised the very power of Christ for the lifting of men and the bringing in of His Kingdom.

CHAPTER XXV

HOLINESS: HINDRANCES

Ye were running well; who did hinder you that ye should not obey the truth?

GALATIANS 5:7.

THIS IS AN OUTBURST OF APPEAL IN THE MIDST OF AN ARGUment, and incidentally reveals a failure which has many other causes and manifestations than those with which this particular letter deals. The causes in this case were Judaizing teachers. The manifestations were that these people were going back into bondage, putting their neck under a yoke from which they had been set free. The actual failure the apostle described in the words: "Ye were running well; who did hinder you?" There had been a slackening of the pace, a relaxing of endeavor. These people were characterized by dimness of vision, weakening of virtue, and absence of victory. Their Christian life was not what it ought to be, and that fact troubled the heart of the apostle. He was never anxious about orthodoxy of intellect, except as it affected orthodoxy of heart and of life. If he was eager that the one and only Gospel should be preached, with an almost fierce invective cursing the men who preached "another Gospel," it was not an intellectual anger growing out of a conviction that he alone was right, but an anger born of his conviction that when men ceased to obey the truth the fine bloom was brushed from their characters, and they themselves suffered deterioration.

HOLINESS: HINDRANCES

In this final study in the subject of holiness, let us give ourselves to personal examination, turning from theory to experience. We have defined holiness as that rectitude of character which issues in rectitude of conduct. We have declared that we believe holiness of character to be possible because it is the will of God for His children, because the work of Christ was in order to produce it, and because the ministry of the Spirit is for the administration of the work of Christ, and so for the realization of it. We have declared that the New Testament teaches that the conditions are those of renunciation of known wrong, the absolute surrender of the life to the Lordship of Jesus, and quiet, restful trust in Him. We have, moreover, considered the character of holiness in contrast to that of the man who lacks it as the selfless life, Christ-centered, and therefore love-centered and light encompassed, the character full of beauty.

Immediately we turn from theory to experience we face the fact of how far we are from realizing the character of holiness. We have seen the vision, but we have not gained the victory, and Paul's inquiry is one that we may pertinently apply to ourselves, "Who did hinder you?" In other words, if holiness be necessary to righteousness, if holiness be possible in the economy of God, if holiness be possible on the fulfilment of conditions, if holiness of character be that fair and gracious attitude of spirit which the New Testament reveals, and we lack it, why do we lack it?

In attempting to answer this inquiry, I propose first to deal with some of the answers commonly given, and, second, to examine the suggestiveness of Paul's inquiry as revealing the true answer.

It is often affirmed that *the teaching of Scripture does*

not warrant the expectation that such character is possible to us here and now.

That statement is already answered by the teaching of the New Testament which we have considered. Nevertheless, the position is maintained on the supposed authority of certain passages of Scripture which do seem to call in question the possibility. I cannot, in the course of one brief study, touch on all of these passages, but there are three principal ones which we may take by way of illustration. There is, first, the passage in the Roman letter at the close of the seventh chapter in which the apostle says: "I am carnal, sold under sin. . . . To me who would do good, evil is present." All the statements of that closing paragraph are constantly quoted, and are sincerely and honestly adduced as arguments against the possibility of having holiness of character here and now. I hope I am making myself clear that in any attempt to deal with this objection I approach the subject in sympathy with those who feel the difficulty. Some of the sweetest Christian people I have ever known have quoted that paragraph to prove it was impossible to be holy even while they were already holy.

Then there is the autobiographical message, in which Paul distinctly and clearly says: "Not that I have already obtained, or am already made perfect . . . I count not myself yet to have apprehended . . . but I press on, if so be that I may apprehend that for which also I was apprehended by Christ Jesus," thus disclaiming perfection.

And, finally, there is the passage in which John says: "If any man sin, we have an Advocate with the Father, Jesus Christ, the righteous One."

How shall we answer the sincere and honest difficulty of such as refer us to these or similar statements? First, by declaring, as a canon of interpretation, that no isolated passage or passages of Scripture can contradict its general teaching. If for a moment we could stand clear of examination of isolated passages, and think of the one message of the Bible to men, what would it be? *"Ye shall be holy: for I the Lord your God am holy."* Or if we could gather up into one brief and comprehensive sentence the whole force of Christ's message to men, to His own disciples, how should we express it? *"Ye therefore shall be perfect, as your heavenly Father is perfect."* I also have quoted isolated passages, but I have done so because I believe they express the whole burden of the message of the Word to men. Never from beginning to end does it excuse anything sinful in the life. It tells the story—thank God that it does—of men of like passions with myself; and it tells the story of their sin. It is one of the peculiar beauties of the Bible that if it presents a man, it presents him as he is. When an artist painted Cromwell, and painted out all the roughnesses on his face, he daubed the canvas, and said: "Paint me blotches and all, or paint me not at all." In the Bible men are painted blotches and all. But if the experience revealed in the Bible is the experience of men who failed and fell, how do we know that they failed and fell? What do we mean by failing and falling? We see the failure because we also know the ideal which the Bible reveals. All the things which in the lives of these men were wrong we know to be so because the standard set up is that of perfection. Dr. Margoliouth, in his book, *Lines of Defence of the Biblical Revelation*, has a remarkable passage about David, as being a man after God's own heart. Dealing with those who declare that a man who sinned as David sinned with Bathsheba could not have been a man after God's own heart, he asks if it is conceivable that any other Eastern monarch of that particular age would have taken up the position of penitence and contrition that David did, and declares that the excellence of David is seen in his attitude in the presence of sin.

The application of that illustration in the present argument is that we know the sin of David because we know the purity of the Divine ideal for him. His action is counted sinful by men who accept the Divine standard of holiness. We know the wrong of every man whose life story is told in the Bible, because we know also what God's thought for man is.

The Bible presents one Figure, Whose humanity was according to the Divine purpose and pattern, and I see the failure of all others because they stand in the fierce light of the purity and the holiness of that Life.

While that is the revelation of Scripture, taking it in its entirety, it cannot be that any single passage to be found in all its course can contradict that great ideal, or declare to men that the holiness which the Bible demands is not possible to them.

But there is another way in which this difficulty is answered. If we take each of these passages carefully, we shall see that none of them really contradicts the teaching of the Bible. It is very unfair to read the closing part of the seventh chapter of the letter to the Romans without running right on into that which follows. I read the solemn words: "I am carnal, sold under sin. . . . That which I do, I know not: for not what I would, that do I practise"; and so on and on, until at last the whole agony of the experience described expresses itself thus: "O wretched man that I am! Who shall deliver me out of the body of this death?" But the passage does not end there. The answer is immediately given. "I thank God through Jesus Christ our Lord." Then going back, and summarizing the whole description that has preceded that answer, the apostle writes: "So then I myself with the mind serve the law of God, but with the flesh the law of sin." Yes, but the apostle does not end even there. Read right on: "There is therefore now no condemnation to them that are in Christ Jesus. For the law of the Spirit of life in Christ Jesus made me free from the law of sin and of death." We are perfectly well aware of the fact that expositors differ entirely as to whether, in the closing part of the seventh chapter, Paul is describing an experience prior to regeneration, or an experience after regeneration. For a moment I do not care which. I admit the experience at the closing part of the seventh chapter. There is an experience which a man voices thus: "To me who would do good, evil is present. For I delight in the law of God after the inward man; but I see a different law in my members, warring against the law of my mind"; but it is not the ultimate experience of Christianity. The ultimate experience of Christianity is this: "The law of the Spirit of life in Christ Jesus made me free from the law of sin and of death." We have no right to quote as descriptive of the normal Christian life a passage that describes an experience from which the next passage declares deliverance to be possible. The apostle is leading us through the struggle that we all know to the revelation of the victory that we all may know if we will.

Again, in the Philippian passage, whereas it is true that the apostle says, "Not that I have already obtained, or am already made perfect . . . I count not myself yet to have apprehended," he also says: "One thing I do, forgetting the things which are behind, and stretching forward to the things which are before, I press on toward the goal"; and holiness is perfectly described in those words. When he says he has not yet apprehended, what does he mean? Follow his statement to its end, and the answer is given. "Who shall fashion anew the body of our humiliation that it may be conformed to the body of His glory?" That is to say, the work of Jesus Christ in a man will never be ultimately perfected until he sees Christ face to face with no veil between, with all the limitation of the present life forever over. The ultimate in my Christian character lies beyond this life in the spacious and far-reaching mystery of the life to come. Holiness today is not perfection of consummation, but it is perfection of condition. It is the right attitude of a human life. Holiness does not mean that there can be no advancement. Holiness is the condition for advancement, that health of the spiritual life which makes growth possible. And this is what the apostle is teaching in the Philippian letter; he is healthy, but not full-grown; holy, but not glorified.

Or if we turn to the passage in the letter of John, it is quite true John wrote words of comfort, even for sinning believers: "If any man sin, we have an Advocate with the Father, Jesus Christ the righteous"; but is it fair to make an "if" a permission? What are the words immediately preceding? "My little children, these things write I unto you, *that ye may not sin*." I submit to you, and leave my argument at that point, that it is quite unfair to quote the gracious provision made for sinning souls as an argument in favor of the impossibility of holiness. Constantly I have to thank God that it is written, "We have an Advocate with the Father"; but if I make—hear me patiently and carefully—if I make the fact of the advocacy of Jesus an excuse for sin, I am guilty of the most terrible treachery and blasphemy. "These things write I unto you that ye may not sin"; but the "if" which follows is not an argument, declaring that sin is necessary.

It is declared by others *that the experience of Christian people does not warrant the expectation.*

I speak to my own heart as also to yours when I say, in answer to that declaration, that it is a reflection on those who make it. If we say that we do not believe holiness to be possible because we have never met people who are really holy, in all kindness but in all earnestness I declare that declaration to be a reflection on the company we have been keeping, or a revelation of our own spiritual blindness. I think that is the difficulty very often when a man says he has never known men and women who lived holy lives. There was a day when a prophet, depressed by overwork, said: "I only am left. I am not better than my fathers." And what was the answer? "Yet will I leave me seven thousand . . . which have not bowed unto Baal." Let us make no mistake. There are multitudes of holy men and women—men and women of beautiful, Christly character, the very salt of the earth, its gracious light. How is it, then, that people say there are no holy men and women? No one will deny that Jesus of Nazareth was holy; yet the men of His own time said of Him: "Behold, a gluttonous man and a winebibber, a friend of publicans and sinners!" What was the meaning of such criticism? An ancient prophet of Israel declared, concerning the coming Messiah, "There is no beauty that we should desire Him." Do you imagine for a moment that the prophet meant the Messiah would lack beauty? By no means. What then? That men would be so blind that they could not see it. Paul, in writing to the Corinthians, declares that the spiritual man is spiritually discerned; and if you have seen a holy man, it was because his holiness was discerned of your own spiritual life. If you fail to discover the beauty of holiness, it is because you are unholy.

I have seen a novice in an art gallery criticizing a picture by a great master, and I have been sure of this, that while he thought he criticized the picture, the picture really criticized him. When I am told that there are no saints, I reply that the saints are close by our side, living in our home, touching us every day; but we are color-blind, and the blue and the scarlet and the purple and the fine-twined linen have no loveliness for us because the dust of death is in our eyes.

But even if it were true that holy men and women are not to be found, then remember this, that prevalent imperfection is no justification of imperfection. Is there no holy man in your circle of acquaintance? Then you be the first. Oh, but it is objected, what other men have not been we cannot be. That we do not believe in any other realm of life. If our argument is that what no man has done, no man can do, then no master picture will ever be painted, no mountain will ever be climbed, no discovery will ever be made! All high things are made possible by the men and women who lead, who make highways, who blaze their way through forests that have never before been traversed. Be a pioneer and leader. Dare to stand alone. All the resources of God are at your disposal. Take hold of them, or, rather, let them take hold of you and be the first.

There are others who say that *holiness is not a condition to be professed; that if they had the experience they would not talk about it.*

My answer to that is this: Holiness does not need to be talked about; it talks. You remember Emerson's words—I do not quote the *pisissima verba*, but the spirit of what he said— "I cannot hear what you say for listening to what you are." I repeat, holiness does not need to be talked about; it talks. I quite agree with you that the nearer a man lives to his Lord, the less he announces his nearness in actual words; but the more evident it is in tone and temper, and these are the things of holiness. But I pray you, do not urge the fact that if you possessed it you would not talk about it as an indication of the impossibility of possessing the character of holiness. Holiness is a rare and beautiful spirit which permeates and pervades the whole life, and sheds its fragrance everywhere. I remember twenty years ago, in a home in which I was staying, that in one room I always detected the fragrance of roses, and I said to my host one day, "I wish you would tell me how it is that I never come into this room without seeming to detect the fragrance of roses." He smiled, and said: "Ten years ago I was in the Holy Land, and while there I bought a small phial of otto of roses. It was wrapped in cotton wool, and as I was standing here unpacking it, suddenly I broke the bottle. I took the whole thing up, cotton wool and all, and put it into this vase." There stood a beautiful vase, and he lifted the lid, and the fragrance of the roses filled the room. That fragrance had permeated the clay of the vase, and it was impossible to enter the room without consciousness of it. If Christ be in us, the fragrance of the Rose of Sharon will pervade and permeate our whole life. We need not talk about it; but if there be no fragrance, the reason is not that if there were you would not talk of it.

There are yet others who say that *they have no desire for the character described.*

That is a most terrible confession. The death of desire is the prelude of death. Let any who lack desire ponder carefully the words of Jesus: "Blessed are they that hunger and thirst after righteousness, for they shall be filled."

In conclusion, let us examine the actual wording of Paul's inquiry. Mark well the preliminary affirmation: "Ye were running well." That to me is a most suggestive statement, and it is true of every Christian man and woman. The beginning of Christian life is ever characterized by desire and endeavor after holiness. When we begin to live a Christian life we see the goal, and we take a corresponding attitude. The men and the women who to-day decide for Christ hand their lives over in order to be what? That they may be holy. There is vast territory to be subdued, enemies to be fought and mastered, much to be done; but they see the vision, and they fall in line.

"Ye were running well." What is the trouble with you? You are a member of a church, you are still a Christian man, I do not question it for a moment, but all the bloom has gone from your character. You have become hard and mechanical and indifferent. There was a time when you sighed over your own shortcoming and failure, but not now. Why not?

"Ye were running well." Every man who first sees the face of Jesus enters into a measure of the experience of holiness. The vision of His face, the glory of His own purity is in itself an inspiration which is of the nature of holiness. Why the failure?

Now, notice the apostle's final admission, *"that ye should not obey the truth."* In that phrase you have the revelation of the whole secret of arrested development and failure. If I—who have seen the face of Jesus, and have desired to be like Him, and have set my face in the attitude He demands—am faltering in character, it is because I have refused to fulfil the conditions. There is something in my life that I retain which I know is unlike Him, and contrary to His will. There is some command He has laid on me which I have not obeyed. There broke on my vision some morning a great light on the hills, calling me to climb and leave the valleys, and I lingered in the valleys until the light on the hills had faded. That is the secret. The new-born soul possesses the character of holiness; but let that new-born soul turn the back on light, disobey in any particular the Word of the Lord, turn for a moment the face from the gleaming glory of the ultimate ideal, and the result is a weakening and a relaxing of effort, and the character suffers deterioration. The blame is never on Him; it is always on us.

Thus we end this whole series with the central inquiry of this text. "Who did hinder you?" That is a purely personal inquiry. I can do none other than repeat it in your hearing. You must answer it alone. Perhaps *"Who* did hinder you?" Perhaps *"What* did hinder you?" Perhaps "Who?" Some person, some friend, father, mother, wife, child, lover, partner in business? "Who did hinder you?" Or perhaps what? What enticement of the world, the flesh, the devil? Some short cut to a kingdom of power, some deft manipulation of truth that was not all a lie, some lowering of the high standard of the ideal in order to make a momentary gain which was wholly of the dust. What did hinder you?

I repeat, the preacher can only inquire. It is not for me to hear the answer, but the answer must be given in the light and in loneliness. But I pray you remember this, that holiness is not merely a privilege, it is a duty. To fail is to fail of the realization of your own life. I mention that only to dismiss it, for it is the lowest argument of all. The most weighty argument is that to fail of holiness is to defame Christ on the highways and in the city. You name His name, but if your children see in you unloveliness of temper, God help you; you had better quit naming His name, and give your child a chance.

That is the terror of this whole matter. I do not know; sometimes I wonder whether I am quite right about this, but

I cannot help it. I must be true to conviction. I am more and more anxious that men should see that the reason of their Christianity is not their salvation, but their influence on other men. You defame Christ if you name His name and sing His song, and do not realize His character. And to fail of holiness is to wrong the world, to dim the only light it has, and make the salt, the aseptic salt that should give goodness its chance, savorless. And mark the infinite satire of Christ. "If *the salt* have lost its savor, wherewith shall *it* be seasoned? It is fit only to be cast out and trodden under foot of man." And that is what happens to Christian men and women who name the name of Christ, and are not salt. They are trodden under foot of men; they are despised by their day and generation. The world itself holds us in supreme contempt if we profess to be Christian and are not holy.

What, then, ought to be the immediate outcome of this series of studies? That we should answer this question, Who or what hath hindered you? that in some hour of quiet meditation and loneliness we should drag into the light the thing that hinders—friend, habit, or enticement—and that we should put it away. To that exercise may this series of studies lead very many of us for the glory of Christ.

CHAPTER XXVI

CLEAN, FOR SERVICE

Be ye clean, ye that bear the vessels of the Lord.
ISAIAH 52:11.

THESE WORDS REVEAL A PHILOSOPHY OF SERVICE FOR THE people of God. They define the responsibility which constantly rests on those who bear His name, that responsibility being indicated in the words, "ye that bear the vessels of the Lord." Moreover, they declare the conditions on which this responsibility may be fulfilled, that, namely, of cleanness in the full sense of that great word.

Bible history reveals the long conflict between two opposing principles, represented by two words, Babylon and Israel; the one standing always for self-centered life, and the other for life which is God-centered.

It is not for us to stay now to trace with any minuteness of examination the conflict between these two principles as it is revealed in the Scriptures of Truth. We may, however, call to mind the landmarks in the case of each. Babel, Babylon, Babylon the great, the mother of harlots. These words serve as indices, and cover the whole movement in the Bible. Over against them we may think of the landmarks on the other side, Abraham, Israel, and Jerusalem, coming down out of heaven from God for the establishment of the Divine order in the world.

In the first case we trace a movement, based on rebellion

against God's government, and issuing at last in uttermost confusion as the great word of the Apocalypse indicates, "Fallen, fallen is Babylon the great." On the other hand, we trace a movement based on loyalty to God's government and issuing at last in eternal stedfastness. The realization of the Divine order among the sons of men is indicated in that word of the Apocalypse, "Behold, the tabernacle of God is with men, and He shall dwell with them, and they shall be his peoples."

Ever and anon in the history of the people of God as recorded in the Scriptures, they are seen yielding to the spirit of Babel, and always as a consequence sharing its confusion. The picture of Jehovah presented, when one takes this outline view, is that of One Who broods over His people, and forevermore attempts to woo them back toward Himself, and He does that because by their complicity with the spirit of Babylon they injure themselves, and, infinitely worse, because by their complicity with the spirit of Babylon they injure the nations round about them.

In this prophecy of Isaiah, and especially in this part from which our text is taken, we find ourselves in the midst of this conflict, where the two principles are clearly evident. As a matter of fact, at this time Israel, as viewed by the prophet, was in actual captivity in Babylon. Yet there was evident among them a Divine movement toward return to loyalty to God, and consequently toward establishment in their own land. It is impossible to understand this text without recognizing that it forms part of a greater whole. At the fifty-first chapter we have the commencement of the prophet's appeal, "Hearken to me, ye that follow after righteousness, ye that seek the Lord." There were among the people of God those who were following righteousness, who passionately desired it, and were seeking the Lord. As we read on we find that the people were aroused as the result of the prophet's appeal, and they lifted a cry to God in these words, "Awake, awake, put on Thy strength, O arm of the Lord." Then we come to the answer of God to the cry of the people. It is found in the opening words of the chapter I read to you, "Awake, awake, put on thy strength, O Zion."

The people of God were captive in Babylon. I pray you notice carefully the suggestiveness of it. The people who stood for loyalty to God, and ought to have borne that testimony to the world, were slaves in Babylon, which represented antagonism to the government of God. Yet amongst them in slavery were those in whom was the consciousness of all they were failing to do, and the sigh after something nobler expressed itself in that prayer to God, "Awake, awake, put on Thy strength, O arm of the Lord." To them the answer of God, if I may reverently put it into other words, was this, Why do you cry to me to awake? I am awake. I am not asleep. It is for you to awake and put on strength, and put on your beautiful garments.

Then follows the strange movement which chapter fifty-two describes. The prophet's vision is a remarkable one. He sees the people in their captivity, and he sees messengers crossing the mountains between Jerusalem and Babylon, and the burden of the cry of the messengers to the people in captivity is this, "Thy God reigneth."

It had seemed to these captive people as though God had resigned the throne of government, and they had said, "Put on Thy strength." His answer is, It is for you to put on strength, and the watchman on the heights, and the messengers that traversed the roads between Jerusalem and Babylon cried to the captives, "Thy God reigneth." That cry was answered by a great song of hope, and the people are seen preparing to leave Babylon and return to Jerusalem.

At last the call came, "Depart ye, depart ye, go ye out from thence." The captives were called to leave the place of captivity and to take their way again to the city of their established government. As they were about to obey, this solemn word was uttered, "Be ye clean, ye that bear the vessels of the Lord."

They had suffered through the Babel spirit, under the influence of which they had passed. They had passed into captivity to Babylon, because they themselves had bent the neck to the spiritual conception of Babylon. Now revival was beginning in the sigh after God and the proclamation of His continued reign; and they were turning back again to the place of blessing. On the eve of departure the solemn warning was uttered, "Be ye clean, ye that bear the vessels of the Lord."

Such is the background. In the foreground is this clear enunciation of abiding principle. Those who bear the vessels of the Lord must be clean. Let us then quietly and solemnly consider the two thoughts already indicated; first, the responsibility of the people of God; and second, the condition on which they are able to fulfil that responsibility. That responsibility is suggested in the words, "Ye that bear the vessels of the Lord." The condition on which it is possible to fulfil that responsibility is indicated in the command, "Be ye clean."

This principle of responsibility is enforced from the beginning of Bible history, and has been enforced over and over again by the prophets and interpreters of the ages, and yet, as Christian men and women and as a Christian Church, it is a principle we are always in danger of forgetting. The principle is that the people of God exist, not for their own sakes, but for the sake of the peoples who are not the people of God.

God's people are ever intended to be channels of communication, through whom He may reach others in blessing. Bible history does not exhaust the possible illustrations, but I am content to confine myself within this limitation. The keyword of God's communication to Abraham was this, I will bless you, and you shall be made a blessing. "I will make of thee a great nation . . . and in thee shall all the families of the earth be blessed." As we watch the building up of that peculiar people—who are to-day scattered and peeled, but retain with singular and remarkable persistence their national loneliness, even though they no longer have a national constitution*—as we watch the growth of that nation we see God's method for reaching other nations. Israel to-day is a people scattered and peeled over the face of the whole earth, because they forgot the meaning of their making, and failed to understand that they were created, not in order that God might have a people on whom He might lavish His love in forgetfulness of other peoples, but in order that they might become the instrument through which He would reach other peoples. An illustration of the principle outside that of the covenant people is found in this prophecy of Isaiah in the words of Jehovah concerning Cyrus, "I will gird thee, though thou hast not known Me." Trace the history of all national life through the ages and the same principle is discoverable. God makes a nation for a purpose. The moment that nation becomes self-centered, there comes disaster; He destroys the nation He has made. As the nation He makes realizes its responsibility for all the rest He maintains its strength.

The principle is most remarkably manifest in the life of

* Written long before the free state of Israel was established.

the Church of God. The Church is the depository of the treasure of God for the race. The Church of God is not an institution which holds within itself treasures for its own enrichment. Said the great apostle, whose peculiar phrase, "my Gospel," referred to the Church, "I am debtor." I am in debt to men. In what did his debt consist? In that he had received the great evangel, in that he had perfect understanding of the provision of the grace of God for men, wrought out into his own experience. Not for his saving only was he saved, but in order that he might be the instrument through which God might reach other men for their saving.

To the Church is committed a threefold responsibility. She stands for the manifestation of God to the world. She exists for the reconciliation of the world to God. She has within her fellowship the living means of grace. Some of you may say that is very high-church doctrine. It is the highest of the high, because it is the New Testament doctrine of the Church. She stands first for the manifestation of God. Hear this great word of the New Testament, "Ye are an elect race, a royal priesthood, a holy nation, a people for God's own possession, that ye may show forth the excellencies of Him Who called you." In other words, the Church exists to manifest God. Not through the Word alone will the world find the Father, but through the Word incarnate in the lives of people who have been obedient to it. Only through those who share His nature can His name ever be known.

We bear the vessels of the Lord. The world can find its way to the Saviour only through the Church. Do not misunderstand me, I mean through the Church's proclamation of this Evangel. If you take the widest outlook you see at once what I mean. He cannot reach the heathen people save through the contact with them of His own people. I am neither attempting to discuss the economy of God or to account for it. I declare it as a fact revealed and demonstrated by experience. The world is not waiting for salvation because God is unready to save, but because the Church is not wholly at His disposal to carry the message of salvation. Knowledge of God can come to men finally, fully, completely, only through the Church. He has committed to us the responsibility of revelation. We bear the vessels of the Lord.

The ministry of reconciliation is ours. We fulfil it by the revelation of His love, the revelation of the meaning of His atoning work, and the revelation of the power by which He remakes humanity. All these things are committed to the Church, and men can know them only through the Church.

The means of grace are committed to the Church, the inspired Word for its interpretation, the sacred activities of worship for explanation, and, infinitely more, and without the more these things are of no avail, that service of pity and of power which brings life to the dead, love to those who are lonely, and light to such as sit in darkness. All the treasures of God are deposited with the Church. I do not mean any organized ecclesiastical system, but the whole Catholic Church, made up of men and women who share the life of Christ and walk in the light He brings. We bear the vessels of the Lord.

The one message of God is that of love. God's love message is, that because He seeks the highest good of man He is the implacable foe of sin. All the vessels of the Lord under the old economy symbolized this truth, and called for the perfection of humanity. The ministry of the Church in the world is with this end in view, that the works of the devil should be destroyed, and the ideals of God realized.

To go back again to the simplest statement of the truth.

The world can find God only through His people. Or let me make that statement in quite another form. The only use God has for His people in this world is that the world may find Him through them. The Church of God exists to-day for the bearing of the vessels of the Lord, for the revelation of the truth concerning Him, the opening to men of doors to fellowship with Him. The great deposit of the Church creates the great responsibility of the Church.

Let us hear what this text suggests to us concerning the conditions on which the Church may fulfil her responsibility. We need to hear them because a statement such as this must bring to us consciousness of our own failure. You speak to me of the indifferent city. I tell you the reason for it is the faulty Church in the indifferent city. We cannot realize our responsibility without knowing our failure. With that thought in mind let us listen to what the prophet said concerning the conditions on which the responsibility may be fulfilled. "Be ye clean." It is a very, very simple word. It is a very searching word. The word itself of which the prophet made use is suggestive. Its first intention is that of clarifying through and through. It is a word which suggests the idea, not of water, but of fire; not of something which deals with the external, but of something that searches through and through. I have been very interested in tracing through the whole of the Old Testament the use of the word here translated *clean*. The result of that survey is this: I find that it is never used of merely ceremonial cleansing. There are other words used in that sense, but this one never. It always has reference to moral cleanness. When the psalmist says, "The Lord rewarded me according to my righteousness; according to the *cleanness* of my hands hath He recompensed me"; "Therefore hath the Lord recompensed me according to my righteousness, according to the *cleanness* of my hands in His eyesight"; "With the *pure* Thou wilt show Thyself *pure;* and with the perverse Thou wilt show Thyself froward," he in each case uses the same word. Perhaps the verse that helps us most to see the force of this word is that mystical and symbolic word in the Canticles,

> Who is she that looketh forth as in the morning,
> Fair as the moon,
> Clear as the sun,
> Terrible as an army with banners?

Clear as the sun, that is pure as the sun, clean as the sun if you so will, and the figure of that verse explains the real thought of the word "clean"; it means clarified as with burning heat. "Be ye clean, ye that bear the vessels of the Lord." Be ye of that fire nature in which no imperfect or impure thing can live. Be ye of that nature which consumes the unworthy, and purifies that which is worthy. Be ye of the very nature of God Himself, of Whom it is written, "Our God is a consuming fire." The great picture of the testing of the Church's work in the Corinthian letter comes to mind in this connection: He shall try our work as with fire. If you will allow your imagination to help you, look at the great picture of the Christ which is given in the Apocalypse by the seer of Patmos, "His eyes are a flame of fire." With eyes of flame he glances over the work of the Church. With what result? Watch the work. Some of it is burnt, destroyed; it shrivels and becomes dust, and is gone; all that is hay, wood, stubble. Some of it loses only its dross and flashes in beauty as the fire of His glance rests on it; all that is gold, silver and precious stones. These are the things that live in fire. These are the things of the fire nature, even though when you touch them they seem to be cold. They are fire nature, for fire cannot destroy them. In the ancient prophecy is this remarkable word, spoken to the king of Tyre, "Thou hast walked up and down in the midst of the *stones of fire*," stones that live in the midst of fire.

If we read the word, "Be ye clean," as though it referred only to some ceremonial cleansing, and inculcated certain ceremonial ablutions, we have not caught the force of the prophet's meaning. You bear the vessels of the Lord. You are to be responsible for His revelation to men. You are the people among whom He has deposited the truth for which the world is waiting. "Be clean," be clarified as by fire, be such men and women as that there is nothing in you that fire can destroy. Be such men and women that all the things fire can destroy are destroyed in your own life. "Be ye clean." Our word "clean" may mean so little when it ought to mean so much. That great Hebrew word of which the prophet made use, which is used with such marked carefulness in all the language of the seers and psalmists of long ago, is a word which suggests cleansing in its profoundest sense: cleanness from complicity with Babylon. You have been in captivity to Babylon. You are sighing after the higher and nobler. "Thy God reigneth." God is calling you back to the place and position of power. Leave Babylon behind you when you turn your back on Babylon. Do not carry with you as you come again to the place you have lost any of the spirit that destroyed you before. The emblems of the holiness of the Divine government must be borne by holy men. "Be ye clean."

www.ingramcontent.com/pod-product-compliance
Lightning Source LLC
Chambersburg PA
CBHW052143300426
44115CB00011B/1498